Information Design

Information Design

edited by Robert Jacobson

The MIT Press
Cambridge, Massachusetts
London, England

First MIT Press paperback edition, 2000
©1999 Massachusetts Institute of Technology

This book was set in Stone Sans and Stone Serif by Asco Typesetters, Hong Kong.
Printed and bound in the United States of America.

Library of Congress Cataloging-in-Publication Data

Information design / edited by Robert Jacobson.
      p. cm.
    Includes bibliographical references and index.
    ISBN 978-0-262-10069-4 (hc. : alk. paper) — 978-0-262-60035-4 (pb. : alk. paper)
    1. Communication in design. 2. Communication—Technological
innovations. I. Jacobson, Robert E., 1948–
  NK1510.I53   1999
  302.2—dc21   98-53665
                                                                        CIP

10   9   8   7

Contents

Foreword*

Richard Saul Wurman

Well, there's today & there's tomorrow.

Today we have things called *search engines*—a strange kind of mechanistic, industrial-age term for information tools—with funny names like Hotbot & Alta Vista, where you type a name or a subject & you have huge numbers of hits, which are rated by the search engine on how close to your name or word the original references are.

This is certainly better than nothing, but these mechanisms are not what dreams are made of. What are our dreams about information? What are our dreams about wisdom & knowledge?

For the first time in history, we can actually dream & expect some of it to happen. And, since dreams are described by human beings, they are constituted out of the fabric of what is deemed at any moment possible & what is deemed as possible is available in new combinations.

When I told the story about Michelangelo & viewing the piece of stone before the hammer and chisel was invented, and all that Michelangelo was able to mouth was his admiration & observation that it's a big piece of stone; whereas, when somebody slaps a hammer & chisel in his hand

---

* Adapted from a presentation made at the 1998 Technology, Entertainment, and Design Conference (TED).

upon the event of the invention of those technologies—of tool making, metallurgy—he then, because of the availability & possibility, thinks of the creative opportunity & shouts, "I must let Moses out!"

Let's hear it for tomorrow!

Now is the time to start shouting about having smart engines that know who you are & anticipate the things you might be interested in. We need smart software & smart hardware in combination which suggests sparklers in a birthday cake, amazing connections between thought & thought, braiding & weaving ideas, overlapping to help you create creative thoughts, new thoughts, artful thoughts, new patterns which are yours. Tomorrow is about personal journeys through data creating patterns that you own, trips that are only yours, journeys & voyages that profile who you are, fantasies of flying through information that is constantly accessible & understandable, that tickle a random thought until it becomes an idea & combines ideas until they become inventions & packages those inventions so they become available for others. Now is the time to dream.

Let's also hear it for books like this collection edited by Bob Jacobson. Books give laurels to the people with passion about understanding. After dreaming comes doing. These words will help start people doing.

The President says to the Vice President, & the Vice President tells the nation, "Gee, children would learn so much more, if only we could repair the schools." If we take that thought further along we can feel in our bones how much better Lincoln would have been if he didn't have to read by candlelight in his log cabin, if only he had improved bricks & mortar.

I must say this is the worst of the educational bureaucracy, a bureaucracy that focuses—if it isn't on bricks & mortar then it's on teacher's salaries, & if it isn't on teacher's salaries it's on crime in the schools, & if it isn't on crime in the schools then it's on strange tests called SATs & PSATs that measure your ability in a pressure-driven situation to fill out a multichoice questionnaire.

I wonder about the correlation between the creatively wonderful people in our society & SAT scores. I wonder what the correlation is between who these people are & the urgencies of an educational bureaucracy. I wonder what is being done to trace, both backwards & forwards, the process of learning that pulls it out of the fever of short-term memory, bulimically put on a piece of paper called a test, & this memory shortly erased because of the requirement for still another load of uninteresting facts to be put once again down on a piece of paper & forgotten the following week. For most of us, that's the cycle of our educational experience.

What of the moments of learning, of understanding ourselves, our human form, our sense, our insides & our outsides? Isn't this the logical place to begin? Within a 5 minute walk of where we get up in the morning, from the electrical system & the plumbing, the sewage system & the structure, the quality of air & water, the insides of our pancreas & the outsides of the roof, the street curve & the traffic flow, the peristaltic action of a traffic jam & the swallowing mechanisms of our esophagus, the cutting of a piece of bread & the chewing of some gum, the digestion of food & the rotting of our teeth, the sloughing off of skin & the budding of a tree. All within view, all free, all within a 5 minute walk, all there for the taking, all for the questioning, we need a guide, we don't need a SAT test, we don't need a metal detector, as we walk in this garden of knowledge.

Yesterday, I was in one of those terrifying blank moments when you aren't certain if your eyes are opened or closed, dreaming, as the poet Robert Graves calls it, "the waking dream" about how little I know about almost everything. I think I went off in this dream-state reading the Sunday *New York Times*. With an image of my mind as I read these lines of type, as if each line was on a curling piece of cellophane which blew off irretrievably.

Then my stomach gurgled, & I realized that I don't even know anything about my own body. I don't know if the sharp pain in my chest is a signal that I'm about to die, or I ate beans, or I stretched my arm the wrong way in a more & more unforgiving musculature.

So, in these moments of sheer, empty anguish—of literally being the Zen empty bucket—the waterfall opportunity of understandable stuff, of lazily rolling around in the warm mud of clarification, of the celebration of connecting a most minor revelation to almost anything else, the ooh-aahs that occur infrequently, within the midst of all this terror came a gleeful happiness that I'd always have something to do, I'd always have something to work on. I'd always have something to make understandable.

There are an infinite number of journeys to take through the design of understanding. First a little walking path through a field connecting to a towpath by a canal, journeys, roads, walkways, resting places & parking lots & harbors, highways and cloverleafs, all navigated in some personal and self-owned journey through information, organized by signs showing me where I am, when something took place, what category of knowledge it is, some sort of organization by importance or size, & indexed by the strange, artificial 26 letters of our life called the alphabet.

The business of America in the next century without doubt will be the learning business, directed at children of all ages, taking place in the Age of Also, through parallel systems of learning, through parallel systems of media, real-time conversation, the pressing of the flesh, the eyeball conversation, new ideas of books, smart television & smart searching mechanisms, through smart computer/tv machines, entertainment informing us as we recognize the utter joy that occurs as we are entertained into understanding, learning, & then wisdom. We are going to learning this way & also that way. We are going to surf the net & also read books, CD-ROMs & DVDs, video & cinema, conversation & music. Also & also. All the design of understanding. All learning. All personally owned & directed.

It is now quite clear that the technology business, the entertainment industry & the design professions have now tied the knot. Their tying of the knot—perhaps in a more flowery way—the bow of that knot is their more recent focus on many emerging parallel systems of learning, independent of the educational bureaucracy. Clearly, the most creative & talented individuals in our society, particularly the young, talented & creative individuals, are joining the ranks of these three businesses. They bring to this braid of backgrounds, not only their creative ideas, but a means of distributing these ideas & an attitude that's focused on learning.

What a wonderful moment this is.

What a wonderful moment to have the catastrophe or the perception of the catastrophe as it effects a bankrupt educational system, come at the same moment when technology & entertainment, or what I call technotainment, & information, or what I call Information Architecture, have a raison dêtre, a purpose, a reason for being, an exciting need to develop their wings, to stretch their arms, to shake their fingers & to think up things that they can only think up now because of the availability of an information technology & a network for distribution & accessibility.

This is a cornucopia of the future.

A future where learning—the design of learning, the design of understanding—becomes a major business. It also happens that at the time when it's indeed the only force in American that can lead towards at least a partial leveling of the playing field between the have-mores, the have-nots & what seems up to now to be the never-gonna-haves. This will constitute not only the great American business in the 21st century but its growth to intellectual greatness.

These businesses, whose foundation will be the design of understanding, will be a cornerstone in the creative economy in the decades to come. Isn't it wonderful: that designers, instead of only applying mascara & fashion, leaning on the crutch of esthetics, rewarding only each other, will now find rewards & purpose in the society as a whole? This is an exciting moment & the explosion of individuals across this country & the world, who now live & breath, think & ruminate, about making things understandable is growing exponentially each year.

Isn't it wonderful that information technologists & the entertainment industry will be able to dance a dance that matters—not just an obsession with bandwidth, storage capacities & bells & whistles.

Their dance can be heated by the warmth that comes from understanding measured by human memory & creative learning connections. Information in its highest form is both an art & an entertainment.

This book is dedicated to the memory of Steven Holtzman, an intellectual pioneer—and a friend.

Preface

This anthology began and was completed at a time of considerable professional and personal turmoil for the editor. I was changing jobs, changing professions, changing lifestyles, changing, well, almost everything. What I hear from my friends and family tells me I am not unusual. Everyone I know is having similar adventures. Change, magnificent in its sheer magnitude, imposes itself on every aspect of our lives. We are co-conspirators in its onslaught. For every action there is a reaction, no less in matters of the intellect than in flashes of fire and movements of ice.

Information Design is our collective reaction to those changes and to the ad hoc emergence of a new discipline. In its form and acceptance it is, we hope, a harbinger of positive changes to come.

I've tried to locate the conceptual ground-zero for information design in order to pay homage to its precursors and formative voices. My thoughts have constantly returned to familiar names: William James, Marshall McLuhan, Gene Youngblood, J. J. Gibbons, and, especially, Richard Saul Wurman (who contributed the Foreword). Undoubtedly there are others. A complete listing of those working in art, design, and the social sciences— all our long-lost intellectual cousins—would take up a book in its own right. In time, many will be recognized as great thinkers, and all will be seen as pioneers of the new field. Two of the contemporaries bringing us together are Yuri Engelhardt, who moderates the InfoDesign computer mailing list (*infodesign@wins.uva.nl*), and Raghu Kolli and his team at the Technical University of Delft, who created and maintain the UI-Design Web page (*www.io.tudelft.nl/uidesign*).

Many individuals have cooperated to cajole *Information Design* into being. (Perhaps *yanked* would be a better word.) There were times when this reluctant editor might have succumbed to weighty problems unrelated to its creation, times when the sheer number of changes I had to juggle was almost too much. Those who urged me on—the contributors, the MIT Press staff, my friends and family—deserve the lion's share of credit for whatever merits this publication may possess.

Bob Prior, computer science and engineering editor at MIT Press, provided the invitation that got this book going. His patience is equaled only by his wise direction to novices like me. Sarah Speare, former executive director of the Society for Environmental Graphic Design, along with Paula Reese and Linda Soukop, coordinated SEGD's 1994 annual meeting in Seattle, where I recruited this anthology's initial contributors.

The cofounders of my erstwhile virtual worlds design company, Worldesign Inc.—Avi Bar-Zeev, Chet Dagit, and Peter Wong—offered me insights of great value. I also benefited from the ideas of Shannon Smith, who joined us later.

My family has been supportive throughout; I thank each one of them. My former wife, Sandra Kay Helsel, and her son, Aeric, put up with more than the usual author's family. Not only were we separated in time but also in space, for literally years. During those times apart, my housemate, Bruce Cherry, provided help with the dishes and personal wisdom.

Above all I thank the information designers, every one of them, whether they are practicing a formal trade or just making the world a little more understandable. They hold our future in their hands.

1 Introduction: Why Information Design Matters

Robert Jacobson

This book is for information designers. And because all of us, all of the time, are both producers and consumers of information, it is for you.

Throughout history, people have systematically designed and delivered information in an effort to share their perceptions of the world and persuade others to reach the same conclusions. The Nazi version of history that propaganda chief Joseph Goebbels twisted around the minds of the German people, as well as the television cartoon version of the Gulf War bear grim witness to the possibilities for coercing perception. In the 1930s, as Franklin Roosevelt's "Fireside Chats" were buoying the spirits of depression-torn America, animation pioneer Walt Disney was cheering moviegoers and beginning to build an entertainment empire around the zany antics of a cast of fantasy figures. But information design has far more distant roots: some of the earliest efforts to subjectively craft human experience lie in the mythologies and tales told by the priests, poets, and playwrights of the ancient world.

What makes our current discussion of information design so exciting is its emphasis on two interrelated concepts: edification and commutativity. *Edification* is the process of personal enlightenment, while *commutativity* is the process of mutual change. Contemporary information designers seek to edify more than persuade, to exchange ideas rather than foist them on us.

We have learned well that the person who issues designed information is just as likely as its intended recipients to be changed by it, for better or for worse. This new awareness has been forced on us by ever more powerful technologies of communication, media that dramatically highlight and shorten the links between those who generate information designs and those who receive and act on designed information.

The fact that information design is so pervasive reminds us to be careful and deliberate in the way we apply the power inherent to this new process. That is, really, the purpose of this book: to show us how to be both cautionary and hopeful, to offer us visions of how information design can be practiced diligently and ethically for the benefit of consumers and producers alike.

The information designers in this book acknowledge the systemic nature of communication. As the old saw has it, what goes around comes around. Everyone has a part in the story. That is the meaning of interactivity. The best information design acknowledges and uses the interactive nature of communication to convey meaning and heighten understanding among all parties involved in an activity or event.

These statements may seem like truisms. But only a decade ago concepts like *edification*, *commutativity*, and *interactivity* were found exclusively in scholarly tomes parked on dusty shelves marked "Philosophy," "Psychology," and "Communications Studies." Now they are being talked about on the Internet!

Five years ago, when we conceived the idea for this book, information design was still little known in North America, Asia, and Europe. It was practiced by small bands of believers concentrated in the United Kingdom and the Netherlands. Today, although the term is still exotic, the practice of applying design to information—or as one contributor, Jef Raskin, notes, applying design to the media through which information flows— is becoming widespread. The problem now is, how do we conceptualize information design so that it can be improved upon by future generations of practitioners?

The answer is not as easy as it might seem. As the contributions to this book argue, there is no agreement that a practice called *information design* actually exists. Even those who acknowledge its existence find a unitary definition elusive. In order to systematize and pass along our knowledge about "how to design information" or "how to be an information designer," we need a reliable lexicon and a tried-and-true theory backed up by case studies. At present, the theory is sketchy and the case studies are scarce. Too few studies of information design have been carried out to support any broad generalizations about its practice.

Nonetheless, I did not permit the contributors to this book, proponents as well as critics, to rest easy! Instead, I cajoled, pleaded with, and persuaded them to seize the bull by the horns and prognosticate, based on their experience, intuition, and expectations. After all, they are among the leading practitioners and commentators in the field: what they think is important and is quite likely to be accurate.

The experts whose opinions are offered in this book truly run the gamut, from those who deny that there is such a thing as information design to those who believe they have been practicing it for a lifetime. Readers will have to decide about the reliability of these pronouncements for themselves, based on their current understandings and the evolving state of the art. Every designer must accept this challenge, not only about information design but about design itself. We are fortunate in this regard: our field changes as fast or faster than we do. We will never be bored.

This book has germinated slowly. It originated with a series of presentations made at the 1994 Seattle annual meeting of the Society for Environmental Graphic Design (SEGD). SEGD now boasts a professional membership of over a thousand individuals and organizations whose practices are built on the design of objects in multidimensional space. These objects range from signage (the original focus of environmental design) to highly elaborate exhibitions and commercial applications, some of which are described in this book. SEGD's 1994 meeting was an especially fertile setting in which to consider the nature of information design, because the society was then involved in its own reevaluation of the meaning of design.

I signed up the core group of contributors to this book at the SEGD event and asked them three questions:

1. Is there such a thing as information design?

2. If there is, what might constitute a formal theory of information design?

3. How can we implement this theory in a systematic practice that can be described to others and taught to new entrants to our field?

The contributions that resulted are among the finest expositions on information design as a discipline. Their contributions range the full ambit of information design.

Information design makes its mark in both the traditional arena of two-dimensional graphics and in the postmodern domain of interactive, computer-driven media. In these fields I was fortunate to find the individuals whose insight, creativity, and unique perspectives enrich this book.

I also recruited to our effort experts on the act of communication itself, people whose studies transcend the preoccupations of the sectoral practitioners. I trust that their divergence from the usual practice-oriented discourse on information design will serve as a touchstone for the claims made by ardent advocates and provide a way of envisioning the future of the profession.

Having asked the three questions of the authors, I must attempt my own answers, so that the reader can sense as I do the ambiguities that the contributors met and conquered.

My own belief is that there is a unique design practice that can be identified as *information design*. Its purpose is the systematic arrangement and use of communication carriers, channels, and tokens to increase the understanding of those participating in a specific conversation or discourse.

One of information design's virtues is that its products, at least at the moment of their conception, are unencumbered by traditional media limitations. The information designer initially works with fields of meaning, not with the materials used to transmit meaning. Other designers may quibble about this point, but in most cases they work with "stuff," concrete or electronic materials that impose a priori design constraints.

Designing with information (whether during its assembly, transmission, or receipt) is a heady affair. The quickly relevant constraints pertain mainly to our finite human sensory and cognitive capacities. All too quickly information design can degenerate into chaotic, random brush strokes on the recipient's cognitive canvas. Because the success of information design is so context-dependent, there is almost no way to predict scientifically for any particular setting what will work and what will not. Each design rises or falls according to factors that are difficult to replicate: the setting in which the transfer of knowledge occurs, the individuals involved, the medium or media employed, and the original and ultimate purposes of producers and consumers.

Perhaps there are broad patterns of correlation between certain types of information design and their effectiveness in particular settings. If so, we must make generalizations ten miles wide to cover all the variations in between.

Which leads me to my second question about theory. When I began this book, I believed we could construct theories about information design from the hypotheses presented and tested by the contributors, as well as by others who have researched the subject. I am no longer so hopeful. The studies of methods that apparently work, like *Sense-Making* (described by Brenda Dervin, its inventor, in chapter 3), are usually context-specific. Could Sense-Making be applied beyond the social milieu—for example, to navigate complex collections of computerized data? I suspect it can, but most studies pertain to human social behavior and interactions among human beings. A similar objection applies to my other favorite method of information design, *wayfinding*. Wayfinding (as described by Romedi Passini in chapter 5) is beginning to provide answers for such unusual challenges as navigating the Web, but it's been almost exclusively studied and used by architects for conceptualizing building spaces.

Unless we are willing, like social psychologists, to construct arbitrarily simplified contexts and then "test" information designs within them, we may have to do without a compelling theory of information design, at least for awhile.

Is information design, then, not a design profession but an art that simply lacks the time-tested foundations of other arts? Does its fluidity make it any less teachable? I believe not, on both counts.

It may be true that, as practitioners of a young profession, information designers haven't collected enough objective, subjective, or even anecdotal information to create a coherent corpus of rules or principles a novice can obey. Nonetheless, the skilled information designer and the trainee with an aptitude will be able to distinguish between what works—what makes sense—and what does not. The more training he or she receives, the more skilled the information designer will become. This method of learning describes a profession in its youth, a craft as it were, devising compacts and curing "bad ethers," as in the early days of jurisprudence and medicine.

We know it is possible to learn a craft. Students can learn carpentry or masonry of a very high order without knowing the real science behind mortar's strength or why flying buttresses permit soaring cathedral walls to stand erect. Apprentices can learn information design in a similar way. The painful corollary to this analogy, of course, is that many structures have fallen because of shoddy workmanship based on lessons ill learned. There are only so many genuine masters.

While it's difficult to ascribe to information design all the desired characteristics of a mature profession, there is clearly movement, if not yet toward professionalization, then toward standards. Criticism of information systems that do not convey information well—whatever their technical fireworks—is commonplace. In fact, one need only look to the popular press (print, broadcast, or digital) to discover a new army of critics whose sole occupation is commenting on the informational value of technologies and systems. Not only information designers but also those who critique their work are increasingly conscious of the design process and aware of its importance. The effect of such criticism will be to hammer practitioners of information design into professionals, if not yet scientists.

The most scientific study to date of designs intended to convey information, *Marks of Distinction* by the respected Danish designer Per Mollerup, attempts to classify trademarks according to various matrices. Mollerup points out that successful trademarks have similar characteristics. Nonetheless, despite all the incredibly expensive research conducted to rationalize trademarking, most trademarks are designed by individuals whose creativity is unencumbered by overt rules. Yet for the design historian and student, even post hoc studies of information design are useful. They impart sense to an apparently chaotic process.

It has been said that living is the best method of learning. If so, how the contributors to this book, and information designers generally, came to their professional role has meaning. I am thinking of the pioneers of modern information design, Charles and Ray Eames. For four decades, beginning in 1940, first Charles alone and then with his wife Ray worked in every conceivable medium, including puppets, film, and furniture. (The famous Eames chair with footstool remains the epitome of contemporary functional, comfortable design.) Later they turned to designing information. Perhaps their most famous contribution to information design is the timeline mural, a linear river of historical currents and events. There were timelines before, of course, but none possessed the information-carrying capacity of the Eameses' version. Using the timeline as a central organizing principle, the Eameses worked like busy ants constructing brilliant commercial and nonprofit exhibitions—including the IBM Pavilion at the New York World's Fair and "The World of Franklin and Jefferson" exhibition that toured during the American Revolution bicentennial year. These exhibitions employed not only styles of presentation then in fashion but also whatever other combinations of graphics, text, photography, and film fulfilled the need to quickly and lucidly convey information.

The Eameses' method of design was highly systematic. First they decomposed a design program into its myriad components and subcomponents, a hundred subtasks for every major task. Then they analyzed the smallest parts one by one, striving with each successive evaluation to choose the one design alternative that equaled or surpassed in quality the choices made before. Meticulously the Eameses arrived at the best of the small parts and then, just as rigorously, assembled these unit by unit, until the resulting product represented the sum of a thousand excellent decisions. Paradoxically, the result frequently stunned Charles and Ray themselves, since the effect of their method was indeed often greater than the sum of its parts.

And yet, the Eameses were also masters of intuition, for the process of taking apart the pieces and putting them back together again was conducted in a context of simple elegance and beauty whose rules resided in their minds alone. If the final products of their labors were honed and fine-tuned to within an inch of excess, still the conception of these products was an act of creation unique to the Eameses' sense of proportion and propriety and their overall genius.

In our own time, many designers of information and objects seek to emulate Charles and Ray Eames. Though some succeed, we live, for the most part, in an era when craftsmanship is usually honored in the breach. There is no time for most things, including information, to be designed well. The quality we cannot attain we make up in quantity: kilobytes, megabytes, gigabytes, terabytes—so many bytes that we may need a data muzzle. This deluge of information, as Richard Saul Wurman notes in *Information Architects*, is contributing to a crisis of understanding on every front. It's a common design cliché that "less is more," but good information design isn't a matter of more or less. Rather, it results from harnessing the determination to engender better understanding to the appropriate skills for doing so.

All told, I think, this volume's collective effort succeeds on several levels: for the novice, the practicing professional, and the student of information design. For those of us in the field or considering working in our nascent profession, this anthology provides a slice of the information design life, mirroring our community as it exists today. For those on the outside, it offers a selection of vista points overlooking a varied terrain, a map against which other descriptions of information design can be checked and registered. Despite the aspirations of its contributors to maintain their personal visions and not be forced to fit a Procrustean standard, this book has not deviated far from its original path. The authors' wishes have been respected: the book is eclectic but strives throughout to make the concept of information design more understandable to its readers.

The truest test of the hypotheses the authors advance will be the reception the book receives from those who define themselves as information designers and, even more, from the changes it evokes in their practice. Abstract discussions of tangible practice—in all fields, not just design— often degenerate into academic jargon. I trust this will not happen with information design. Conferences and journals produced by information designers are taking up the debate and giving it a welcome practical bent.

These developments will have an effect. The only question is, how profound? Will the field of information design race ahead and outdistance the publication of *Information Design*? Or will this text become a benchmark for the profession's further development? The authors had to address the three questions we started with because they are inevitable. Our effort may be a wild stab or a milestone. Time will tell.

For you, the reader, information design (whether under that name or another) will have increasing meaning. If you practice information design, you will discover that we are no longer an exotic breed able to mystify our means and motives. There are enough bona fide information designers, and critics, to engender a lively critique of each others' work in the months and years ahead. If you consume designed information (through any information media), you will probably notice greater sophistication in the quality of your experience.

I conclude on an optimistic note. Information design, whatever its label, will enhance our society's ability to collect, process, and disseminate information and to produce understanding. We may not yet fully appreciate how this is happening, but the contributors to this book make a good start toward explaining it.

Remember, too, that a book is a designed medium. Did we, professional information designers and students of information design, succeed in our purpose? Let me know. I can be reached by e-mail at *bluefire@well.com*. It will be my greatest pleasure to share with the contributors and publishers your comments and reflections. After all, it is your understanding of information design that we have worked hard to enlarge.

I *Theoretical Foundations of Information Design*

Where do we find information design and how can we identify it when we see it or experience its effects?

Design theory provides a substantial infrastructure of formal knowledge about the practice of design. It explains, through abstractions, how design works and how it can be made more effective. A workable theory, however, requires something more: an adequate knowledge of the phenomena to which the theory pertains. The experiments and observations necessary for constructing a theory cannot be made at random. We have to know where to look and what to look for. Interestingly, the contributors to this section almost unanimously direct us to the realm of power relationships as the source of all information design. They could be right. The investments now being made in information design certainly suggest that there is more to the practice than simply getting out a neutral message on this or that mundane matter.

There is also a consensus among the contributors to this part of the book that information design is real and not an intellectual chimera. Nevertheless, as long as the theory is still problematic, practitioners and observers will need to enunciate for themselves compelling arguments for the concept of information design. And each argument must rest on its own laurels. Part I presents four positive statements for the reader's evaluation.

Bob Horn's historical review of information design (chapter 2) describes several continuing themes associated with the practice. These include the strong interpretive responsibilities assumed by past information designers as part of their overall mission to elucidate and clarify the meaning of things. In this sense, information design has a moral as well as a practical responsibility. How effectively the designer communicates a particular viewpoint may be subordinate even to this larger purpose when he or she begins work on a project to inform, educate, or propagandize. Horn presupposes that the information designer will be alert to this interpretive power and aware of the inherent moral question reposing in any assignment. Of course, this isn't always the case, but when it is designers are truly put to the test and compelled to fashion their own internal guidelines.

The moral dimension of information design is even clearer in Brenda Dervin's discussion of power relationships and their consequences for information designers (chapter 3). The designer, she suggests, gets to choose between serving power and having many resources at one's disposal, or taking a more radical position and working with far fewer resources. Presumably, the more the information designer identifies with the dispossessed —those currently without access to the information necessary for bettering their lot, those for whom the world is eternally in informational chaos— the cleverer and better skilled he or she must be to succeed. This is the context for Dervin's methodology of *Sense-Making*, which is a powerful tool widely used by libraries and other institutions whose job it is to distribute information equitably. But Sense-Making is also a moral guide that could be cynically misapplied.

Mike Cooley is an information designer who has been through a moral meat grinder, apparently to good effect (though it must have been very unpleasant at the time). In the 1970s, Cooley led a designers' strike as part of a general labor action at the British manufacturer Lucas Ltd. The designers came up with hundreds of new-product ideas they hoped could be used as intellectual capital to fend off an unfriendly acquisition and the subsequent downsizing. Unfortunately, the strike failed and the designers were let go. Cooley, freed of his corporate responsibilities, became a staunch advocate of design education based on tacit knowledge and the guild model of learning (chapter 4). He has since successfully incorporated his theory of design—centered on the human subject—into several important industrial initiatives being undertaken by the European Commission and European Union.

The architect Romedi Passini concludes our pursuit of a formal information design theory by examining how *wayfinding*, an architectural methodology, can be applied to information design (chapter 5). Wayfinding as a practice embodies a modern architectural ideal: helping people find their way through the built environment (by, for example, color coding the signs in hospital complexes). Passini argues that information designers can help them navigate through information environments too. Interestingly, Richard Saul Wurman, who provides the Foreword for this volume, sees an even closer identity between the theories of information design and architecture, which he fuses in the unified concept of *information architecture*. Although the term has been appropriated by computer database designers, it is a more apt description of Passini's work.

2 Information Design: Emergence of a New Profession

Robert E. Horn

Egyptian scribes sat every day in the marketplace and wrote hieroglyphic letters, reports, memos, and proposals for their clients. At least since then, the business of assisting others to make their communications more effective has flourished. Specialists in communication already abound in our society: ghost writers, technical writers, advertising writers and art directors, public relations writers, and marketing consultants are only the most obvious ones. In any field of human endeavor there is a process of, first, specialization and, then, increasing professionalization. Information design is the most recent manifestation of the age-old profession of communications assistance.

What Is Information Design?

Information design is defined as the art and science of preparing information so that it can be used by human beings with efficiency and effectiveness. Its primary objectives are

1. To develop documents that are comprehensible, rapidly and accurately retrievable, and easy to translate into effective action.

2. To design interactions with equipment that are easy, natural, and as pleasant as possible. This involves solving many problems in the design of the human-computer interface.

3. To enable people to find their way in three-dimensional space with comfort and ease—especially urban space, but also, given recent developments, virtual space.

The values that distinguish information design from other kinds of design are efficiency and effectiveness at accomplishing the communicative purpose.

Need for Information Design

Why has information design emerged as a profession? First, managing information in our complex modern society requires sophisticated computing and communication devices and networks that operate with ever-increasing efficiency and effectiveness. Simply storing large amounts of information on computers and retrieving it does not solve our information needs. In fact, gigantic storehouses of information overload us with too much information and burden us with navigational problems that have sometimes make us feel that we are "lost in cyberspace." What we need is not more information but the ability to present the right information to the right people at the right time, in the most effective and efficient form.

The second factor behind the recent push for the professionalization of information design is the increasing cost of time: management, technical, and professional. Much of what most managers and technical professionals do every day is process information. If the information is poorly designed, they operate inefficiently and their organizations are not as effective as they might be. I once hired a secretary who had previously worked as one of four secretaries to a IBM vice president. Three of the secretaries were kept busy full time just summarizing the information coming into the office so the vice president could use it.

Information Design: Not an Integrated Profession

Information design is not yet a fully integrated profession. Its practitioners have quite different views of the profession—even different names for it.

In newspaper and magazines it is called *information graphics*; in business, it's *presentation graphics* or *business graphics*; and in science, it's known as *scientific visualization*. Computer engineers refer to *interface design*, while conference facilitators use the term *graphic recording* and architects talk about *signage* or *wayfinding*. Graphic designers just call it design. While these practitioners no doubt have distinct interests that might warrant different names, many of their core concerns and practices are similar. The different terms simply indicate that information design is still mostly characterized by separate groups that have little or no contact with each other. Even so, there is undoubtedly an increasing tendency to march under the new banner of information design. This book is an example of that tendency. Moreover, in the last decade, a number of design and consulting companies have begun to assemble their marketing messages around the concept of information design.

History of Information Design

It is beyond the scope of this chapter to trace the history of the information design movement in each of the professions mentioned above. Nonetheless, we can look at the history of information design as a profession in itself by considering some of those who contributed to its development (see figure 2.1).

Inventors

One of the unusual aspects of information design as a profession is that we can identify many of those who invented particular classes of communication units (e.g., bar charts, pie charts, or time lines). There are towering figures in the history of information design invention and use. William Playfair, who lived at the time of the American Revolution, invented several major types of graphs and charts and popularized them use through his writings on political and economic topics. In addition to her contributions to medicine, Florence Nightingale is credited with inventing new types of statistical graphs and being one of the first to use information design in a public policy report, a massive 800-page document on

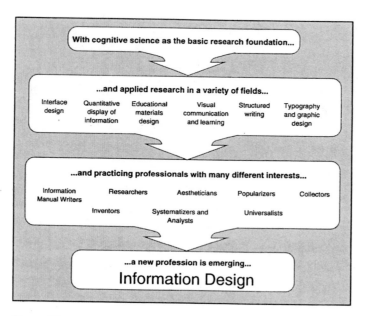

Figure 2.1

Contributors to the Emerging Information Design Profession.

hospital administration she prepared for Prime Minister Palmerston during the Crimean War (Cohen 1984). Although Michael George Muhall invented pictorial statistics just before the turn of the century, it was Otto Neurath, the Austrian social scientist, who developed a methodology for displaying them effectively (1973). David Sibbet (1980) has devised a set of techniques for graphically recording the process of group dynamics as they develop during a meeting. James Beniger and Dorothy Robyn (1978) provide a list of the inventors of quantitative charts, and H. G. Funkhouser (1938) usefully summarizes the early history of statistical graphics. I devote a chapter of *Visual Language* to the history of these innovations (Horn 1998).

Systematizers and Analysts

The systematizers have tried to bring all the pieces of the graphic language together to analyze them from a particular point of view. Jacques Bertin developed a comprehensive semiotic analysis of large portions of information design in his *Semiology of Graphics* (1983). Another early pioneer in this areas was Gui Bonsiepe (1966), whose early studies demonstrated that the visual language of graphics has analogues to many traditional rhetorical devices. Scott McCloud's *Understanding Comics* (1993) and Will Eisner's *Comics and Sequential Art* (1985) are excellent analyses of one "dialect" of visual language, the comic book. William Bowman (1968) produced an important early taxonomy of graphic communication, while Michael Twyman (1973) has provided an important analysis of how many types of static information design direct eye movement. My own book, *Mapping Hypertext* (1989), is not only an introduction to the world of on-line applications for information design but also (in its three central chapters) an overview of the structured analysis of subject matters and structured writing (see below).

Universalists

From time to time, individuals have hoped that purely visual communication, without the use of words, could become an international auxiliary language. A purely iconic language could substitute in certain situations, such as travel, for normal spoken language. In the optimistic era that followed World War II, the movement for iconic language attracted advocates like the eminent anthropologist Margaret Mead and her principal graphic-language compatriot, Rudolf Modley (1952). E. K. Bliss (1965), who developed an enormous and extremely clever iconic language of upwards of ten thousand symbols, was a prolific inventor and supporter of universalism. Like Mead, Modley, and Neurath, Bliss wanted to devise a purely iconic common language to free humanity from the tower of Babel created by its thousands of spoken languages. Purely iconic languages do not usually catch on, however, except in the field of transportation, which now uses internationally recognized symbols for all aspects of transportation and travel.

Collectors

Once any profession starts to grow, writers and publishers bring out reference books about it. Information design has its share of these. Among the more interesting, from a systematic point of view, is that of Henry Dreyfus (1984), who collected all the specialized icons from several dozen fields and incorporated them into a still-valuable reference book. Thompson and Davenport (1980) put together an engaging visual dictionary of the images and metaphors found in contemporary advertising.

Writers of Instruction Manuals

Once a profession thinks it knows something that others do not know, a spate of how-to books appears. At Stanford University, Robert McKim (1972, 1990) pioneered in demonstrating that visual thinking is not solely a means of artistic expression but is also a powerful tool for problem solving in many professions. Stephen Kosslyn's recent book on designing graphs and charts (1994) is a good example of a practical information design instruction manual. Gene Zelazny (1991) has written a similar book on business charts. Gary Glover's introduction to the new field of clip art (1994) will enable many more people to use icons and illustrations in their information design. A book by William Horton on icon design (1994) is another excellent example of an instruction manual on a limited topic.

Aestheticians

Information design has great variability in style and quality, which often affects its usefulness to researchers concerned about issues of precision and clarity. Foremost among the aestheticians is Edward Tufte, whose concepts of *data-to-ink ratio* and *chartjunk* stand as enduring signposts in the skillful and graceful use of visual language. His three books, *The Visual Display of Quantitative Information* (1983), *Envisioning Information* (1990), and *Visual Explanations* (1997), have provided the field of information design with pioneering studies in how communication can be both beautiful and useful.

Popularizers

In recent decades, magazines and newspapers have been leaders in the popularization of information design. Stephen Baker's (1961) book, *Visual*

Persuasion, is an extraordinary window into methods advertising designers have long known about and practiced to make information attractive and persuasive. Nigel Holmes, longtime art director at *Time*, is an acknowledged teacher and pioneer in this area. He recognized, in particular, how design attractiveness affects whether readers will actually read and use information. Recently he described these "infotainment" values in several books (Holmes 1984, 1991, 1993). David Macaulay's *The Way Things Work* (1988) is another brilliant example of information design at work. We must also credit Richard Saul Wurman with raising public awareness of the importance of information design in his books, *Information Anxiety* (1989), *Follow the Yellow Brick Road: Learning to Give, Take and Use Instructions* (1992), and *Information Architects* (1997).

Researchers

Research on communication, education, learning, human factors in technology, computer interface design, and perception all bear on the use of information design. However, most of the research does not use that term, even as an indexing category. To locate citations relevant to information design on research databases, therefore, we have to check many other keywords. But, as information designers begin to bring this research together, they can build on such firm foundations as the work of William Cleveland (1985), who has made important discoveries in the field of understanding quantitative graphics and charts. The research in structured writing (summarized in Horn 1993) is another area that is providing more secure foundations. Excellent summaries of the research on diagrams and other methods of presenting information graphically can be found in Winn (1982, 1990) and Horton (1991).

The British Information Design Society

In the history of information design a unique place must be reserved for the Information Design Society. As far as I can tell, this group invented and popularized the term *information design*. Its conferences have brought together users from several disciplines: design practitioners, researchers in psychology and education, computer graphics specialists, and teachers. Many practitioners of information design in the United States are members of this organization, as there is no comparable association in their own country. The society's *Information Design Journal*, currently edited by Paul Stiff, has been a major source of coherence for development of the profession.[1] Great Britain has also led the United States in the development of interdisciplinary university programs in information design. The program at the Department of Typographic and Graphic Communication at Reading University, chaired by Michael Twyman, is an outstanding example of such a program.

Research Foundations for Information Design

Although there has always been a component of skilled practitioners thinking analytically about information design, research is becoming increasingly specialized—and fundamental. Compared to other professions, however, information design has barely begun to develop and integrate its own research community; it still draws on other fields for its research base. Fortunately, more and more researchers are becoming interested in the problems information designers must solve.

Information design rests, therefore, on a variety of research foundations, including such disciplines and subject areas as human factors in technology, educational psychology, computer interface design, performance technology, documentation design, typography research, advertising, communications, and structured writing. Some of the more important summaries of the research in these areas are

- Interface design: Smith and Mosier (1986), Shneiderman (1987, 1992)

- Educational materials design: Fleming and Levie (1993)

- Typography: Evans (1974), U.S. National Bureau of Standards (1967), Tinker (1963)

- Visual communication and learning: Goldsmith (1984), Pettersson (1989), Horton (1991)

- Quantitative display of information: Cleveland (1985)

Research in cognition, which provides both a theoretical base and experimental data, is becoming fundamental to all of these fields (see, e.g., Eysenck and Keane 1990). In medicine, information design research and applications parallel work carried out in many of the above-mentioned research domains, under the name *medical informatics*.

Foundational Research: Structured Writing

Structured writing (called Information Mapping® in its commercial applications) is foundational to some areas of information design.[2] It provides a systematic way of analyzing any subject matter to be conveyed in a written document. Production of a written communication (such as a report, memo, proposal, training manual, procedural or operations manual, or electronic performance-support system) requires a method for ensuring that all relevant subject matter has been obtained and is presented in the form the user needs. Structured writing is such a method. It consists of a set of techniques for analyzing, organizing, sequencing, and displaying the various units of information.

One of the insights gained from structured writing is that the paragraph is too poorly defined to be a basic unit of the analysis. Instead, structured writing divides information into domains in which basic units—called *information blocks*—can be precisely described. Forty such information blocks can be used to sort 80 percent of the sentences found in writing about most relatively stable subject matters (such as the sentences found in training manuals and introductory textbooks). The ability to provide such precise functional descriptions has been used in the design of various training and reference documents. Although this is not the place for a full description of structured writing, we should point out that it is a mature methodology based on over twenty-five years of research and business implementation (Horn 1989, 1992a, 1992b, 1993, 1997). It has more than 200,000 users in the business and technical writing professions and has become part of the democratization of information design. So far, structured writing has been used primarily by writers. Information designers working in other fields are only now beginning to understand the importance of using structured writing as one of the secure foundations for analyzing the subject matter of documents.

Failure to Fully Integrate Research

It is symptomatic of a recently self-conscious profession that its knowledge of itself, its practices, and its research foundations are only partially known to practitioners. Many information designers have not read much of the research relevant to the profession. Perhaps one example will show what I mean. There is widespread interest among information designers in devising iconic signage for public places, even though research has cast doubts on the viability such an enterprise at this point in history. In one study of 108 international symbols (32 of which are widely used), fewer than half of the respondents clearly understood what 86 of them meant. Only three of the symbols were understood by more than two-thirds of the sample (Easterby and Graydon 1981, summarized in Sless 1986).

Other studies producing similar results induced me to advocate the use of what I call VLicons™ (Visual Language icons) rather than icons. VLicons integrate words and images in the same small communication unit (Horn 1998) and often perform some of the same important semantic functions as icons. They identify, they focus attention, they help set a mood, and they may aid in retrieval.[3] But they differ from icons in that they do not attempt the task of full communication with images alone. Instead, VLicons take advantage of the best aspects of words and images and integrate them tightly to convey meaning. They utilize the possibility that words and images effectively combined can disambiguate each other. Information design is still to some degree the prisoner of an old either-or paradigm in which words and images exist in completely separate domains of use.

Tensions in Information Design

As a profession, information design is currently experiencing a variety of tensions. Often these result from the clash of different ideologies or

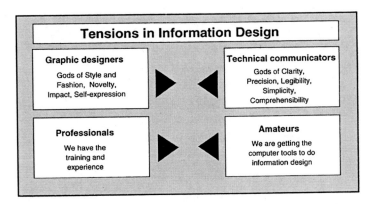

Figure 2.2
Tensions among Practitioners of Information Design.

value positions that have grown up in the course of solving particular problems and have been extended to uses beyond their original boundaries (see figure 2.2).

Value Differences

There is, for example, a considerable tension between (1) graphic designers —who learn in art school to worship the gods of Style and Fashion, Novelty, Impact and Self-expression—and (2) technical communication people—who worship the gods of Clarity, Precision, Legibility, Comprehensibility, and (often) Simplicity. The graphic designers grew up in schools where Advertising and Fashion were the Senior Deities. The technical people's Senior Deity is Communication. Some graphic designers fall in love with a particular typeface and size and use it at the expense of clarity of communication. Many graphic designers assigned to help the training and documentation organizations of a company appear to be incapable of imagining that someone else might have a different set of values. When I was CEO of an information design consulting company, I often asked documentation and training managers to state their major problem. I expected to hear that it was tight budgets or short deadlines for producing documents (especially in the software industry). This is what they told me: "Graphic designers are my biggest headache, because they simply won't produce simple illustrations for our manuals. They won't listen."

The information design community is just beginning to create a self-identification. As a result, working relationships among the different professions out of which it is growing are often uneasy. Practitioners sometimes see themselves, first and foremost, as engineers, architects, graphic designers, or illustrators (or as psychologists, educators, or writers) and only secondly as information designers. Nonetheless, when asked about their problems, they usually point to common issues. They also admire a common set of books (many of which are cited in this article). What they get excited about is information design, not the problems of their particular profession.

The tension between the graphic designers and researchers is also important. Researchers tend to avoid trying to measure style, novelty, and self-expression, partly because it is very difficult and partly because their research grants and contracts usually come from organizations whose major commercial priority is evaluating the clarity, legibility, and efficiency of communications. This tension sometimes also grows out of the vastly different social, economic, or moral values of designers and researchers working in advertising, and information designers and researchers in more technical communication fields.

Democratization

Every profession has the problem of trying to exclude those who "don't know what we know." The professional says, "Let us do it. We're the professionals. We have secret knowledge. You don't really know how to do it right." This possessiveness is to be expected. Information design has already begun trying to defend its boundaries. Unfortunately, some information designers perceive a threat in the democratization of information design that has resulted from putting information design features into computer software.

Already, there are business graphics and statistical packages advertising that the charts and graphs they produce follow principles researched and outlined by information design pioneers Edward Tufte and William Cleveland. This is occurring even though some people who call themselves information designers have not yet heard of Tufte and Cleveland!

Other software packages being designed today are gobbling up various areas of information design expertise. There is software that incorporates publishing and page-design principles commonly taught in art school. Some software packages provide templates that automatically incorporate principles of color combination, so that a user only needs to choose a cluster of colors that work together. When you can describe rules and guidelines with sufficient precision and stand behind them with sufficient research, you can put them into software so that anybody who buys the software can use them.

The ubiquity of the computer prevents us from even asking whether further democratization of this nascent profession should be welcomed. We do not have a choice. The computer provides millions, if not tens of millions, of people with the capacity to do at least a modicum of information design in the everyday documents they prepare. Thus tensions between a profession trying to emerge and consolidate and the multitude of amateurs performing many of the same tasks are likely to continue.

Information Design and Visual Language

Information design can be thought of as the professionalization of another communication phenomenon: the emergence of a new language. Visual language is defined as the tight coupling of a words, images, and shapes into a unified communication unit (Horn 1998). "Tight coupling" means that you cannot remove the words or the images or the shapes from a piece of visual language without destroying or radically diminishing the meaning a reader can obtain from it. In diagrams, for example, you cannot remove the boxes or arrows without severely damaging or destroying the communication. Words and images are tightly integrated in most business slide presentations and in many examples of information graphics used by newspapers and magazines. Similarly, tight integration is apparent in the words and images in comic books, in most advertising, as well as in most video, film, and animation. A great many publications, both in paper and on-line, are now composed least partly of visual language.

Visual language is a language, I maintain, because one cannot understand its syntax, semantics, or pragmatics by using only the linguistic concepts developed to analyze spoken languages. Nor are the tools of analysis used by either the visual arts or linguistics sufficient to analyze what is happening in visual language. To create a true linguistics of visual language we need new concepts that focus on how words and images work together.

Visual language has emerged just as other languages have—by people creating it and speaking it. It has evolved, I believe, because of the urgent needs of contemporary individuals and organizations to deal with complexity. Many ideas are best expressed with visual language, and others can only be expressed by visual language.

Along with information design, visual language has also developed rapidly in the past decade because of the personal computer and, especially, the widespread availability of computer graphics programs—software that allows the user to draw, paint, and present quantitative information in chart form. In many ways, practitioners of information design have been the inventors and first users of visual language. They have helped it spread. And, as visual language has become democratized into what some now call our *visual culture*, many people have realized that there is a great need for more professionalized information design.

Changes in the Ratio of Visual Elements to Words

One major shift to which research has called attention is the dramatic increase in the image-to-word ratio in documents of all kinds (Horn 1998). Many publications that in the past might have used one illustration per article now have one illustration per page. Thus the sheer volume of visual elements has changed. But that is not all. In my characterization of visual language, I focus attention on the tight integration of words and visual elements, whereas in the old document paradigm, words and images are separated. Images were referred to as *figures* and often did not even appear on the page on which they were discussed. That practice is changing; more and more, words and images are coming together.

Also underway is "the Great Sorting Out of the Functions of Words and Images When They Are Tightly Integrated." In the Sorting Out, we study what words do best and what it is that the visual elements do best when the two are tightly integrated; that is, we are developing the functional semantics of visual language. It turns out that we need a whole set of new guidelines and rules for understanding this tight integration, principles that are quite different from those used when words and images operate separately (Horn 1998). As we understand this integration more comprehensively and deeply, we apparently increase the integration of our own words and images. This has happened in my own work on the analysis of the words and images in diagrams: they have become more integrated. The functional semantics of visual language can now be extended to fully effect the tight integration of visual elements and words.

Conclusion

In ancient times, scribes had to invent the papyrus on which they wrote. Over many centuries they modified writing symbols from ideographs to phonetic script to meet the changing needs of their times. Their modern counterparts, tomorrow's information designers, will also have to improve the tools and techniques of their trade to meet the even more rapid and complex changes of the twenty-first century.

The profession may well develop along the lines taken by medicine, where training in the foundational sciences is combined with internships, residencies, and practice to train the effective professional. In many ways we already see this kind of training emerging in the field of interactive interface design (Winograd 1996).

If the profession becomes more unified and practitioners understand that it rests on a multifaceted foundation of both creative design and rigorous research, it will continue to make major contributions to solving human communication problems. This future will require greater professional self-consciousness, the development and sharing of good practices, and increased incorporation of research findings into the design process. And, finally, it will require all of us to accept the democratization of information design.

Notes

1. Current research on the use of information can be found in many sources, including Special Interest Group on Graphics (SIGGRAPH) and Special Interest Group on Computer-Human Interaction (SIGCHI); All publications of the Association of Computing Machinery (ACM); research journals in human factors engineering and the graphics arts; and, especially, the *Information Design Journal* (address: Information Design Association, PO Box 239, Reading RG6 2AU, England; e-mail: ltstiff@reading.ac.uk) and *Visible Language* (U.S.A.), published by the Rhode Island School of Design (R.I.S.D., Graphic Design Dept., 2 College Street, Providence, R.I. 02903).

2. The primary source of training in structured writing is Information Mapping, Inc. (address: 300 Third Avenue, Waltham, Mass. 02154; telephone: 617-890-7003). Information Mapping is a registered trademark of Information Mapping, Inc.

3. VLicon is a trademark of the visual language and information design work of Robert E. Horn, 2819 Jackson Street #101, San Francisco, Calif. 94115. For a complete discussion of the functional semantics of VLicons, see Horn 1997.

References

Baker, Stephen. 1961. *Visual Persuasion*. New York: McGraw-Hill.

Beniger, James R., and Robyn, Dorothy L. 1978. Quantitative Graphics in Statistics: A Brief History. *American Statistician* 32, no. 1 (February 1978): 1–11.

Bertin, Jacques. 1983. *Semiology of Graphics: Diagrams, Networks, and Maps*. Madison: University of Wisconsin Press.

Bliss, E. K. 1965. *Semantography*, 2d ed. Sydney, Australia: Semantography Publications.

Bonsiepe, G. 1966. *Visual/Verbal Rhetoric*. Dot Zero.

Bowman, William J. 1968. *Graphic Communication*. New York: John Wiley.

Cleveland, William S. 1985. *The Elements of Graphing Data*. Pacific Grove, Calif.: Wadsworth and Brooks/Cole.

Cohen, I. Bernard. 1984. Florence Nightingale. *Scientific American* 250, no. 3 (March): 128–37.

Corel Corporation. 1994. *Corel Gallery Clipart Catalog*. Ottawa.

Dreyfus, Henry. 1984. *Symbol Source Book: An Authoritative Guide to International Graphic Symbols*. New York: Van Nostrand Reinhold.

Easterby, R. S., and Graydon, I. R. 1981 Comprehension/recognition tests. *AP Report* 100 (January 1981). (Birmingham, England: University of Aston.)

Eisner, W. 1985. *Comics and Sequential Art*. Tamarac, Fla.: Poorhouse Press.

Evans, Harold. 1974. *Handling Newspaper Text*. London: William Heinemann.

Eysenck, M. W., and Keane, M. T. 1990. *Cognitive Psychology: A Student's Handbook*. Hillsdale, N.J.: Lawrence Erlbaum.

Fleming, M., and Levie, W. H., eds. 1993. *Instructional Message Design*, 2d ed. Englewood Cliffs, N.J.: Educational Technology Publications.

Funkhouser, H. G. 1938. Historical Development of the Graphical Representation of Statistical Data. *Osiris* 3: 269–404.

Glover, Gary. 1994. *Clip Art: Image Enhancement and Integration*. New York: McGraw-Hill.

Goldsmith, Evelyn. 1984. *Research into Illustration: An Approach and a Review*. Cambridge: Cambridge University Press.

Gombrich, E. H. 1960. *Art and Illusion*. New York: Pantheon.

Holmes, Nigel. 1991. *Pictorial Maps*. New York: Watson-Guptill.

Holmes, Nigel. 1993. *The Best in Diagrammatic Graphics*. Mies, Switzerland: Rotovision.

Holmes, Nigel. 1984. *Designer's Guide to Creating Charts and Diagrams*. New York: Watson-Guptill.

Holmes, Nigel, and DeNeve, Rose. 1985. *Designing Pictorial Symbols*. New York: Watson-Guptill.

Horn, Robert E. 1989. *Mapping Hypertext: Analysis, Linkage, and Display of Knowledge for the Next Generation of On-Line Text and Graphics*. (Available from Information Mapping, Inc., 300 Third Avenue, Waltham, MA. 02154. Telephone 1-800-627-4544 or 617-890-7003.)

Horn, R. E. 1992a. Clarifying Two Controversies about Information Mapping's Method. *Educational and Training Technology International* 2 (no. 29): 109–117.

Horn, R. E. 1992b. *How High Can It Fly? Examining the Evidence on Information Mapping's Method of High-Performance Communication.* Lexington, Mass: The Lexington Institute.

Horn, R. E. 1993. Structured Writing at Twenty-five. *Performance and Instruction* (Feb.): 11–17.

Horn, R. E. 1997. Structured Writing as a Paradigm. In *Instructional Development, State of the Art*, Charles R. Dills and Alexander Romiszowski, eds. Englewood Cliffs, N.J.: Educational Technology Publications.

Horn, R. E. 1998. *Visual Language: A Global Language for the 21st Century.* Bainbridge Island, Wash.: MacroVU®, Inc. (Available from the publisher, Box 366, 321 High School Road, Bainbridge Island, WA 98110.)

Horton, W. 1991. *Illustrating Computer Documentation—The Art of Presenting Information Graphically in Paper and Online.* New York: John Wiley.

Horton, William. 1994. *The Icon Book: Visual Symbols for Computer Systems and Documentation.* New York: John Wiley.

Kosslyn, Stephen M. 1989. Understanding charts and graphs. *Applied Cognitive Psychology* 3: 185–226.

Kosslyn, Stephen M. 1994. *Elements of Graph Design.* New York: W. H. Freeman.

Macaulay, David. 1988. *The Way Things Work.* Boston: Houghton Mifflin.

McCloud, Scott. 1993. *Understanding Comics: The Invisible Art.* Northampton, Mass.: Kitchen Sink Press.

McKim, Robert. 1972. *Experiences in Visual Thinking.* Monterey, Calif.: Brooks/Cole.

McKim, Robert. 1980. *Thinking Visually: A Strategy for Problem Solving.* Belmont, Calif.: Wadsworth.

Modley, Rudolf, and Lowenstein, Dyno. 1952. *Pictographs and Graphs.* New York: Harper.

Neurath, Otto. 1973. ISOTYPE: International System of Typographic Picture Education. In *Empiricism and Sociology*, M. Neurath and R. S. Cohen, eds. Dordrecht, The Netherlands: D. Reidel.

Pettersson, Rune. 1989. *Visuals for Information: Research and Practice.* Englewood Cliffs, N.J.: Educational Technology Publications.

Playfair, William. 1786. *The Commercial and Political Atlas.* London

Sibbet, David. 1980. *Fundamentals of Graphic Language: Practice Book*. San Francisco: Graphic Guides.

Sibbet, David. 1981. *I See What You Mean!* San Francisco: Sibbet & Associates.

Shneiderman, Ben. 1987, 1992. *Designing the User Interface: Strategies for Effective Human-Computer Interaction*. Reading, Mass.: Addison-Wesley.

Sless, David. 1986. *In Search of Semiotics*. London: Croom Helm.

Smith, Sidney L., and Mosier, Jane N. 1986. *Guidelines for Designing User Interface Software*. Bedford, Mass.: Mitre Corporation.

Thompson, P., and Davenport, P. 1980. *The Dictionary of Graphic Images*. New York: St. Martins.

Tinker, Miles A. 1963. *Legibility of Print*. Ames: Iowa State University Press.

Tufte, Edward. 1983. *The Visual Display of Quantitative Information*. Cheshire, Conn.: Graphics Press.

Tufte, Edward. 1990. *Envisioning Information*. Cheshire, Conn.: Graphics Press.

Tufte, Edward. 1997. *Visual Explanation*. Cheshire, Conn.: Graphics Press.

Twyman, Michael A. 1979. Schema for the Study of Graphic Language. In *The Processing of Visible Language*, P. A. Kolers, M. E. Wrolstad, and H. Bouma, eds. New York: Plenum.

Twyman, Michael A. 1990. *Early Lithographed Books*. London: Farrand Press.

U.S. National Bureau of Standards. 1967. *Legibility of Alphanumeric Characters and Other Symbols, II. A Reference Handbook*. Washington, D.C.: U.S. Department of Commerce.

Winn, William. 1990. Encoding and Retrieval of Information in Maps and Diagrams. *IEEE Transactions on Professional Communication* 33 (no. 3): 103–107.

Winn, William. 1982. *Design Principles for Diagrams and Charts in the Technology of Text*, pp. 277–99. Englewood Cliffs, N.J.: Educational Technology Publications.

Winograd, Terry, ed. 1996. *Bringing Design to Software*. Reading, Mass.: Addison-Wesley.

Wurman, Richard Saul. 1989. *Information Anxiety*. New York: Doubleday.

Wurman, Richard Saul. 1992. *Follow the Yellow Brick Road: Learning to Give, Take and Use Instructions*. New York: Bantam.

Wurman, Richard Saul. 1997. *Information Architects*. New York: Watson-Guptill.

Zelazny, Gene. 1991. *Say It With Charts*. Homewood, Ill. Business One Irwin.

3   *Chaos, Order, and Sense-Making: A Proposed Theory for Infomation Design*

Brenda Dervin

The writers represented in this volume offer the term *information design* as a designator for a new arena of activity. Their underlying assumption is that as a species we face altered circumstances that demand a new practice. They further assume that prior to the advance of the new communication technologies there was no pressing need for information design; without these increasingly unnatural channels, people effectively distributed information through existing channels in natural ways.

Information Design: Something New, Something Old

While granting that others have drawn many strong arguments from these assumptions, I want in this chapter to challenge the central idea that information design is a new idea. Reducing the issues briefly to a polarity, it is useful to start by considering two ways to conceptualize information. One way, implicit in the above assumptions, is that information is something that describes an ordered reality and has some knowable, or at least idealized, isomorphic relationship to that reality (i.e., it represents in an identical way the form and content of reality). In short, information instructs us, this assumption says, about the nature of the world we live in: its history, its future, its functioning, our place in it, our possible actions, and the potential consequences of those actions. Information, conceptualized in this way, can only be seen as inherently beneficial, for it offers enormous survival value. Clearly, such a set of assumptions makes the economic and effective distribution of information an uncontested mandate.[1]

Intrinsic to this way of conceptualizing information is the implication that the "something" labeled *information* can be readily distributed, like concrete objects, from time to time, place to place, and person to person.[2] To follow this metaphor to its conclusion, we must put aside temporarily any misgivings we may have about the capacities of human beings to act as observers. Aside, then, from needed improvements in human powers of observation, in this metaphor we see information as a natural thing potentially movable from place to place by natural means. In our current circumstances, therefore, only the fact that unnatural forces are at work demands that we create a new practice: information design.

A second, alternative view of information contests this scenario. Evidence is accumulating that we are using the enormous capacities of the new technologies to do what we have already done in the past—though on far larger scales, much faster, at greater distances, and with much greater frequency. Further, taking a hard look at fundamentals and setting aside issues of scale, I argue in this chapter that the information design thus far offered by the new technologies is not that much different from that made possible by the old technologies or, since early history, by nontechnological human practices.

In order to consider these fundamentals in detail, however, we must start with an alternative assumption about information itself: that there is nothing natural about information. Information, no matter what it is called—data, knowledge, or fact, song, story, or metaphor—has *always* been designed. This alternative assumption about information is what drives this chapter. In it, I argue that assuming information design to be a new practice can only deter us from facing head-on some alternative conceptualizations of what that activity could be about.

In the succeeding sections of this chapter, I develop this argument by first presenting a brief history of our treatments of the concept *information* and discussing the implications of these treatments for a practice called *information design*. I then extract from this discussion guiding principles important for theorizing about the practice of information design. Next, I present an exemplar theory, methodology, and practice called Sense-Making, which embodies these principles. I conclude with several illustrations of how Sense-Making can be applied to practical situations.

Concepts of Information: A Brief History

It is beyond the purpose of this chapter to dig deeply into the historical roots of our treatments of the concept *information*. Rather, my goal here is to provide briefly a context for the alternative I am presenting. We can simplify a complex history by tracing the treatments of information in the western tradition through seven roughly chronological narratives.

1. Information describes an ordered reality.

2. Information describes an ordered reality but can be "found" only by those with the proper observing skills and technologies.

3. Information describes an ordered reality that varies across time and space.

4. Information describes an ordered reality that varies from culture to culture.

5. Information describes an ordered reality that varies from person to person.

6. Information is an instrument of power imposed in discourse on those without power.

7. Information imposes order on a chaotic reality.

While I present these narratives in the rough chronological order of their appearance in the philosophical literature, the chronology is really cumulative, in the sense that all narratives are present in our time in various combinations and in both commensurate and highly contested arrangements. We could describe the narratives extensively in terms of their philosophic underpinnings. For present purposes, however, we need provide only just enough of the basic ideas behind them to give foundation to my argument. Essentially, the argument is this. Historically, information was conceptualized as a natural description of natural reality. This way of seeing information remains the dominant conceptualization assumed in the design of information systems—and it is heavy baggage. Most of our ideas about information design attempt to achieve narrative No. 1 while struggling with narratives Nos. 2 through 7.

There are three themes that run through the chronology of narratives. One focuses on the nature of reality, one on the nature of human observing, and one on the involvement of power. Briefly, the chronology suggests that over time conceptualizations of information's capacity to describe reality (i.e. its ontological assumptions) have first been tempered and then directly contested. The tempering came first with a growing understanding of the limits of human observation (as in No. 2); then with a growing understanding of the impacts of time and space (as in No. 3). Ultimately, the very foundational assumptions of reality were shaken (as in Nos. 6 and 7). At one extreme we have an ordered and universal reality; at the other, a chaotic and inaccessible reality.

The second theme focuses on human observing, which, the chronology suggests, was historically assumed to create "informations" that were isomorphic with reality (as in No. 1). Over time, this conceptualization evolved: first to incorporate the idea that information needed a way to correct and control the potential biases and errors of human observing (as in No. 2); and then, in chronological steps, to accept the relativistic notion that observing differs according to contextual, cultural, and personal perspectives (as in Nos. 3, 4, and 5). Finally, most recently, it integrated the belief that human observing is a product of discourses of power (as in No. 6). At one extreme, therefore, we have an epistemology assuming a universally applicable ability to observe an ordered reality and at the other an entirely relativistic, solipsistic (i.e., unique to each person), or tyrannical view of observation.

The third theme focuses on the involvement of power in information. This theme is more subtle, because it does not permeate the movement across narratives but rather bursts forth suddenly in No. 6. In earlier assumptions, power was irrelevant; information was assumed to have a universal character based on an assumed capacity to precisely mirror reality. Moving through the narratives, however, we can see the impact of historical struggles with power: cultural relativity, for example, applied to ideas about information argues for the right of peoples' observings to differ, not only across time and space (as in No. 3), but also across cultures (as in No. 4). But people within cultures differ as well, and when individual voices demand to be heard we see the emergence of personal relativity (as in No. 5) and, ultimately, the concept that all attempts to formalize information are bounded within discourses of power (as in No. 6).

We have drastically abbreviated a great deal of philosophical history in the above paragraphs. The important point for our purposes here is this: we can think of narratives Nos. 2 through 7 as resulting, in part, from struggles to maintain narrative No. 1. Nested within the narratives are a host of polarities that plague the design and implementation of information systems—not to mention the very construction of our societies. Alternatively, however, we can reconceptualize the narratives as subordinate parts of a larger picture. Sometimes, this view assumes, information describes an orderly reality; sometimes it requires specialized observing skills and technologies; sometimes it varies across time and space, and from culture to culture and person to person. Sometimes it represents the imposition of power; sometimes it imposes order on chaotic reality. If one accepts all the narratives as useful, the difficulty becomes how to transcend the seemingly inherent contradictions among them. For these purposes, therefore, I propose an eighth narrative:

8. Information is a tool designed by human beings to make sense of a reality assumed to be both chaotic and orderly.

The Alternative Narrative and Its Implications

It is possible to look at narratives Nos. 2 through 7 as a struggle with two ideas inherent in narrative No. 1—the notions of a fixed and orderly reality and of *a human power to observe that can accurately perceive that reality*. As the historical narrative unfolds, increasing complexities are introduced into the assumptions underlying the nature of observing, while assumptions about reality are reduced to an impossibly simple choice—either reality is orderly or it is inaccessible and chaotic.

Narrative No. 8 builds on the earlier narratives most clearly in its position on observing at the same time as it attempts to transcend the impossible choice by accepting both the ordered realities of narratives Nos. 1 through 5 and the imposed/chaotic realities of narratives Nos. 6 and 7. Thus narrative No. 8 posits that humans live in a reality that sometimes manifests itself in orderly ways and sometimes manifests itself in chaotic ways.

The importance of this ontological position lies in its implications for how systems handle human differences in information-making. Narratives Nos. 1 through 5, after presenting all the reasons why people see the world differently, cannot resolve the differences or find a way to ameliorate them except with a tautology: people see the world differently because they differ. Thus there is no mandate (nor any possibility) for one person to learn from another. At this point, therefore, the solipsism becomes unbearable, and we retreat for resolution to narrative Nos. 1 and 2. But each chronological advance in our theories of information makes this retreat more and more difficult, and it becomes ultimately impossible, as narrative No. 7 demonstrates.

In contrast, narrative No. 8 forces us to a different resolution, one with profound implications for information design. The resolution is that in the face of differences we must look for differences not in how humans, individually and collectively, see their worlds but in how they "make" their worlds (i.e., construct a sense of the world and how it works). This view is more than just a mandate to understand how others see the world; it makes that understanding an ontological necessity. For if we conceptualize the human condition as a struggle through an incomplete reality, then the similar struggles of others may well be informative for our own efforts.

Notice here how much traditional baggage we must jettison—the idea, for example, that there is a given amount or kind of information that can fully instruct us about a given reality. Instead, this narrative assumes that movement through a given time-space (as well as gaps in physical, natural, and/or social reality) introduces an inherent inability to be completely instructed (i.e., to attain complete information). By assuming ontological chaos as well as order, we force ourselves to understand that it may be more useful to conceptualize human beings as information designers rather than information seekers and finders.

Sometimes the information designing seems suggestive of a reality that is ordered; when, for example, a consensus regarding observing—process, product, and consequences—yields an informative outcome we call *fact* because its application to material conditions produces reliable and useful outcomes. But the only way we can account for the overbearing evidence that today's fact is tomorrow's folly, or worse the cause of tomorrow's rebellion, is to reconceptualize what is involved in facts. *Fact*, as a word, has traditionally had an essentialist meaning: a fact describes a reality that *is*. On the other hand, *factizing*, as a verb, suggests that among the many ways in which people make their worlds is a proceduring, a designing called *making facts*. There are many other words that can be used as verbs in this way. A suggestive list might include, besides *factizing: emoting, comparing, concluding, predicting, consequenting, avoiding, communing, creating, opinioning, socializing, imposing, terrorizing, inculcating, challenging, resisting,* and *destroying*.

With this simple idea—that whatever it is that humans make informationally of their worlds, they are always involved in acts of design—we can pull together the threads offered by the discussion above. The result is a view of humans who are themselves ordered and chaotic moving through a reality that is ordered and chaotic. Humans make sense individually and collectively as they move: from order to disorder, from disorder to order.

This narrative refocuses our attention away from information as such to the constant design and redesign of the sense by which humans make and unmake their worlds. Because of its emphasis on information as designed and redesigned—as made, confirmed, supported, challenged, resisted, and destroyed—this approach positions power as a primary consideration rather than as afterthought. Borrowing from narrative No. 6, this narrative requires that the power inscribed in information be subject to continuing deconstruction (i.e., constant analysis and reanalysis). One possible consequence of doing so would be a capacity in information-system design to avoid the ways in which systems now build in inequities. In essence, our current design situation is one in which information is assumed to be natural but is in fact designed. And, because it is designed without attention to design, it fits the needs, struggles, and resources of the designers. This puts all others at a disadvantage.

Theories that explain why the others don't make use of these valuable design systems can take a variety of forms. Nonetheless, they can be summarized in the argument that humans are too chaotic and overwhelmingly various to make responsive system designs possible. Yet, if in fact we have developed theories of information and system designs based on narratives Nos. 1 to 5, then we know that, ultimately, difference can always be measured against a standard. The system is X; people who cannot or will not use it are not-X. Research efforts to understand these recalcitrant non-users seem to show that they lack both understanding of and interest in what is deemed by the designers to be appropriate use of the system. This finding, in turn, leads some to conclude that information design must be reduced to the lowest common denominator and, in turn, to theories of madness or badness that locate the source of problems in users' defects. Such theories persist despite ample evidence to the contrary.

Some Principles for a Theory of Information Design

Each of the earlier narratives about information moves us away from the idea that seeking and finding information does not involve design. What emerges in narrative No. 8 is a conceptualization of information that, although informed by the complexities of narratives Nos. 6 and 7, does not abandon the human potential for observing implied by the earlier narratives.

For purposes of our discussion, I label narrative No. 8 a *communication perspective on information*. The central idea here is that information is made and unmade in communication—intrapersonal, interpersonal, social, organizational, national, and global. With this view of information, information design cannot treat information as a mere thing to be economically and effectively packaged for distribution. Rather, it insists that information design is, in effect, metadesign: design about design, design to assist people to make and unmake their own informations, their own sense. Some of these metadesigns may pertain to human activities amenable to fact transmission, though studies suggest that relatively few human uses of information can be addressed solely in a factizing mode. The theory behind narrative No. 8 also contends that metadesign must deal with the entire complex range of what humans do when they make sense, when they construct their movements through what is assumed to be an ever-changing, sometimes chaotic, sometimes orderly, sometimes impenetrable time-space.

Narrative No. 8, then, mandates a particular kind of theory, one that focuses on information as made and unmade in communication; as designed by all humans, individually and collectively, in struggle and mediation; as relevant to both making and unmaking order and chaos; as theoretically incomplete and always open to potential challenge; as relevant not only to the centered human but also the decentered human; as pertinent to the human heart, body, and spirit as well as the human mind.

Further, this theory of information design decrees that we create an information system to assist people in designing their own information and, in particular, in sharing with each other the ways in which they have struggled individually and collectively to both create order out of chaos and create chaos out of order when order restricts or constrains them. Such a theory would demand that we redefine the standards by which we judge something as informative: in essence, redefine what we mean by success and failure. The system would allow not only the factizing that permits regimentation as a sometimes useful way of making sense but also the myths and storytelling that permit us to tolerate and muddle through diversities and seeming incompletenesses.

Sense-Making: An Exemplar Theory, Methodology, and Practice

The Sense-Making approach, which has been twenty-two years in development, is in actuality a set of assumptions, a theoretic perspective, a methodological approach, a set of research methods, and a set of communication practices. The approach was originally developed to assess how patients/audiences/users/clients/citizens make sense of their intersections with institutions, media, messages, and situations and to apply the results in designing responsive communication/information systems. Since its early development, the approach has been applied in a variety of contexts (e.g., political communications, everyday information seeking, health communications, organizational images, mass media, and telecommunications). It has been used at various levels of analysis (e.g., individual, group, organization, community, culture) in both quantitative studies with sample sizes as large as a thousand and in qualitative studies with as few as twenty participants. Work resting on the approach has been published and cited, primarily, in the various communications, information, and library science fields, with some secondary usage in other fields.[3]

The phenomena of interest for Sense-Making is *sense-making*, which we define broadly in terms of the set of assumptions about reality, observing, and power suggested by narrative No. 8. Sense-Making starts with the fundamental assumption of the philosophical approach of *phenomenology* —that the actor is inherently involved in her observations, which must be understood from her perspectives and horizons. What differs in the Sense-Making formulation is the explicit acceptance of a reality assumed to be both orderly and chaotic. Sense-Making, then, brings these assumptions together by asserting that—given an incomplete understanding of reality (ontology) and an incomplete understanding of what it is to know something (epistemology)—we arrive at an uncompromising problematic for the human species: how to bridge persistent gaps in existence (gaps between self at time 1 and time 2, between person 1 and person 2, between person and society, organization and organization, and so on).

From this reasoning, Sense-Making extracts two assumed mandates for the species: one is to make sense without complete instruction in a reality, which is itself in flux and requires continued sense-making; the second is to reach out to the sense made by others, in order to understand what insights it may provide into our continuing human dilemma. Sense-Making emphasizes the importance of the latter requirement in particular, for it is not rooted (as most calls for understanding difference are) only in a relativistic epistemology but rather in the assumption that humans *must* muddle through together and that their usual tools assuming a wholly ordered reality are inadequate for making sense of all their experiences in a world that is both ordered and chaotic.

Setting this understanding within the common polarities of social theorizing today, Sense-Making explicitly enters the research situation in the "in-between" spaces between order and chaos, structure and individual, culture and person, self 1 and self 2, and so on. Sense-Making focuses on how humans make and unmake, develop, maintain, resist, destroy, and change order, structure, culture, organization, relationships, and the self.

The Sense-Making theoretic assumptions are implemented through a core methodological metaphor that pictures the person as moving through time-space, bridging gaps, and moving on. Sense-Making thus requires theorizing based on concepts relating to *time*, *space*, *movement*, and *gap*. It also rests on a theory of the subject that is consonant with its ontological and epistemological assumptions: the human is conceptualized as centered and decentered; ordered and chaotic; cognitive, physical, spiritual, and emotional; and potentially differing in all these dimensions across time and across space. Sense-Making assumes that the rigidities in information use implicitly hypothesized by demographic, personality, and many constructivist theories pertain only to a subset of human possibilities. As humans move across time-space, both rigidities and flexibilities are possible. Sense-Making assumes that one of the reasons why our theories of information use and their potential applications to design have been so weak is that they have focused primarily on predicting patterns in rigidities, rather than patterns in flexibilities.

One way in which Sense-Making differs markedly from other approaches is that it explicitly, and necessarily, privileges the ordinary person as a theorist involved in developing ideas to guide an understanding of not only her personal world but also collective, historical, and social worlds. Sense-making must theorize about the individual human in this way because of narrative No. 8's acceptance of ontological incompleteness. If reality is incomplete, then movement through it must be guided by theory, not merely by fact. Further, in its attention to movement, Sense-Making requires us to focus on power by attending to forces that facilitate movement and forces that inhibit and constrain movement.

While Sense-Making relies heavily on concepts of time, space, movement, and gap, we must emphasized that these are not set forth as if sense-making were merely a purposive, linear, problem-solving activity. Instead, they are posited as merely a subset of human possibilities. The Sense-Making metaphor must be understood as a highly abstract framework. Similarly, while Sense-Making focuses on the human individual, it does not rest on an individualistic theory of human action. Rather, it assumes that structure, culture, community, organization are created, maintained, reified, challenged, changed, resisted, and destroyed in communication and can only be understood by focusing on the individual-in-context, including the social context. Note, however, that this is not the same as saying that the only way to look at the individual is through the lens of social context; this kind theorizing would imply that the individual is entirely constrained or defined by that social context, which would admit no room for resisting, changing, inventing, or muddling through.

In the context of both research and applications, Sense-Making is implemented within the Sense-Making *triangle*, which encapsulates the Sense-Making metaphor in a picture of the human (individually or collectively) moving from a situation (time-space) across a gap by making a bridge, and then moving onto the other side of the bridge. The three points of this triangle, therefore, are situation, gap/bridge, and outcome.

In the research context, for example, the Sense-Making metaphor may be implemented in interviews in several ways, ranging from brief interviews of twenty to thirty minutes to in-depth interviews lasting from one or two hours and up to six hours. The foundational interviewing approach, the one most aligned with Sense-Making's theory, is called the *micro-moment time-line interview*. In this approach the interviewer asks the respondent to describe one or more critical situations in detail: first in terms of what happened first, second, third, and so on; then, for each time-line event, in terms of the situations (e.g., barriers, constraints, history, memory, experience), gaps (e.g., confusions, worries, questions, muddles), bridges (e.g., ideas, conclusions, feelings, opinions, hypotheses, hunches, stories, values, strategies, sources), and outcomes (e.g., helps, facilitations, hurts, hindrances, outcomes, effects, impacts). Since Sense-Making provides only a theory of the interview and not a script, actual implementation can take myriad forms, depending on the purpose of the study (e.g., needs assessment, evaluation, audience reception, etc.). In an alternative approach, the respondent is examined in detail about the basic time-line and then asked to choose the most important event, or question, or contact, and so on. Some interviews begin with the situation, others with the gap, the bridge, or the outcome.

It is important to note that Sense-Making conceptualizes the research situation as itself an applied communication situation involving attempts to understand how others have designed their senses of their worlds. In this situation, the researcher is involved in a metadesign focusing on design. Similarly, in application to what is commonly called *practice*, Sense-Making posits a theory of practice, a metadesign for design. In this way, there is no discontinuity between Sense-Making as a research approach and Sense-Making as an approach to the design of practice. In the following sections of this chapter I present some illustrations of applications to practice and draw some conclusions from those applications.

Some Applications

To date, as Sense-Making has been applied primarily in research contexts, most of the applications to practice have been hypothetical. There have been, however, a number of actual practice applications. We can use these applications, along with several hypothetical cases, to show how the theoretic guidance offered by narrative No. 8 translates into a theory of the practice of information design and, ultimately, to metadesign. The illustrations that follow are presented in no particular order; their selection has been guided only by a wish to present variety.[4] While only a few of the examples described are highly technologized, it is a fundamental assumption of Sense-Making that the enormous flexibilities the new technologies offer make implementation of Sense-Making in practice potentially powerful.

In implementing such systems, fundamental questions would need to be answered, such as: How much diversity is sufficient to trigger user sense-making? How can we serve factizing needs without cutting-off challenges to factizing and without retreating to a conceptualization of information as a thing to be transferred? How do we handle vested interests? Can a profession serve the sense-making needs of users without being subject to the powerful influences of other professionals who have vested interests in particular kinds of sense? Given the enormity of these questions, some might contend that the illustrations presented are exercises in impractical idealism. One alternative point of view, however, suggests that there is a large space in society for professional facilitators of sense-making. Yet another suggests that the myriad challenges we see to nation-states, organizational systems, and all kinds of experts are manifestations of the failure of these structures and experts to be informationally useful to people.

Sense-Making the Reference Interview

The most extensive application of Sense-Making to date has been at the library reference desk. An estimated five hundred professional librarians at several locales have been trained to use the Sense-Making approach in the reference interview. Some reference librarians report that they have changed entirely to this approach, while others say they combine Sense-Making with other techniques. Librarians using this approach as a dialogic interface between librarian and patron focus on developing a picture of the user's sense-making triangle. To do so, they ask such questions as: What led you to ask this question? How do you hope to be helped? If you could get the best possible answer, what would it be like? What are you trying to do?

Journal Authors as Sense-Makers

In a small test application, abstracts of ten journal articles were prepared for students in two classes. Traditional abstracts and keywords were presented to one class. In the second class, in addition to these traditional elements, students were given authors' answers to such Sense-Making questions as: What was it that you hoped to accomplish with this article? What led you to write it? How did writing it help you? How do you think it will help others? What was your major struggle with the article? What remains unresolved? Students were asked to rank the articles in terms of their potential usefulness and were then given copies of the actual articles to use in writing term papers. Three months later they were asked to rate the articles' actual usefulness. The actual and potential usefulness rankings of the students who received the Sense-Making abstracts were significantly closer than those who received the traditional abstracts. The implication is that author abstracts guided by Sense-Making provided more potential bridges of connection to readers.

Sacrificing the Coherent Journalism Narrative

In this small-scale test application, journalism students were taught to sacrifice the coherent narrative that is the foundation stone of journalistic practice and, instead, to surround their phenomena of interest within the kind of circling of reality mandated by Sense-Making. The students were taught to ask themselves questions such as: What leads me to care about this? Who else cares? What leads them to care? What different groups of people care? Within groups, what disagreements might there be? What would be alternative views of the reasons for the dispute? Is there consensus across groups/people on any points? What explains this? The student journalists were also taught how to select for observation and interview people at five or six maximally different sites, taking into account issues of power and difference, and, within sites, to seek out both conflict and consensus and people with and without power. In writing up the results of their efforts, the students were to display the results as a number of incomplete, sometimes overlapping, sometimes disparate narratives rather than as one coherent narrative. To assess the results, a group of student readers talked with the student journalists, focusing the discussion on such questions as: Given that a journalist cannot present all viewpoints in an article, what degree of difference among interviewees—and within the minds of individual interviewees—would be sufficient to trigger the reader's own sense-making processes? How could technologies be used to implement this kind of journalism?

Transforming a Professional Stereotype

Interested in the level of activity around its video desk, a public library asked users to explain how the videos they watched helped them. The results transformed how the librarians thought about their video collections. Users reported a range of life-enhancing and survival outcomes that ran counter to the stereotype of video as an entertainment medium. As a result, the library both increased its video budget and developed programmatic connections between the video collection and literacy training.

How Books Help

At another library, readers were invited to post their answers to the following questions on a bulletin board: How did the book you are returning today help you? What leads you to say this? Librarians observed that patrons stood at the board for long periods reading other readers' responses. They also noticed an increase in demand for several books that ordinarily had low circulations.

Student Sense-Making

A trial Sense-Making system was developed for a college class. First, researchers interviewed students who had taken the class in the past. Using Sense-Making, they asked the former students to describe the sense-making they had applied to writing their term papers. After analyzing the situations, gaps, bridges, and helps the students reported, researchers structured them into an interactive computer program so that new students could plot their own paths through the input on an as-needed basis. A large number of paths were possible; students could enter through situations, gaps, bridges, or helps. For example, a student might start by choosing a situation description ("I hate this class"), a bridge ("What's the best resource on this topic?"), a gap ("How can I choose a topic when I'm so confused"), or an outcome ("What's the easiest way to do this?"). Once through the gate of each entry, additional gates were offered, again developed inductively based on the actual sense-making needs of those who had gone through the experience in the past. Students could, for example, ask a question and then select the kind of answer they would like—for example, what a librarian said, what the teacher said, what a good student or a selection of different students said. Users could also add their own comments if they found that their own sense-making needs were not well enough represented.

Information Presentation at a Blood Donating Center

At a blood center, donors' needs for information usually arise within the context of a sequenced movement of intake, testing, preparation, donating, and recovering. Most attempts to inform donors about the process, however, occur before they come to the center. A Sense-Making study showed that there are reasonably well-demarcated sequences of sense-making that can address donors' information needs and questions at particular points in the process. Results also suggested that donors often had information needs they could not easily articulate publicly; these could be handled with a donor-controlled, interactive, path-flexible sense-making system. The research results also indicated that donors were well aware of disagreements and differences of opinion among health professionals that sometimes produced different answers to their questions, and they wanted the information system to address these varying perspectives.

Information Sheets for Patients

In a small-scale application at a cancer clinic, patient information sheets concentrated on the major questions raised during Sense-Making interviews. Each sheet focused on one question. Since patients' interviews showed that they were very concerned about conflicts in information, the sheets placed major emphasis on those issues. The typical question was followed by answers from three or four doctors, one or two nurses, and several patients. The answers were followed with comments that circled around the conflicts, each source explaining her or his understanding of what accounted for the differences.

Surveilling an Organization

In an organizational context, a leader used Sense-Making to begin every staff meeting by asking each staff member to talk briefly about the preceding week's work. What successes did you have last week? What successes did we collectively have last week? What made these successes possible? What barriers or struggles did you face last week? What barriers or struggles did we collectively face last week? What do you see as leading to these barriers/struggles? What do you think would help overcome them? The leader reported that participants resisted the process at first but that over time it become a meeting highlight. In addition, the leader noted that consensus-building became much easier and that staff members became more and more tolerant of and cooperative with each other. Further, critical needs for information collecting became more clearly apparent, and people's efforts to answer the questions grew less wasteful and better focused.

Constructing a Research Community

Much the same approach was used in a research community where each participant presented his or her work for group discussion. Presentations were kept brief—no more than thirty minutes—and no interruptions were allowed. At the end of the presentation, each listener was asked to speak for three or four minutes in answer to these questions: What was helpful to you about this presentation? How did it help? What connections do you see between your work and this presentation? What leads you to say that? What confused you about this presentation? What would have helped you handle that confusion? What would you have liked to see in this presentation that was not there? How would that have helped you? After this round, the subject was opened up for general discussion. Evaluations by both leader and participants suggested that the process helped everyone enter more easily into constructive dialogue and find ways to connect with and assist each others' work.

Self Sense-Making

In this application, people used the detailed micro-moment time-line interview to ask themselves about a situation of struggle or confusion or threat. Following the usual approaches to the interview, the self-interviewers described what happened in detail and then examined each time-line step in terms of what conclusions or ideas or thoughts had arisen, what emotions or feelings they felt, and what confusions or worries they faced. Each conclusion, idea, thought, emotion, feeling, confusion, worry was then probed. What led to it? How does it connect to the rest of my life? Did it help me or facilitate my efforts? Did it hurt or hinder me?

How? What constraints or barriers or forces are at play? What explains these? Over the past twenty years more than a thousand people have conducted these self-interviews. Many have observed increases in their understanding of not only themselves but also others and the conditions and events that affect them. Further, they have reported improvements in understanding how and what information from others could be helpful in similar situations.

Conclusions

In this chapter I have traced briefly the history of theories of information design and have proposed that we must change our theory if we are to pursue a practice that is maximally helpful to the human condition. I have also presented an exemplar approach called Sense-Making, whose theory and methodology calls for looking at information design as a dialogic circling of reality, a reality that can be reached for but never touched, described in gossamer but never sculpted. This practice focuses on meta-design—design about design—and explicitly acknowledges that its work involves not merely transferring information from here to there but assisting human beings in their information design.

If we are to pursue this challenge, we will have to examine our use of terms traditionally held to be fundamental to information processes—*fact, knowledge, data*—and, even, the concept *information* itself. Our views of information are challenged by what many observers call the most important philosophic rupture of our time, with order on one side and chaos on the other. Traditional views of information define it as serving the former and threatened by the latter. What I propose in this chapter is a reconceptualization that chooses both order and chaos and that focuses on the ways humans individually and collectively design the sense (i.e., create the information) that permits them to move from one to the other. Some may see this reconceptualization as diminishing the role of information design, but an alternative view suggests that it may enrich that role to one of far-reaching consequences for the human species.

Notes

1. Since the mandate for this volume is to write for a diverse audience, I present the arguments in this chapter in as accessible language as possible without arduously tracing the roots of ideas and supplying detailed footnotes. Citations are reduced to the bare essentials and to only the most recent work by scholars whose ideas I have relied on. Readers who wish more detailed and extensive presentations—albeit developed for different purposes—are directed to Dervin 1993, 1992, 1989a, 1989b, 1994. I owe particular gratitude to Richard F. Carter (1989, 1991), whose work has informed my own thinking more than any other.

2. In this chapter, the terms *information, knowledge, knowing, data,* and *truth* are used purposely without any attempt to distinguish precisely among them. The intent is to point out the ways we use these terms without definition in everyday discourse, even everyday scholarship. It is a major premise of this article that most of the conceptual edifices constructed to distinguish one term from another in fact posit *truth*—defined as statements isomorphic to reality—as the criterion for knowledge and information.

3. In this presentation, Sense-Making the approach is distinguished from sense-making the phenomena by the use of two capital letters.

4. More complete descriptions of most of these examples can be found in Dervin 1992, Dervin 1989a, and Dervin and Dewdney 1986. More information can also be obtained from the author.

References

Best, S., and Kellner, D. 1991. *Postmodern Theory.* New York: Guilford Press.

Bruner, J. 1990. *Acts of Meaning.* Cambridge: Harvard University Press.

Carter, R. F. 1989. Reinventing communication, scientifically. In *World Community in Post-industrial society: Continuity and Change in Communications in Post-industrial Society,* vol. 2. Seoul, Korea: Wooseok.

Carter, R. F. 1991. Comparative analysis, theory, and cross-cultural communication. *Communication Theory* 1: 151–58.

Clifford, J. 1986. Introduction: Partial truths. In *Writing Culture: The Poetics and Politics of Ethnography,* J. Clifford and G. E. Marcus, eds., pp. 1–26. Berkeley: University of California Press.

Dervin, B. 1989a. Audience as listener and learner, teacher and confidante: The sense-making approach. In *Public Communication Campaigns,* 2nd ed., R. Rice and C. Atkin, eds., pp. 67–86. Newbury Park, Calif.: Sage Publications.

Dervin, B. 1989b. Users as research inventions: How research categories perpetuate inequities. *Journal of Communication* 39: 216–32.

Dervin, B. 1992. From the mind's eye of the user: The sense-making qualitative-quantitative methodology. In *Qualitative Research in Information Management*, J. D. Glazier and R. R. Powell, eds., pp. 61–84. Englewood, Colo.: Libraries Unlimited.

Dervin, B. 1993. Verbing communication: Mandate for disciplinary invention. *Journal of* 43: 45–54.

Dervin, B. 1994. Information ⟷ democracy: An examination of underlying assumptions. *Journal of the American Society for Information Science* 45, 6 (July): 369–85.

Dervin, B., and Dewdney, P. 1986. Neutral questioning: A new approach to the reference interview. *RQ* (Summer): 506–13.

Fraser, N. 1989. *Unruly Practices: Power, Discourse, and Gender in Contemporary Social Theory*. Minneapolis: University of Minnesota Press.

Freire, P. 1970. *Pedagogy of the Oppressed*, M. Bergman Ramos, trans. New York: Herder and Herder.

Foucault, M. 1972. *The Archaeology of Knowledge*, A. M. Smith, trans. New York: Pantheon. (Original work published in 1969).

Gandy, O. H. 1988. The political economy of communication competence. In *The Political Economy of Information*, V. Mosco and J. Wasko, eds. Madison: University of Wisconsin Press.

Geertz, C. 1975. On the nature of anthropological understanding. *American Scientist* (January–February): 8–14.

Giddens, A. 1989. The orthodox consensus and the emerging synthesis. In *Rethinking Communication: Paradigm Issues*, vol. 1, B. Dervin, L. Grossberg, B. J. O'Keefe, and E. Wartella, eds. Newbury Park, Calif.: Sage Publications.

Giddens, A. 1984. *The Constitution of Society: Outline of the Theory of Structuration*. Berkeley: University of California Press.

Habermas, J. 1972. *Knowledge and Human Interests*, Jeremy Shapiro, transl. Boston: Beacon Press.

Hayles, K. N. 1990. *Chaos Bound: Orderly Disorder in Contemporary Literature and Science*. Ithaca: Cornell University Press.

Lather, P. 1991. *Getting Smart: Feminist Research and Pedagogy with/in the Postmodern*. New York: Routledge.

Lukes, S. 1974. *Power: A Radical View*. London: Macmillan.

Lyotard, J. F. 1984. *The Postmodern Condition: A Report on Knowledge*, G. Bennington and B. Massumi, trans. Minneapolis: University of Minnesota Press.

Mouffe, C., ed. 1992. *Dimensions of Radical Democracy: Pluralism, Citizenship, Community*. London: Verso.

Theunissen, M. 1984. *The Other: Studies in the Social Ontology of Husserl, Heidegger, Sartre, and Buber*, C. Macann, trans. Cambridge: MIT Press.

4 Human-Centered Design

Mike Cooley

It is said that we learn from history. The evidence, however, is not entirely convincing and frequently indicates that the opposite is true. We often seem determined to slavishly repeat the mistakes made at earlier historical stages. It would be unfortunate indeed if we were to use information technology to do to intellectual work what we have already done at such terrible cost to skilled manual work. Thus when we talk about *information design* a little caution and modesty are in order.

What do we mean by *design* and how do you design information? The notion of design arose during the fourteenth and fifteenth centuries in Europe and connoted the separation of thinking and doing. That is not to suggest for a moment that designing was a new activity. Rather it was separated out from a wider productive activity and recognized as an activity in its own right. Design can be said to constitute a separation of hand and brain, of manual and intellectual work, of the conceptual part of work from the labor process. Above all it indicated a process called *designing* that was to be separated from *doing*. It is clearly difficult to locate a specific historical turning point at which it occurred. Rather, it should be viewed as a historical tendency.

Up to the stage in question, great structures, which to this day define our twenty-first century, were "built" by master builders. Subsequently the structures were "designed" by architects and the construction was then undertaken by builders. Whereas earlier, site drawings conveyed an intentionality or purpose, which would then be interpreted within a tradition and cultural context, the drawings at later stages became merely a set of instructions. In this, we can already detect, in embryo, the central tenets of Taylorism. Frederick W. described it thus: "In my system the workman is told precisely what he is to do and how he is to do it and any improvement he makes upon the instructions given to him is fatal to success" (cited in Cooley 1993).

These processes went hand in glove with—some would say were a consequence of—our notion of science. For a process or a design to be scientific it must display the three predominant characteristics of the natural sciences: namely, predictability, repeatability, and mathematical quantifiability. This, by definition, precludes intuition, subjective judgment, tacit knowledge, dreams, imagination, and purpose.

That narrow scientific view is obsessed with the notion of "the one best way" (witness the mathematics of convergence or Leibniz's attempts at an exact language) and with rule-based systems. All of this is deeply problematic. For example, any active trade unionist will tell you that an effective way to stop anything in its tracks is to "work to rule." It is all the little things we do outside the rules, through our sense of purpose, that keep everything going.

It may be held that these concerns, if they are relevant at all, apply only in the field of manual work. Yet one of the founders of computing, Charles Babbage, maintained: "We have already mentioned what may perhaps appear paradoxical to some of our readers: that the division of labour can be applied with equal success to mental as well as to mechanical operations and that it ensures in both the same economy of time" (cited in Cooley 1993). Not surprising, then, that some of our German colleagues refer to new information-technology environments as "the production line in the office" (*Fliessband im Büro*).

What we see on all sides is a tendency to automate those who work—whether manually or intellectually—rather than to *informate* them. In the meantime, we still tend to confuse the potential of these technologies with their realities. Perhaps as the millennium draws precariously to its close it will also provide the stimulus to look creatively at information design and so structure our systems as to enhance and celebrate the most precious asset of any society, which is the skill, ingenuity, creativity, imagination, and commitment of its people.

This Extraordinary Millennium

The year 2000 marks the end of the most extraordinary millennium in human history. During it, humanity has witnessed the decline of feudalism, the growth of capitalism, and the weakening of religion as the leading edge in European society. We have facilitated the emergence of Cartesian science, the concentration of populations into modern cities, and the development of earth-shrinking transport systems. Above all, there has been the growth of industrial society. We have allowed the great storytelling traditions to all but wither away. We have devised the means of flying, declared Jackson Pollock a great artist, bounced on the moon, and killed forty million people in just one war.

We clearly perceive ourselves to be an upwardly mobile species. Yet at no time in human history have so many of our citizens felt alienated from and threatened by the society that we have created. Through our science we have become the first generation of the only species to apparently have it within its power to destroy not only itself but life on the planet as we know it. We have become far too smart scientifically to survive much longer without wisdom.

We should reflect upon the beauty and upon the devastation we have wrought on our own two-edged way to the twenty-first century. The delinquent genius of our species has produced the beauty of Venice and also the hideousness of Chernobyl; the playful linguistic delights of Shakespeare and the ruthlessness of British imperialism; the musical treasures of Mozart and the stench of Bergen Belsen; the caring medical potential of Roentgen's X-rays and the horrific devastation of Hiroshima.

The last century of this millennium has been characterized by a convulsed and exponential rate of technological change in which our speed of communication has increased by 10^7, our speed of travel by 10^3, and of data handling by 10^6. Over the same period our depletion of energy resources has increased by 10^4 and weapon power by 10^7.

We have seen the polarization of wealth and activity. In developed countries there are computer programs to help people diet, while out of the 122 million babies born in developing countries in 1982, 11 million died before their first birthday and an additional 5 million died before their fifth birthday. In some countries it is more today!

At the end of the millennium we appear to stand as the masters of nature. We scrabble millions of tons of material around each year, and in doing so we shift the equivalent of three times the sediment moved each year by the world's rivers. We mine and burn billions of tons of coal each year, so venting the waste—which includes carbon dioxide, the principal contributor to the greenhouse effect—into the atmosphere. In many parts of the world we have turned the soil into a craving junkie incapable of producing without its next fix.

Stimulus

Symbols in turn determine the kind of stories we tell and the stories we tell determine the kind of history we make and remake.
—Mary Robinson

The year 2000 could, and should, provide a powerful stimulus to examine where, as an industrial society, we are going. To do so at the macrolevel, we will require the perspective of a historian, the imagination of a poet, the analytical ability of a scientist, and the wisdom of a Chief Seattle. We shall have to be capable of thinking holistically, working in multidisciplinary groups, coping with change, and developing systems and products that are sustainable and caring of nature and humanity. Our current educational systems are fundamentally inappropriate and woefully inadequate to address this historical task. In relation to manufacturing and industry, it seems self-evident that developing the skill and competence necessary in the twenty-first century will require nothing short of a cultural and industrial renaissance.

To come about, this will require citizens possessed not just of knowledge but also of wisdom. It will require the courage and the dignity to ask simple questions of profound significance. Why is it that if we grow our own lettuce and repair our own car, the gross national product (GNP) goes down, whereas if there is a pile-up on the motorway and in the carnage scores of people are killed and piles of cars are destroyed, the GNP goes up? What compels us to design products to fall apart after five years? What is the deranged mentality of the expert in artificial intelligence who said on the BBC that human beings will have to accept their place in the evolutionary hierarchy of animals, human beings, and intelligent machines?

These are key issues as we approach the twenty-first century, and our educational system should be preparing people to discuss them in an informed, creative, and imaginative fashion.

The Industrial Future

If you can look into the seeds of time and say which grains will grow and which will not ...
—William Shakespeare

There is a growing recognition that the future cannot merely be an extrapolation of the past. We cannot assume it is possible to have an ever-increasing rate of production and consumption. The mass production of throwaway products based on energy-, capital-, and chemical-intensive forms of production, whether in manufacturing or in agriculture, is no longer possible nor acceptable. The ecological damage we are doing is now making this clear to growing numbers of concerned citizens. Furthermore, these intensive forms of production are also giving rise to political and social tensions and are contributing significantly to growing structural unemployment worldwide. The so-called lucky ones who retain their jobs are increasingly involved in new technologies resulting in processes not only stressful for people but which frequently reduce them to mere machine appendages. A European Community report highlighted these issues and advocated *anthropocentric systems* as a long-term, sustainable alternative (EEC 1990). The report suggested that industrial society needs to move from an economy of scale to an economy of scope and on to an economy of networking and thus that there is an urgent need for a society of proactive, creative, involved citizens at all levels. It made the point that society will gradually become one of "continuous innovation," where the capacity to design and build prototypes and to have skill-based, short-batch manufacturing capabilities will be of growing importance.

It advocated that linguistic, cultural, and geographical diversity (regarded by some as a weakness) should in the future be perceived as an advantage and a source of innovation. In addition, technological and educational support systems should enhance that diversity rather than diminish it. Anthropocentric systems, which I prefer to call Human-Centered Systems (HCS), are the appropriate context for these new developments to flourish.

Human-Centered Systems (HCS)—An Overview

My own conclusion is that engineering is an art rather than a science and by saying this I imply a higher, not a lower status.
—H. H. Rosenbrock (1990)

The HCS approach rejects the mechanistic paradigm of technological and societal development. HCS provides a powerful alternative philosophy for systems design and broader educational and societal development. It strongly questions the basis of the scientific methodology, which accepts only the predictable, the repeatable, and the mathematically quantifiable. This is because the scientific methodology excludes intuition, subjective judgment, and tacit knowledge.

HCS also rejects the notion of the "one best way" and the "sameness" of scientific ideas and suggests instead forms of science and technology that would be culturally specific. A great emphasis is put on the importance of diversity, providing a motivation to reflect and enhance cultural, educational, and even product diversity. HCS envisages quite different forms of human-machine interaction resulting in a human-machine symbiosis. It regards the social and cultural shaping of technology as central to the design and development of future technological systems and society as a whole.

This challenges much of the given wisdom about the information society, emphasizing knowledge, wisdom, and action rather than data and information. A dialectical interaction is necessary between the subjective and the objective, challenging the appropriateness of the narrow technocentric and cognitive-engineering approaches to systems design and emphasizing new forms of "emancipatory technology" with new mechanisms for user involvement.

The initial debate on HCS systems concentrated in the main on the human aspects of production and skill in an industrial setting. Recently, the concept has begun to be used to address socioeconomic and cultural issues that are becoming central to the industrial and social development of Europe as it approaches the twenty-first century. The Forecasting and Assessment in Science and Technology project (FAST) has recently carried out a survey of the potential for anthropocentric developments in most of the countries of the European Union (EU) (EEC 1990, 1991). In order to test in practice the concepts of HCS systems, the European Strategic Programme in Information Technology (ESPRIT) funded a major research and development project (directed by the author) to design and build the world's first human-centered, computer-integrated manufacturing system. Partners from Germany, Denmark, and Britain were involved (Cooley 1993).

A Tool Rather than a Machine

When the fact fails him, he questions his senses; When the fact fails me, I approve my senses.
—Robert Graves

Our aim was to provide an advanced system in which the human being would handle the qualitative subjective judgments and the machine the quantitative elements. It involved a radical redesign of the interface technologies. At a philosophical level, the objective was to provide tools (in the Heideggerian sense) that would support human skill and ingenuity rather than machines to objectivize that knowledge.

One of the main processes of current technological development is to render systems active and human beings passive. Our project's objective was to demonstrate that it is possible to design forms of technology that reverse this process, thus enhancing the activity and dominance of the user. It meant providing powerful analogical systems in which it was possible to program the devices according to the traditional ways of working while enhancing them by providing very modern software and hardware tools.

In the context of high-level intellectual work (in this case designing), it was necessary to challenge the concept of menu-driven systems. These frequently reduce the designer to being like a child with a LEGO set. The child can make a pleasing pattern of predetermined elements but cannot change those elements. To overcome this, an electronic sketchpad was designed which restores to the designer the creative freedom of a Renaissance artist. The system is now being tested at a number of major European companies, including Rolls Royce and BICC in Britain and BIBA in Germany.

The whole project has raised very important questions for education at every level. The skill and competence at every level of the organization is changed and expanded. So also is the worker's perception of himself or herself. On the shop floor, those who functioned and thought of themselves as *machine operators* metamorphized into *cell managers*. They can take an overview of the functioning of the cell and acquire additional competences in the fields of planning, costing, and systems maintenance (figure 4.1). They are provided with powerful support tools through workstations with adaptive interfaces. Such interfaces acknowledge and celebrate traditional craft skills and provide for graphical programming and

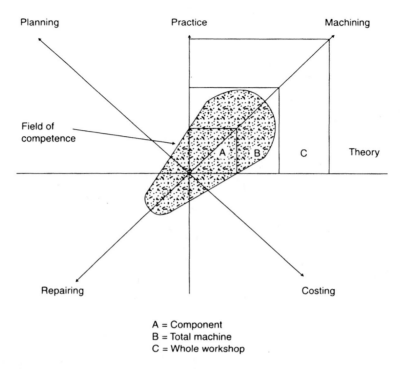

Figure 4.1
(© Cooley 1992)

sketchpad input devices and ensure that the absurd QWERTY keyboard does not get in the way of the real domain competences.

Experience in a number of countries demonstrates that those able to make best use of such systems are those who emerge from a quasi-apprenticeship system and therefore start from a high "competence platform." The whole process is one in which the operator "builds on the familiar to create the new." Part of the competence and some of the skills required to work in such environments will be the capacity to

1. Absorb new knowledge and transform it

2. Draw conclusions about the unknown from the known

3. Take initiatives

4. Make decisions

5. Work with a team

6. Adopt a systematic, analytical approach

7. Plan independently

8. Take on responsibility

The German company manager who identified these requirements for the future tellingly observes: "It will go without saying that in the majority of cases these skills cannot be taught in isolation during instruction or in the classroom but only in conjunction with technical exercises and concrete practical problems at the workplace."

Those involved in systems design will need to be competent in the design of adaptive tools that accord closely with the traditions and practices of the domain area (see figure 4.2). Furthermore, they will need to be competent in the design of systems and organizations that display the following characteristics.

Coherence The embedded meanings, if not immediately evident, at least must not be cloaked or obscure. A related concept here is *transparency*, which means rendering highly visible what is going on and what is possible.

Inclusiveness The system should be inviting and tend to invite you in and make you feel part of a community of activities with which you are familiar and on friendly terms.

Malleability A possibility to mold the situation to suit, to pick-and-mix and sculpt the environment to suit one's own instrumental needs, aesthetic tastes, and craft traditions.

Engagement A sense that one is being invited to participate in the process and which creates a feeling of empathy.

Ownership A feeling that you have created and thereby own parts of the system. A sense of belonging and even companionship as traditional craftsmen may feel with a favorite machine tool.

Responsiveness A general sense that you can get the system to respond to your requirements and your individual needs and ways of doing things. A

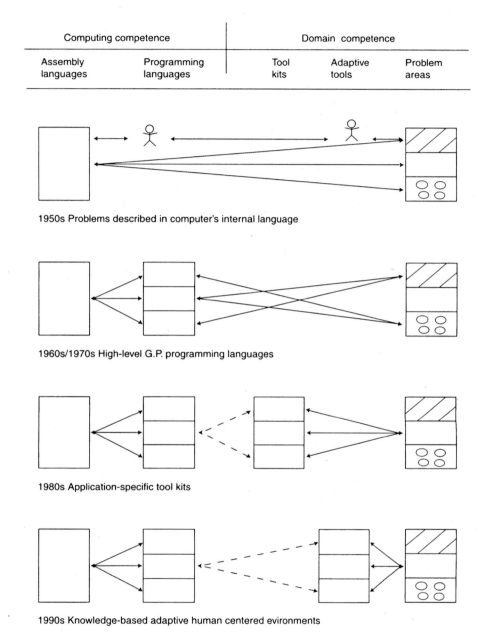

1950s Problems described in computer's internal language

1960s/1970s High-level G.P. programming languages

1980s Application-specific tool kits

1990s Knowledge-based adaptive human centered evironments

Figure 4.2
(© Cooley 1992, after Fischer)

system that makes visible its own rules and then encourages one to learn them and to change them at will.

Purpose Meant in the sense in which Rosenbrock describes it. The system is capable of responding to the purpose the user has in mind and then encouraging him or her to go beyond it.

Panoramic Most current systems tend to encourage the user to converge on narrower activities. Good embedded systems should also provide windows or apertures through which one can take a wider or more panoramic view. This encourages the acquisition of *boundary knowledge* and allows the user to act more effectively and competently by locating what he or she is doing in the understanding of a wider context.

Transcendence When operating the system, the user should be encouraged, enticed, and even provoked to transcend the immediate task requirements. The possibility of acquiring boundary knowledge and a macrolevel vision of the process as a whole should be self-evident.

Initial Results

Hard-nosed industrialists and their compliant foot soldiers, industrial engineers, have tended to regard the type of systems described above as being at the best a diversion from "the real world of industry" or at the worst, "dangerous liberal waffle." But times are changing. A crisis in many of the rigid, hierarchical large organizations is forcing a radical re-examination of much of the given wisdom. At an economic level, a multidisciplinary report on the future of U.S. industry pointed out, "We have tended to treat our workforces as a cost and a liability, whereas our major competitors have treated them as an asset whose skills should be ever enhanced" (Dertouzos et al. 1989).

Professor Anthony Hopwood has highlighted the need for accountants to re-examine their arid thinking. They spend 75 percent of their time in dealing with direct labor costs, though direct labor costs now only constitute about 10 percent of the total costs if one considers industry as a whole. On the other hand, material, which accounts for 50 percent of the cost, is subject to only 10 percent of accounting effort (Hopwood 1990).

At the technical level the case is even more compelling. In machine-based, hierarchical, Tayloristic systems that relentlessly drive toward wall-to-wall automation, there is now a growing recognition that such systems are extremely vulnerable to disturbance. They are typically good at coping with high-frequency, low-impact events, but bad in dealing with low-frequency, high-impact ones—for example, the uncertainty of the real world. Otherwise stated, machine-dependent systems are highly synchronized and coordinated. When one part of the system goes down, the high-level synchronization is turned into its dialectical opposite and one gets massive desynchronization rather in accord with catastrophe theory.

An alternative scenario, as studies in Germany have pointed out, is to have proactive, capable, interventionist workers for whom the system is transparent. These workers can anticipate system failures, take remedial steps, and if downtime occurs know what steps to take to minimize its consequences. Research already shows that such systems are much more robust and capable of handling disturbance. Moreover, the resultant downtime is significantly less than in machine-dependent systems.

Practical tests carried out in the real world of manufacturing are even more compelling. When the British Company BICC tested out a form of cell- or island-based production utilizing human-centered systems with powerful graphical outputs to assist decision making on the shop floor, the results were that on-time delivery increased from 31 percent to 86 percent, manufacturing lead time approximately halved, work-in-progress value reduced by 45 percent, and excess overtime required to meet schedules declined by 75 percent.

In addition to demonstrable economic benefits, there may be long-term advantages in the form of flexibility and strategic capability for innovation. Of equal importance, but less easy to quantify, are social benefits such as a higher quality of working life, dramatically improved motivation, and the liberating of one of society's greatest assets, the skill, ingenuity, and creativity of its people. The resultant flexibility will become paramount in coming years as there are more custom-bound, short-batch production runs and as an economy of networking becomes widespread. Concurrent or simultaneous engineering will further reinforce the need for systems of this kind.

Overstructuring

Management is just a bad habit inherited from the army and the church.
—Danny Conroy-Craftsman

A feature of modern industrial society is its overstructuring. This arises within production from a mechanistic, Tayloristic view of optimum organization. The United States led in this overstructuring of industry and, as a recent report from the Massachusetts Institute of Technology pointed out, it is seriously debilitating because it treats human beings as liabilities rather than as assets (Dertouzos et al. 1989).

Although these lessons are beginning to be understood in industry, the educational system in general—and universities in particular—still seem determined to pursue teaching forms based on factory models. When Henry Ford donated a hundred million dollars to an institution he called the School of the Future, he said, "I have manufactured cars long enough to the point where I have got the desire to manufacture people. The catchword of the day is standardization" (cited in Cooley 1990).

More recently, I have described methods of organizing universities as factories within which the students are referred to as *commodities*, the examinations as *quality-control procedures*, graduation as *delivery*, and the professors as *operators*. They have a Frank Wolf algorithm (computer-based) to work out the rate at which the professors are "producing" (Cooley 1993). The factory model is now all-pervasive. It conditions and distorts every aspect of life in the technologically advanced nations. I am not sure if it was ever true in the Shakespearean sense that all the world's a stage, but it is certainly true that at the close of the twentieth century all the world's a factory—and all of nature that surrounds us is inert material for its remorseless production line.

Paradigmatic changes are already at hand, and within these we will require people with the competence to cope with ill-defined, loosely structured situations that cannot be defined in a unidimensional way and that embody high levels of uncertainty and unpredictability. At a design level, we will have to consider a scientific methodology based on purpose and not one based only on causal explanations (Rosenbrock 1990).

Education, Not Training

Any teacher who can be replaced by a computer deserves to be!
—David Smith

Many of the factorylike universities have ceased any pretense at education and are instead concerned with instruction. In many cases, they are so highly structured that even the instruction becomes mere arid training. Training usually provides a narrow explicit machine- or systems-specific competence that is quickly obsolete with technological change. Education is of a much more durable quality; as one of my German colleagues put it, it is "a state of mind."

My hierarchy of verbs in these matters is that you *program* a robot, you *train* an animal, but you *educate* human beings. Education in this sense is not just what occurs in schools or universities, where, so often, students and teachers are, as Ivan Illich points out, "schooled to confuse teaching with learning, grade advancement with education, a diploma with competence, and fluency with the ability to say something new" (Illich 1971: 9).

Education is merely a subset of the cultural milieu in which it occurs. Thus apprenticeships in the classical sense were the transmission of a culture. They produced the giants who define our European civilization: Leonardo da Vinci, Filippo Brunelleschi, Giotto. A great skill, as we approach the twenty-first century, will be to use the new technologies in such a fashion as to build upon the best traditions of those rich learning processes. In a Developing European Learning through Technology Advance (DELTA) project I directed, we developed a multimedia learning environment that seeks to transmit not expertise but rather the means by which

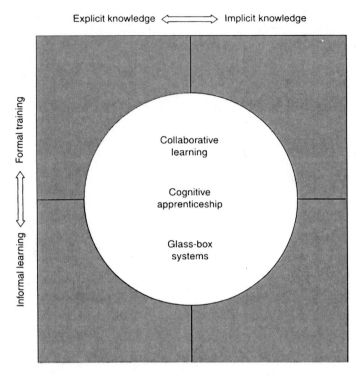

Figure 4.3
(Reprinted with permission from John Seeley Brown, "Toward a New Epistemology for Learning," in *Intelligent Tutoring Systems at the Crossroad of AI and Education*, ed. C. Frasson and J. Gauthiar [Norwood, N.J.: Ablax], 1989)

expertise is acquired. To use a crude analogy, it is to the learner what a flight simulator might be to a trainee pilot.

Over and above this, it provides the basis for a new epistemology of learning. Above all, it embodies a *cognitive apprenticeship* (figure 4.3). It recognizes in the best Polanyi tradition that "There are things we know but cannot tell" (1962) and that the richness of human competence can only in part be reduced to rule-based systems. Further that an interaction must exist between the rule-based core and the heuristics, fuzzy reasoning, imagination, and intentionality that surrounds it. Thus we advocate *emancipatory technologies* (figure 4.4).

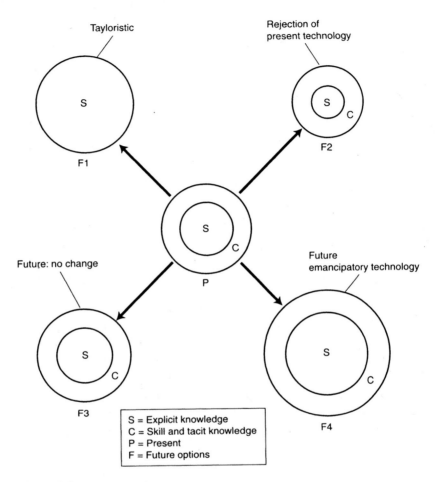

Figure 4.4
(Reprinted with permission from H. H. Rosenbrock, *Designing Human-Centred Technology* [Berlin: Springer], 1989)

In all of these systems, we question the given wisdom that daily advises us that we live in an information society. We may perhaps live in a data society, whereas what is required is the competence to operate at the knowledge/wisdom/action end of the cybernetic loop (figure 4.5). I freely admit that it took us many years and much technocratic rambling to arrive at this rather obvious conclusion. If we had been more fully exposed to the ideas, however ill-structured, of artists or poets, this might have been more obvious. Thus the basic "theory" behind figure 4.5, for example, was anticipated by T. S. Eliot in one of his poems, "Where is the wisdom we have lost in knowledge?/Where is the knowledge we have lost in information?" (Eliot 1990). One might presume to add the line "Where is the information we have lost in data?" Frequently, the big issues in society are prefigured by our poets and our artists, and we diminish ourselves as engineers and scientists if we do not interact with them in a multidisciplinary way. The ability to do so may be an important requirement as we approach the twenty-first century.

In order to transcend the narrow boundaries of existing disciplines, a number of programs have now been implemented throughout the EEC—now the EU—to address these difficulties. An exciting one was stimulated in Sweden. It is entitled "Culture, Language and Artificial Intelligence." Engineers, scientists, musicians, playwrights, dramatists, and master craftsmen all came together for an "event," and in consequence a new book series was launched, poems were written, paintings were produced, and a new journal, *A.I. and Society*, was launched.

All of this is to stimulate a multidisciplinary, multicultural approach to dealing with the problems of industrial society as we approach the twenty-first century. The International Research Institute for Human Centred Systems, an institute without walls, has been founded to facilitate the development of the skills and competences to do so.[1]

Let There Be Enterprise!

They are ill discoverers that think there is no land, when they can see nothing but sea.
—Francis Bacon

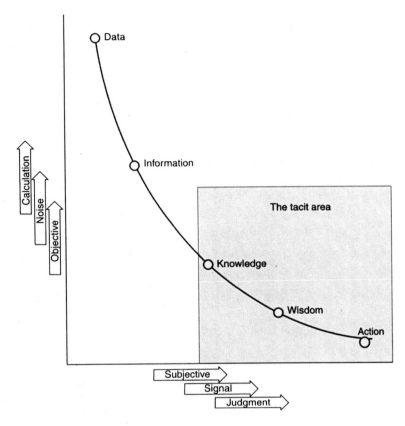

Figure 4.5
(Reprinted with permission from M. Cooley, *Architect or Bee?* [London: Chatto & Windus], 1987)

In this chapter I have concentrated on the abilities that will be required in industry in the twenty-first century. Many of these will be of vital importance in related areas such as product innovation. There are many policymakers, including some key ones in Japan, who believe that the next "Schumpeter shove" will be in the field of ecologically desirable and socially useful products. In this connection, the need for sensitive antennae to identify emerging markets and the ability to develop new markets, social markets, and community projects will be of paramount importance.

We urgently need enterprising, social entrepreneurs! Linked to this necessity will be the important capacity to interact creatively with other designers, innovators, and user groups through organizations such as the EU/SPRINT-supported Technology Exchange.[2] More commonly known as the Product Bank, the exchange has available some five thousand new products in various stages of preparedness from concept through commercialized product. In addition, *pattern recognition*, the ability to identify synergetic opportunities across disciplines—electronics and medicine, multimedia techniques and culture, information technology and education—will be at a premium.

Furthermore, there will be extensive opportunities for those with the capacity to grasp them and link communication technologies with cultural products, in the manner of Village Action Projects in Finland and the "sense of place" and "social citizenship" proposals in Italy. These projects will be particularly important at the periphery of Europe, which still has some of the richest cultures. Furthermore, properly used, they could enhance the language revival in the West of Ireland.

In an overall sense, I advocate entrepreneurial and enterprising capacities that far transcend their traditional concern with narrow, short-term profit maximization. The abilities required in the twenty-first century will subsume these traditional areas and will also stretch into community work and care, urban renewal programs, heritage activities, and social and cultural activities in the wider sense. In this broader regard, the Druid theater in Galway, with its various multiplier effects, should be conceptualized as a very entrepreneurial and enterprising undertaking.

Entrepreneurial skills have to do with motivation, commitment, and imagination. Even in their most straightforward commercial forms, they are not those which can be learned in a university alone (if at all). What I am suggesting here, however, is that part of that motivation in the future will be driven by ecological concerns, a sense of community, and a desire to see technology assist the lame to walk, the blind to see, and the hungry to be fed. It should not be driven by system possibilities alone. This will require taking a human-centered view at an all-embracing level, and already activities are underway that are laying the basis for such developments (figure 4.6).

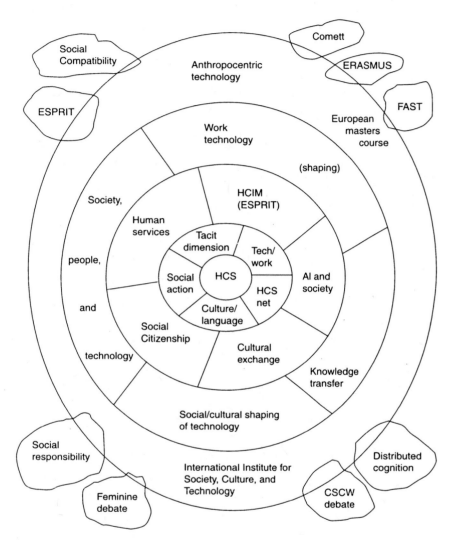

Figure 4.6
(Reprinted with the permission of Dr. K. Gill, International Research Institute for Human-Centred Systems)

Imagination

It stands almost complete and finished in my mind so that I can survey it like a fine picture or a beautiful statue.
—Wolfgang Amadeus Mozart

Industrialization has in many ways reduced and overconcentrated our competences as human beings. We confer life on machines and diminish ourselves. We are gradually becoming observers of life rather than its active participants. Education in the sense in which I use it above should imbue a sense of excitement, discovery, and imagination. We are far too obsessed with narrow facts, details, and exams. Exams essentially find out what people do not know rather than what they do know.

There used to be a tradition in some of the older universities that if you didn't like the examination question you were set, you simply ignored it and wrote your own question. Life in the widest philosophical sense should be about writing one's own questions, and education should facilitate that. It should stimulate and excite our imagination and sense of discovery. The great Einstein on one occasion observed that "Imagination is far more important than knowledge." And, he went on to say, "The formulation of a problem is far more important than its solution, which may be merely a matter of mathematical or experimental skill. To raise new questions, to look at old problems from a new angle marks the real advances in science."

Human-Centered Design provides one exciting context in which to consider these pressing issues "from a new angle."

Notes

1. Details on the journal *A.I. and Society* and the International Research Institute for Human-Centred Systems is available from Dr. K. Gill, Department of Information Studies, Brighton University, Brighton, Sussex BN1 9PH, U.K.

2. The Technology Exchange. Wrest Park, Silsoe, Bedford MK45 4HS, U.K.

References

Cooley, M. 1990. *The New Shape of Industrial Culture and Technological Development.* Tokyo: Keizai University.

Cooley, M. 1993. *Architect or Bee?: The Human Price of Technology.* London: Hogarth Press. (Also available in German, Japanese, and Swedish and forthcoming in Irish. Distributed by Technology Innovation Associates, 95 Sussex Place, Slough, Berkshire SL1 1NN, U.K.)

Dertouzos, M. L.; Lester, R. K.; Solow, R. M.; and the MIT Commission on Industrial Productivity. 1989. *Made in America: Regaining the Productive Edge.* Cambridge: MIT Press.

Eliot, T. S. 1990. "*Choruses* from The Rock." In *Selected Poems*, p. 107. London: Faber & Faber.

European Economic Community (EEC). 1990. *European Competitiveness in the Twenty-first Century: The Integration of Work, Culture and Technology.* Report on Forecasting and Assessment in Science and Technology (FAST). (Available free from FAST, 200 Rue de Loi, 200 B-1049 Brussels, Belgium)

European Economic Community (EEC). 1990, 1991. *Prospects for Anthropocentric Productions Systems.* FAST Reports on EC Member States. (Available from FAST as above)

Hopwood, A. 1988. Production and finance: The need for a common language. In *Proceedings of the New Manufacturing Imperatives Conference*, pp. 79–89. London: Axiom Systems Design.

Illich, I. 1971. *Deschooling Society.* New York: Harper & Row.

Polanyi, M. 1962. Tacit knowing: Its bearing on some problems of philosophy. *Review of Modern Physics* 34 (no. 4): 601–616.]

Rosenbrock, H. H. 1990. *Machines with a Purpose.* Oxford University Press.

5   *Sign-Posting Information Design*

Romedi Passini

In the field of design, new terms are regularly introduced and old ones are put aside. Sometimes old terms are rediscovered and put to new use. Sometimes new terms buzz for short periods and then fall, forgotten. Eventually they are replaced. This semantic play may account for little more than the superficial beautification of old and worn-out design concepts and practice. In such cases a new term, at best, provokes critical reactions; at worst, it dazzles some designers and clients into expectations of wonders that never come to pass.[1]

The introduction of a new term, on the other hand, may be fully justified if it refers to new notions, or if it signifies profound changes in established practice. It then creates its own identity and serves as a symbol, a rallying point for the foundation of a new school of thought and, maybe, the development of a novel design paradigm.[2]

Information design is not a new term, but its popularity has certainly increased in recent years. A number of professional journals, associations, design groups, and even university programs use the information-design banner to proclaim a new identity. A glance at recent publications shows that the phrase is an umbrella term to cover the planning of everything—from user instructions to warning labels, from manuals to timetables, from official forms to invoices, from traffic instructions to traffic signs, from wayfinding signs to maps, from technical information sheets to scientific papers, from simple computer layouts to virtual environments—and the list continues. As used in this paper the term *information design* means communication by words, pictures, charts, graphs, maps, pictograms, and cartoons, whether by conventional or electronic means.

I use it to refer to a design approach that, I believe, is clearly emerging and that promises to evolve into a distinct design practice. The aim of this chapter is twofold: first, to review some basic criteria for this new design practice and, second, to illustrate the importance and the meaning of those criteria in a particular field of application—the design of information for helping people find their way around in complex settings.

Designing Information

Who could dispute the fact that during the last two decades information, its access and its use, has had a strong impact on our society? More and more of our work depends on the effective use of information. New possibilities to access information are affecting our daily lives, not only at work but also at home and during leisure time. Social functions have become more and more specialized, creating greater complexity and, consequently, new needs for information. The urban and architectural environment has also grown more perplexing; just finding our way around our built environment, a trivial task in the past, is now a distinct challenge. Thus the design of information and its efficient communication are more critical than ever before.

In an amusing article, David Sless, after pointing to all the things we sell (including ourselves), asks what else there is to sell *but* information (Sless 1994b). In his view, information is becoming the ultimate commodity and, probably, a profitable line of business. This new focus and promising opportunities create a climate conducive to rethinking the way we produce and present. The emergence of information design as a field of study and practice is a sure sign that something new is in the making.

Distinguishing Characteristics of Information Design

Graphic design is the traditional profession most closely associated with the design of information. The distinction between information design and graphic design might appear tenuous at first. Both are concerned with information displays and with communication, but the distinction makes sense if we look at it in a microhistorical context.

Graphic design over the last few decades has tended to emphasize appearance and give expression to certain contemporary aesthetic values. The profession, as it is still taught and practiced, has its roots in the early twentieth- century Art Deco style, and, to a lesser extent, in Dadaism (Kinross 1992). Information design, on the other hand emphasizes communication and is as concerned with content as with form (Sless 1994a). It has its roots in a variety of disciplines—including information theory and the cognitive sciences—and brings together design and research.

Knowledge Base for Information Design

Any object in existence has the potential for communicating information, and anything we do has the same potential. Although we can refer to some aspects of communication in general terms, I would argue that we need to see information design in the light of a particular field of application. The issues in designing a government document, for example, are not quite the same as those involved in designing a wayfinding system or a warning label. As information serves a specific function (filling in forms, wayfinding, warning, etc.), understanding that function is probably the single most important aspect of efficient information design.

Nonetheless, many functions, even those that have their own characteristics and requirements, have something in common. Whenever people set goals and use information to attain those goals in novel conditions, they engage in a mental activity that can be conceptualized as problem solving. Indeed, filling in a government form and wayfinding are both problem-solving activities. Providing information for problem solving is one of the major tasks of information design. Understanding how people solve problems provides designers with the criteria needed to determine what information is required and where or when it has to be accessible.

If information is the issue, there has to be not only a source and a transmitter of information but also a receiver. Respecting the receiver's information-processing characteristics is fundamental to transferring information. The ways people read and understand messages vary with the task and the individual. They are not the same when confronted with a set of instructions at work and using a sign system to find their way around in a complex setting; nor are they the same when struggling to make sense of a government form and trying to understand a wayfinding map. Understanding the ways we process different kinds of information provides the designer cues to the most suitable forms of presenting that information.

Research and Information Design

Researchers have identified a number of variables that can affect information processing. Having to deal with great quantities of information may lead to overload conditions, which in turn may reduce the processing of information (Arthur and Passini 1992). Cultural, social, and age differences may also make responses to information more complex. The complexity of the messages themselves, combined with information-processing differences among receivers and contextual variables, makes it difficult to predict the effectiveness of an information display. In fact, a strong argument can be made that design solutions can only be properly assessed by potential users—regardless of how confident the designer is about the proposed design.

Adams (1994) distinguishes between two kinds of information-design research: (1) outcome research, which is usually done by specialist investigators, assesses products according to scientific methodology and uses large test samples, while in (2) process research, designers incorporate changes in small, scaled, flexible increments. Though designers prefer the latter type of research because of its accessibility, time efficiency, and freedom to study the issues they consider most important, the practice has its pitfalls, especially if designers do not fully understand the scientific concepts of reliability and validity.

There is also a danger, however, in relying solely on assessment research to build a discipline: it tends to be conservative. Although it produces improvements on present conventions, it is not particularly well suited for generating new ideas and questioning existing assumptions and practices. New approaches and innovations originate in research of a more fundamental nature and can give rise to a rejuvenation that is, I believe, important for information design to survive and develop.

The knowledge base for designing information emerges from the behavioral sciences, in particular from work in cognitive psychology. It is also linked to ergonomics and environmental psychology. Those who question the contribution of these sciences to information design may misunderstand the role of science. Science does not provide solutions, it only provides information and knowledge that designers can use to develop solutions and new approaches. It would be ironical if designers—who design information so that others can solve problems—were to fail to use information to solve their own difficulties.

Pitfalls for Information Design

Some might identify the objective of information design as the production of information, whereas the objective should be to attain a more general design goal. Thus the objective of information design for wayfinding is not to design signs but to help people move efficiently to their chosen destinations. The measure of quality for a design is not simply the designed product but also users' behavior and satisfaction. Information is not an end in itself. If this point is not emphasized, information design could well end up being merely the design of good (i.e., beautiful) information displays. And what would we gain from that?

The term *information design* assumes that what users need is information, when, in fact, other design interventions might be more effective.[3] Rather than designing a label warning parents that a child might be able to push over a high chair if it is placed too close to a wall, we could probably solve the problem more satisfactorily by designing a stable chair. Information design is not the only, and not always the best, design intervention.

Information Design and Wayfinding

In this section I introduce the cognitive and behavioral notions that are key to designing information systems. The concept I use as an illustration is *wayfinding*, defined in terms of problem solving.[4] This concept is essential not only for determining what information is necessary, where it should be, and what form it should take, but also for establishing an underlying design logic.

The Concept of Wayfinding

Wayfinding refers to the cognitive and behavioral abilities associated with purposefully reaching a desired physical destination. It was introduced in the mid-1970s to replace the notion of *spatial orientation*, which referred more specifically to an individual's ability to mentally represent a place.[5] This representation is sometimes referred to as a *cognitive map*.

Wayfinding conceptualized in terms of problem solving comprises three major processes: (1) decision making and the development of a plan of action to reach a destination; (2) decision execution, transforming the plan into behavior at the appropriate place(s) along a route; and (3) perception and cognition (information processing), providing the necessary information to make and execute decisions (Passini 1984, Arthur and Passini 1992).

Wayfinding is distinguished from other types of problem solving by operating in an architectural, urban, or geographic space. It incorporates the mental representation of large-scale spaces (cognitive maps) that characterizes the older notion of spatial orientation. Cognitive maps, in this context, are part of information processing. They are, in addition to being records of direct environmental perception and cognition, possible sources of information for both making and executing decisions.

A major distinction must be made between wayfinding in unfamiliar settings and wayfinding in familiar settings or along familiar routes. On familiar routes, people know what to do to get to their destination. In other words, they have a record of the required decisions and, thus, do not need to make decisions—only execute them. Executing decisions is a less conscious and more automatic process than actual decision making, which accounts for the ease with which people follow well-known routes. They retain decision plans in one form or another and remember or recognize the places where they have to execute specific decisions.[6]

What Information Is Needed

According to our conceptualization of wayfinding, people need information to make and execute decisions. Therefore, the wayfinding decisions they make determine the content of the required information. (So much for internal consistency of the argument!) But what does that mean for the design of information? How can a designer know what decisions future users are going to make?

Two empirical observations help in answering these questions. First, for similar tasks, decisions vary a great deal from one type of setting to another. Second, within the same setting, the decisions of different users tend to be similar for a given task (Passini 1984). These observations suggest that the key decisions are determined more by the setting and its architectural characteristics than by individual characteristics. It also indicates that information, if it is relevant and consistent with the wayfinding task, will be used. The more efficient the support information, the more similar the wayfinding solutions of its various users. It is interesting to observe that settings with poor wayfinding information lead to more exploratory decisions, whose objective is usually to find relevant information.

The issue is slightly complicated by the observation that some users tend to rely more on information of a linear, sequential order that leads them from one point on a route to the next, whereas others are more likely to rely on information of a spatial nature that provides them with an overall picture of the setting.[7] These two wayfinding styles are only partly user-specific; they are also affected by the setting's architectural and spatial characteristics. Most people will rely on a linear sequential style when finding their way in complex underground spaces where cognitive mapping is difficult. This suggests that, as a rule, designers should provide information for both wayfinding styles.

There is a tendency to see wayfinding information only in terms of signs. The analysis of the decisions people make in real wayfinding situations, however, shows clearly that most decisions are actually based on information of an architectural nature—entrances to buildings, transition points from one zone to another, exits, paths, stairs, escalators, elevators—as well as information about overall spatial features—for example, the layout of a building or the pattern of a street system (Arthur and Passini 1992). For this reason, the content of wayfinding information should not be limited to signs but should also include such architectural and spatial features. Each of the three elements depends on the presence and articulation of the others.

To establish a list of decisions for which they have to provide information, designers must first identify the locations of the main access points of a setting and—from the users' point of view—the key functions of the space (i.e., the key destination zones). The principal wayfinding decisions can be established by considering the following user tasks: (1) going from each access point to the destination zone and back; (2) going from one destination zone to another; and (3) circulating within the destination zone. The designer can identify the need for more detailed decisions by recording the points along the circulation routes where the users have to choose among directional options.

Where Information Is Needed

Information is needed when and where users have to make a decision. Information may be needed in the planning stage of a journey. Some people need little information to start with but develop their wayfinding solution as they confront new situations and new information. Others prefer to plan a trip in some detail before embarking on it. To do so, they need more information than the improvisational wayfinder.[8]

Information is also needed when people make and execute decisions at specific points along their way to a destination. The location of an information unit along a path is determined by the location of the corresponding decision point. Graphic designers and building managers often complain, in this regard, that users do not pay attention to signage. People attempting to deal with a complex setting do not take in everything but tend to choose what seems relevant to them; they pay attention to what they need. An information unit located at a place when it is not needed at the time has a good chance of being ignored.

The Question of Form and Presentation

If the content and the location of wayfinding information are determined by users' wayfinding decisions, its form and presentation relate to the way people perceive and recognize information displays. Through experience, graphic designers have developed a design culture incorporating a good deal of knowledge about these issues. It concerns letterforms and styles, spacing, legibility and distance, angular distortions, halation (i.e., the spreading characteristics of light), the use of symbols and colors, the illumination of signs, and even the design of arrows.[9]

At this point it is useful to consider an important methodological design issue often encountered when transferring an information design from the drawing board to the real setting. The readability of a display in the studio may not carry over to its application in the setting. A sign containing many units of information, for example, while easy to read in a quiet, stable setting may be difficult to make out in a complex environment where users are in motion. The reason, in this case, is quite simply that people's habits of perception in complex settings when they are moving are different from when they are motionless in a quiet situation. In a busy street or corridor people typically scan a setting by glancing at particular fixation points for less than two-tenths of a second. Although this perceptual technique is suitable for coping with great quantities of information in complex settings, it is not adaptable to reading many units of written information on a sign.[10]

Understanding environmental perception in complex settings also suggests the design solution: people *are* able to perceive small numbers of written units in a glance. Information obtained from such a quick look is retained in the form of a short-lived iconic memory that can only be read when it has been translated into a more stable memory (Neisser 1967). Although this translation process can only deal with a limited number of words, grouping longer messages into small three-unit packages restores the user's ability to perceive it at a glance. The lesson here is twofold: designers need (1) to know about the basic perceptual and cognitive processes and (2) to test information displays in the real setting with real users, while avoiding generalizing from results obtained in nontypical conditions (drawing board) to real settings.

From Information to Information Systems

Up to this point we have looked at individual decisions and the information required to make them. Decisions, though, are not isolated events. They are linked together, and it is their linkages that give them their full meaning in a problem-solving context. In order to take an elevator to a given floor, for example, the user has to press the call button, enter the elevator, press the destination button on the control panel, keep track of the floors reached, and get out at the desired floor.

We can consider these decisions in the order described as a solution, a blueprint for taking an elevator. In wayfinding terminology we refer to such a blueprint as a *decision plan*. The decisions to press the call button, to enter the elevator, and so on, all lead directly to behavior and thus do not require additional decisions.

The decision to take the elevator to floor *n* was probably not the main wayfinding task but was related to other decisions: for example, to enter

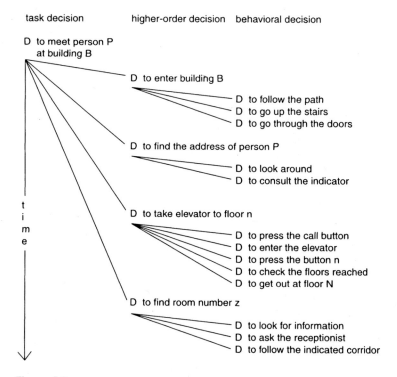

task decision   higher-order decision   behavioral decision

D to meet person P
   at building B

                                    D to enter building B

                                                    D to follow the path

        D to go up the stairs

        D to go through the doors

D to find the address of person P

        D to look around

        D to consult the indicator

D to take elevator to floor n

        D to press the call button

        D to enter the elevator

        D to press the button n

        D to check the floors reached

        D to get out at floor N

D to find room number z

        D to look for information

        D to ask the receptionist

        D to follow the indicated corridor

time (shown vertically along left axis)

Figure 5.1
Hypothetical Decision Diagram. The task decision is at the left while the decisions leading directly to behavioral actions are shown on the right.

the building, to find the address of the desired destination, and, after arriving by elevator at the desired floor, to find room number *z*. These decisions, in this order, constitute a general blueprint (decision-plan) for completing the original wayfinding task, which might be to meet person P at building B (see figure 5.1). The decisions of that blueprint requiring the person to make additional decisions are called *higher-order decisions*. They can be seen as subtasks—just as taking an elevator is a subtask.

Decision-plans are hierarchically structured.[11] At the top (the top-left in figure 5.1) is the original task, which is linked to a series of higher-order decisions describing in a general way how to solve the task. Each of these decisions, if it cannot be directly executed, represents a subtask for which a decision plan has to be developed. At the bottom of the hierarchy are the decisions that lead directly to behavioral actions.

The hierarchical links between decisions signify an *in-order-to* relation. They describe the reason why a decision is made. So, one may read that the decision to press the call button is made in order to take the elevator to floor *n*, and that this decision is made in order to meet person P. A decision-diagram, thus, represents all the decisions in the structured solution to the original wayfinding problem.

Each decision requires information. Posting signs only at intersections tends to ignore the higher-order decisions. If used systematically, they will lead people to a destination, but they do not propose a structured way to solve the problem. Furthermore they can only be applied to a limited number of destinations. Information design should consider all decisions, including those of a higher order. This principle leads to more efficient information design and to more intelligent wayfinding.[12]

The logic that links decisions into a decision plan is the same logic that links information into an information system. In other words, an information system is a structured ensemble of information that corresponds to a way of solving a wayfinding problem.

Information Design and Professional Boundaries

We have already pointed to the fact that architectural design is also concerned with wayfinding. The articulation of entrances to buildings, transition points from one zone to another, exits, paths, stairs, escalators, elevators—all are part of architectural communication and are essential to wayfinding. Architects and architectural planners also intervene, on a different level, by organizing and linking spaces, thus creating overall layouts that include the circulation system. By doing so they establish the wayfinding context, setting the stage and defining the wayfinding problems users have to solve. The circulation system is also a determining factor in the ease or difficulty with which users can form cognitive maps of the setting. It is true that information designers can enhance user's cognitive mapping by finding ways to communicate the layout, including the circulation system; nonetheless, much of the ability to map a setting is inherent in the nature of the layout itself (O'Neill 1991, Passini 1984b).

The conception of the layout and the circulation occurs very early in the design process, and at this point wayfinding considerations are already crucial. To be efficient, wayfinding communication, should not just follow the architectural conception of the layout and be relegated to "mopping up the mess," but should be utilized from the first to define the wayfinding problems future users will have to solve. This poses the intriguing question of who should do what.

The boundaries of design for wayfinding are clearly not in accord with the traditional disciplinary boundaries. Wayfinding design and, more specifically, information design includes behavioral considerations and is thus interdisciplinary in nature. It also overlaps the professional boundaries of at least two congruent design disciplines, architectural planning and graphic design. Relations between the two professions have always been problematic. Architects often see signage as a necessary evil that needs to be controlled so as not to disfigure a building. Graphic designers complain that they are not involved in the design of wayfinding support systems until after the key decisions have been made and the setting is being built. Often they are called in at the last-minute to install some signs before opening day.

The solution to this problem is rather complex, and probably political as well, for each profession wants to maintain its field of influence. At the very least, architects should be made aware of wayfinding and how their architectural conceptions affect it. They should also be aware of the importance of articulating the major elements related to wayfinding (entrances, intersections, horizontal and vertical circulation, etc.). Graphic designers also need to be aware of wayfinding and comprehend its conceptual basis as well as to understand the architectural dimensions of wayfinding design.

This knowledge should be transmitted in schools of design and architecture. It is difficult, though, to assess the feasibility of such a proposal.

Design schools already have more subjects to teach than they can teach adequately during a limited time span, and students may not see the importance of adding yet another subject of study.

It might be more realistic, therefore, to construct a new field specializing in information design and providing a knowledge base in all the related disciplines. Such a specialty would incorporate expert knowledge in a given field, such as wayfinding, with training in basic architectural, graphic arts, and communication skills. The designer would also be trained in behavioral research, not necessarily to conduct complex studies but at least to understand research and to be able to incorporate research into the design process.

This profile corresponds to the previously introduced criteria for an information-design paradigm. It has been our experience over the years that very few complex public settings work in terms of wayfinding. Health care and educational facilities, transportation terminals, and multifunctional settings, old and new, are particularly difficult to get around. This new field might provide an interesting and rewarding professional avenue for designers and give information design the necessary definition and professional standing.

Notes

1. Edward Carpenter, in a similar vein, questioned the term *wayfinding*: "Design breakthrough or trendy buzzword?" (Carpenter 1989).

2. The notion of paradigm in a research context was introduced by Thomas Kuhn in *The Structure of Scientific Revolutions* (1962). The same arguments about its unifying force and its power of generating methods and results can be made for design.

3. Wogalter (1994) discusses several hazard-prevention methods. The design of warnings, he points out, is not the most efficient strategy. The first and best defense against accidents, when possible, is to remove the hazard from the product (i.e., redesign the item).

4. In earlier writing I used the term *wayfinding design* to cover all architectural and graphic aspects of the issue. The phrase *environmental communication* also refers to support information and can be equated with information design.

5. For early references toward conceptualizing wayfinding, see Kaplan (1976), Downs and Stea (1977), and Passini (1977).

6. Cognitive maps of familiar routes also contain information that can be used in taking familiar routes. Little is known about the relative importance and interplay of recorded decision plans and cognitive maps.

7. For an early study of cognitive map typology, see Appleyard (1970).

8. In a study we were able to show that blind people tend to prepare routes in more detail than sighted people (Passini and Proulx 1988).

9. For general references on these issues, see Arthur and Passini (1992), Wildbur (1989), and McLendon (1982).

10. Boersema, Zwaga, and Adams (1989) studied the eye movements and number of fixations of people in settings full of competing advertising signs.

11. Similar hierarchical structures have been proposed for other goal-directed events (Lichtenstein and Brewer 1980).

12. People with reduced cognitive abilities may have special information requirements. In a recent study exploring the wayfinding abilities of patients with dementia of the Alzheimer's type, we found that patients at an early or intermediate stage of the disease, while still able to find their way under certain facilitating conditions, were incapable of developing an overall plan to solve wayfinding problems (Passini et al. 1994).

References

Adams, A. 1994. The role and methodology of testing in information design. In *Proceedings of the International Symposium on Public Graphics*, pp. 13.1–13.20. Utrecht: Stichting Public Graphics Research.

Appleyard, D. 1970. Styles and methods of structuring a city. *Environment and Behavior* 2 (1): 100–18.

Arthur, P., and Passini, R. 1992. *Wayfinding, People, Signs and Architecture*. Toronto: McGraw-Hill.

Boersema, T.; Zwaga, H. J. G.; and Adams, A. S. 1989. Conspicuity in realistic scenes: An eye-movement measure. *Applied Ergonomics* 20 (4): 267–73.

Carpenter, E. 1989. Wayfinding: Design breakthrough or trendy buzzword? *Print* 43 (1): 92–163.

Downs, R., and Stea, D. 1977. *Maps in Mind*. New York: Harper & Row.

Kaplan, S. 1976. Adaptation, structure and knowledge. In *Environmental Knowing*, G. Moore and R. Golledge, eds., pp. 32–46. Stroudsburg, Pa.: Hutchinson and Ross.

Kinross, R. 1992. Conversation with Richard Hollis on graphic design history. *Journal of Design History* 5 (1): 73–90.

Kuhn, T. S. 1962. *The Structure of Scientific Revolutions*. Chicago: University of Chicago Press.

Lichtenstein, E. H., and Brewer, W. F. 1980. Memory for goal-directed events. *Cognitive Psychology* 12 (3): 412–45.

McLendon, C. 1982. *Signage: Graphic Communications in the Built World*. New York: McGraw-Hill.

Neisser, U. 1967. *Cognitive Psychology*. Englewood Cliffs, N.J.: Prentice Hall.

O'Neill, M. 1991. Effects of signage and floor plan configuration on wayfinding accuracy. *Environment and Behavior* 23 (5): 553–74.

Passini, R. 1997. Wayfinding, a study of spatial problem solving. Unpubl. Ph.D. diss. State College: Pennsylvania State University.

Passini, R. 1984a. *Wayfinding in Architecture*. New York: Van Nostrand Reinhold.

Passini, R. 1984b. Spatial representation: A wayfinding perspective. *Journal of Environmental Psychology* 194: 153–64.

Passini, R., and Proulx, G. 1988. Wayfinding without vision: An experiment with totally blind people. *Environment and Behavior* 20 (2): 227–52.

Passini, R.; Joanette, Y.; Rainville, C.; and Marchand, Nicolas. 1994. Wayfinding abilities in dementia: An experiment suggesting generic design ideas. In *Proceedings of the International Symposium on Public Graphics*, pp. 23.1–23.11. Utrecht: Stichting Public Graphics Research.

Sless, D. 1994a. What is information design? In *Designing Information for People*, R. Penman and D. Sless, eds., pp. 1–16. Canberra: Communication Research Press.

Sless, D. 1994b. Information, the first and final commodity. *Communication News* 7 (3): 1–3.

Wildbur, P. 1989. *Information Graphics*. New York: Van Nostrand Reinhold.

Wogalter, M. S. 1994. Factors influencing the effectiveness of warnings. In *Proceedings of the International Symposium on Public Graphics*, pp. 5.1–5.21. Utrecht: Stichting Public Graphics Research.

II *The Practice of Information Design*

The contributors to this volume found it difficult—no, impossible—to remain in the realm of the theoretical and the abstract. They are hands-on people, problem solvers as well as problem definers, and very often they express their ideas better in the media they use every day than in formal philosophical discourse. Presuming that there is an activity called *information design*—even if we can't entirely agree about its components—we can learn several important practical lessons about that activity from the contributors to this section.

Roger Whitehouse is an award-winning practitioner of Universal Design —a design system for getting information to all individuals, regardless of whether their perceptions of the world are conveyed through the tactile sense, sound, sight, or in some other way. In Chapter 6 he makes a strong case for the idea that the information designer must honor each recipient's unique and valuable perceptual point of view. In describing his famous case study of The Lighthouse, Whitehouse provides us with a detailed taxonomy of the devices Universal Design employs to ensure that all groups of individuals, each with its own unique sensorium (deaf, blind, "normal," and so on), have access to an information design experience. Whitehouse has created an impressive succession of inclusive information designs and is one of the relatively few information designers who focus on this problem. It's not that other designers don't acknowledge the need, but they are often so challenged by the simple task of creating the information experience that they forget there are wide differences in the perceptual mechanisms people use to take in information.

In chapter 7 Chandler Screven takes a broad and equally inclusive look at environmental design, deducing from his extensive experience a series of rules that may make it easier to design successful instructive environments. Screven is an avid devotee of the systems perspective: in his worldview, nothing happens in the designed environment that does not affect other processes taking place within that environment. From the first stages of a design idea through it final implementation in concrete forms, this simple acknowledgment requires the information designer to consider many human and environmental factors—for example, the energy level of people attending an exhibit who expect to acquire bits of instructive, long-lasting wisdom as they progress from entry to exit. Unlike other, more common life experiences, attending a particular exhibition is something we generally do only once or, if truly moved, maybe two or three times. The exhibition designer, therefore, gets but one chance to make his or her mark. Screven offers some valuable suggestions on how to do so.

Except perhaps for the design of everyday appliances and clothing, graphic design is the most ubiquitous design modality. In most cases, printed or digital graphics are used in conjunction with other ways of communicating meaning (usually words). Sometimes, however, graphical images alone can become a powerful pattern language (or *ideography*): they not only symbolically represent meanings but also have elaborate meanings of their own. Such is the work of Yvonne Hansen, an information designer whose eclectic forays into a variety of other media inform her central work with graphics as a communication medium of unusual power. Hansen notes that just as there are different spoken and textual languages, so there are different graphical languages. The skillful deployment of these languages, she argues, can accomplish many different ends. Hansen's contribution (chapter 8) offers us insights into how we can use graphics to enhance understanding of complex, often abstract relationships without relying on the normally obligatory captions and textual explanations.

Moving from the printed or electronic page into three dimensionality at once amplifies our ability to design information and complicates the process. Currently, almost every design-industry trade show has a feature on three-dimensional (3-D) design, implying that everyone is doing it. Maybe so, but the fact remains that working in more than two dimensions requires prodigious spatial skills that many designers do not possess, because of sensory and cognitive disabilities or lack of training. In chapter 9, Hal Thwaites, who annually hosts a meeting on 3-D media at Concordia University, takes us on a tour of the vagaries of multidimensionality. We should emphasize that, although Thwaites is concerned mainly with representations in three-dimensional space, many forms of information design— for example, websites and scientific visualizations—regularly employ more than three dimensions by hyperlinking texts and illustrations or by displaying complex relationships involving the dimensions of time and place.

Researcher Tamara Munzer, whose work, regrettably, is not represented in this collection, takes multidimensionality even further, suggesting the use of non-Euclidean geometries to organize information consisting of more than three dimensions. (Munzer's work can be found at *www-graphics. stanford.edu/~Munzer*.) Thwaites shows us, however, that working in three dimensions is tricky enough: what awaits future information designers as they tackle the even knottier problems of conveying four or more dimensions of meaning is mind-boggling.

Yet another dimension relevant to information design is the dimension of human collaboration. In chapter 10 artist and information designer Judy Anderson describes a Seattle collaborative design project that linked not only many individuals but also many organizations in an effort to communicate the unexpected pleasures of sensibly planned public transportation. Her subject is the Puget Sound Metro's program for adding art to travel, to encourage commuters to leave the car at home and take the bus to work. Anderson was central to this project, and her account, which captures so well the enthusiasm of the participating artists, also contains an implicit caution. Every designer knows there is a complex and intimate relationship between design and politics, but the situation becomes even more complicated when ideology is at stake.

6 *The Uniqueness of Individual Perception*

Roger Whitehouse

In a recent project for The Lighthouse in New York, I became more aware than ever of the unique manner in which each of us perceives and processes the environment around us. It's not just a matter of the differences between, say, a sighted and a blind individual—as fascinating and demanding as those differences are when we set about studying them in detail—but of the remarkable variations between one sighted individual and another or among different blind individuals. If information design is to be meaningful, it must be responsible to the full range of perceptual viewpoints.

The essential premise of this essay, then, is that there are unique features of individual perception that have important implications for the design of information. However, as design cannot respond to each person on an individual basis, designers must search for some areas of commonality. Perhaps we can think of these areas as the circles of separate spotlight beams, each encompassing a specific group of individuals. In ideal situations, the beams can be broad and so include a large group of people; in other cases, they must be more tightly focused. The essential lesson for designers, therefore, is that we must be diligent enough in our efforts to understand individual needs to ensure that no one is left in the dark, either inadvertently or through our ignorance.

In the following account from his essay "The Man Who Mistook his Wife for a Hat," author and neurologist Oliver Sacks provides us with an intriguing glimpse into the world of a patient who, in other ways essentially normal, had lost the ability to understand and process what he saw, a condition known as *visual agnosia*.

... Not only did Dr. P. increasingly fail to see faces, but he saw faces when there were no faces to see: genially, Magoo-like, when in the street, he might pat the heads of water-hydrants and parking meters, taking these to be the heads of children; he would amiably address carved knobs on the furniture and be astounded when they did not reply. (Sacks 1985: 7)

In another account, "To See and Not See," Sacks describes the case of Virgil, who, blind from early childhood, had his sight surgically restored at the age of fifty. Suddenly and miraculously he could see but, like an infant, had no way of comprehending what he saw. Tragically, instead of having his universe expanded by these new-found senses, Virgil found himself trapped in a no man's land between two totally inconsistent identities. The comfortable perceptual equilibrium of blindness with which he was familiar was shattered by the raucous intrusion of the visual world.

On the day he returned home after the bandages were removed, his house and its contents were unintelligible to him, and he had to be led up the garden path, led through the house, led into each room, and introduced to each chair.... As Virgil explored the rooms of his house, investigating, so to speak, the visual construction of his world, I was reminded of an infant moving his hand to and fro before his eyes, waggling his head, turning it this way and that, in his primal construction of the world. (Sacks 1995: 127)

I cite these two examples, unusual and dramatic as they are, because they begin to give us an important insight into the nature of perception. They open the door to the notion that our perception of the world is not the same experience for all of us; that reality, like beauty, is perhaps in the eye of the beholder.

These, admittedly, are not everyday examples. What about the rest of us? When you or I see a fire hydrant, our spouse, or a hat, we probably understand them as a fire hydrant, our spouse, or a hat. Can I, therefore, assume that what I see is the same as what you see? Or, more specifically, that what I understand from what I see is the same as what you understand from what you see? What if the way we perceive things is much more individual and unique? What if we each, in effect, have our own special perceptual identity, our own unique "perceptual fingerprint"? Perhaps it is time to take a closer look at how and what we think we see.

At any specific point in our lives, our individual perceptual fingerprint is made up of three essential components. First, it depends on our *sensory mechanisms*, the receptors: such things as the rods and cones of our retinas, which determine whether or not we are colorblind, or the physical construction of our eardrums, which affect how well we hear. Second, it is depends on the *processing* of the information received by the brain. For instance, although we actually see things upside down, we perceive them right side up. If we wear special glasses that invert our vision, our brain, after a short but unpleasant period, corrects the situation and we see right side up again—until we remove the glasses. Then the whole process starts all over again. The specific brain cells allocated to processing sight vary greatly from one individual to another. There is evidence to suggest that in some instances areas of the primary visual cortex of blind individuals may in time be given over to the processing of auditory information, partially compensating them for the loss of sight. The third influence on perceptual individuality is the *meaning* we ascribe to what we see, hear, taste, smell, or touch. This interpretation, in turn, depends on memory, on the culture in which we have been brought up, and on the myriad experiences we associate with what our senses tell us.

Examples of perceptual differences abound. Some individuals who have perfect pitch can identify or whistle middle C or any other note precisely. At the other end of the scale are those who are tone deaf and can't even hold a tune when given a middle C to start with. Others, such as expert wine tasters, have such highly developed senses of taste and smell that they can identify the specific vineyard and vintage of a wine. To some of the rest of us, smell and taste are relatively insignificant aspects of our total sensory universe. In the area of visual perception, similarly, there are those who possess a so-called photographic memory, the visual counter-part of perfect pitch. Some individuals can memorize an entire page from the telephone book at a glance and recall individual numbers from it with apparent ease. (Personally, I can't remember a telephone number long enough to read it from the directory and dial it.)

With regard to the first component of perception, our sensory mecha-nisms, it is worthwhile to remember that nearly 10 percent of the male population—including myself, as it happens—is red-green colorblind. The very term *red-green colorblind*, however, only serves to emphasize and per-petuate the misconceptions we have about perception. In fact, I perceive all colors, including red and green, very vividly. However, I experience them differently than you may. To me they appear less clearly differen-tiated from each other; and reddish and greenish colors become increas-ingly less distinguishable as they become pale or muted or diluted with other colors—as in pastels, browns, or grays.

What about other red-green colorblind individuals? Do they inhabit the same special universe that I do? In fact, red-green colorblindness varies considerably in its intensity. There are also two very distinct types of this condition: one is a function of the red-sensitive receptors of the retina, the other of the green-sensitive receptors. Over the years, I have often had the experience of working in a darkroom under the illumination of a red safelight. I noticed that other people seemed quite nimble at finding their way around, while I can hardly make out anything in the cryptlike gloom. Though it occurred to me that this was probably due to my colorblindness, I noticed that a colleague of mine, who was also red-green colorblind, skipped around in the dark with no apparent difficulty. I was about to abandon my theory when I discovered the answer to the apparent puzzle: I am a *protanope*, and he a *deuteranope*—that is, my eyes are deficient in seeing red, his in seeing green. Notwithstanding the very different con-sequences of our respective sensory mechanisms, he and I are grouped together in the common category of red-green colorblindness.

The second component of perception is the way our brain, in the most basic way, understands and interprets what our senses tell us. In the days when I still practiced architecture in London, I had a very well-educated client, a publisher, who could not understand the drawings for the new house I was designing for him. The floor plans were very explicit and clear, but no matter how I explained them, it became increasingly obvious from his questions that he didn't understand them at all. When I took him to the site of the house and explained what I was proposing, walking around and pointing to this location and that, he understood clearly. He simply did not have the conceptual "software," as it were, to look at the two-dimensional drawings and create a three-dimensional image in his mind.

The third component of perception is meaning: what does your sensory experience mean to you? Past experiences, memory, and cultural influences all affect meaning. For example, those of us brought up in industrially developed cultures may have a rather different system of processing what we see than others do. In Western culture the environment abounds in straight, and frequently parallel, lines: the facades of buildings, streets and sidewalks, railroad tracks—our world is constructed of beams, planks, and panels whose very essence is to be parallel. Moreover, an environment of parallel lines is one rich in natural perspective—the lines of the curb, street, or highway converge toward a point on the horizon.

People in other cultures, such as the Zulu of Africa, see far fewer straight lines. Linear perspective is rarely experienced and so is typically not a developed attribute of their perception. Instead, they inhabit a landscape of plains, hills, and meandering rivers inhabited by trees and animals. Their immediate environment is of circular huts, pots, and baskets. Instead of the linear perspective with which we are familiar, they inhabit a free-form world of organic shapes. As a result, their perceptual experience tells them, size is the clue to distance; perspective is of little consequence.

When given distortion-illusion tests, the Zulu react only slightly to the effects of perspective. By contrast, in industrially developed cultures, the effects of perspective very strongly influence our perception. All the bold vertical lines in figure 6.1a and 6.1b are identical in length. Placement of the bold lines in 6.1a, however, creates a strong illusion that leads people acculturated to perspective to perceive the right-hand line as longer than

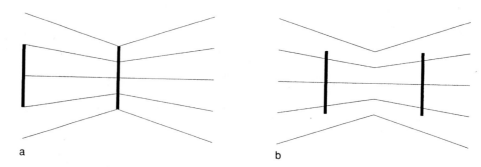

a   b

Figure 6.1

A Distortion-illusion Test. (a) People acculturated to perspective see the right-hand bold line as longer than the left. (b) As the background lines do not suggest perspective, most people see that the lines are the same length.

that on the left; as the background lines in figure 6.1b do not suggest perspective, the fact that the lines are the same length is clearly evident. A Zulu, not having a developed sense of perspective, would probably see little difference between the apparent length of the two bold lines in either diagram.

Not only do our individual perceptual differences distinguish us from one another, but all three components of perception—sensory mechanisms, interpretation, and meaning—also change, often dramatically, over the normal course of our lives. As babies, we leave a womb where we receive little sensory stimulation and, with all our sensory input devices in full working order, emerge into an explosion of light, color, sound, smell, noise, movement, touch—sensations that have absolutely no meaning for us. As newborns we may look at a cat, but we do not perceive "catness." In fact, as infants, we do not see a cat at all, but a confusion of shapes and colors, of light and dark—a meaningless, if interesting, jumble.

From that point on, our brains begin to work overtime, making connections between one thing and another until a coherent picture begins to emerge. One set of movements, patterns, shapes, smells, and tactile sensations slowly evolves into Mom. Another set becomes the cat, yet another the sideboard. We test each one out: feel them, chew on them, focus on them, and evaluate the dramatically different results. Chewing on Mom is good; on the sideboard, not too bad; and on the cat, a disaster. Rapidly, an increasingly complex awareness and understanding of the world around us emerges. We learn to compare and contrast, to sort out our experiences, to make connections and categories. In fact, as the process of perception develops we not only learn how to perceive specific things, but, in doing so, we learn the skill of perception itself. If, as adults, we see a praying mantis for the first time, despite its unusual shape we have now developed the ability to understand it as a creature and identify it as an insect, with a head, legs, eyes, and body. The newborn, in contrast, would simply not "see" it at all.

During childhood and young adulthood our sensory mechanisms, if not impaired, probably reach their peak. My fourteen-year-old daughter can read the small print on the back of an aspirin bottle in a darkened room without any difficulty. When she holds the bottle five inches away from her face, she can focus on it quite comfortably. At this distance, the type creates an adequately large and distinguishable image on her retina.

As time rolls on, many of us begin to notice that we can't focus as closely as we once did. At some point, typically in our mid-forties, holding the newspaper at arm's length is no longer sufficient to enable us to read it; the type just appears too small. After a visit to the opticians, everything is fine again, for a while at least, until, once again, we start holding the paper farther and farther away and have to pay more visits to the optician to get even stronger reading glasses. Then, as the ability of our eyes to focus continues to decrease, we may also need a distance prescription and are introduced to our first pair of bifocals.

As we move through our environment, things become increasingly awkward for us. Going to an art gallery and trying to read the captions becomes frustrating. Because our ability to focus is now so limited, and because indoor light levels make this worse by causing our pupils to dilate, we inch backward and forward, knees half-bent, head thrown back, so that we can squint out of the bottom of our trifocals in an attempt to get the caption on the wall into clear focus. Sadly, our need to indulge in these Neanderthal-like antics—made all the more difficult by stiffening joints—is the consequence of inattentive design. If the labels were at the correct height and angle, of sufficient size, and properly lit, we would not have to suffer this absurd indignity.

By this age, other changes are taking place. Our night vision has become noticeably reduced. In fact, at sixty years of age we need a great deal more light to read by than we did as a teenager. Our ability to adjust from bright to low light has also dramatically decreased, and the afterimage of car headlights in our rearview mirror at night makes night driving increasingly less pleasant and more difficult.

All of these changes, however, are absolutely "normal," and in middle age we are probably at the peak of our productive lives. At our regular visit our ophthalmologist may well pronounce our eyes "in perfect health." We are just experiencing the normal effects of natural aging.

Perception, thus, is a much more personal affair than we might have imagined. In Oliver Sacks's account of both Dr. P. and Virgil, we are surprised to discover that what we see and what we understand are two very different matters. It comes as a shock to realize that perception is not just a simple matter of seeing something and learning what it is. First we have to establish a whole set of, as it were, perceptual beliefs to serve as a framework for interpreting sensory experiences. Our unique perceptual abilities are, in fact, an essential component of our very identity. If we recognize that our individual sensory equipment and our ability to interpret what this equipment tells us also differ—sometimes dramatically—we begin to see perception in a wholly new light.

For designers, this situation presents a special challenge, one to which we have so far largely failed to respond. We seem to have assumed that we are each located at the center of the perceptual universe. We may have done, at best, a good job of responding to the demands of that idealized universe. At worst, however, this attitude has disenfranchised many whose needs we could readily meet. Whereas we could just as easily choose a color palette perceptible to the entire sighted population, we routinely expect the approximately 10 percent of the male population who are colorblind to differentiate among colors that are, to all intents and purposes, indistinguishable and that render most color-coded maps unintelligible. Why do we continue to package dose-critical drugs intended for adults in medicine bottles that display essential information in four-point type and feature childproof caps that only children could possibly read or open? Why do we only erratically and infrequently place street numbers on individual buildings? Apart from making wayfinding difficult for those with good vision, this creates a frustratingly impossible hurdle for anyone with any kind of impaired sight.

The probable answer is *adaptability*, one of our greatest human attributes. We seem to adapt ourselves without complaint to unnecessarily difficult circumstances. Nonetheless, designers should not accept the lowest level of performance as an acceptable design parameter just because people will put up with it. We need to pay much more attention to the real needs of users of all ages and cultural groups. Even then we may not be able to take everyone's needs into account all of the time; but if we are at least cognizant of the full range of perceptual differences, we will probably be able to satisfy a much more inclusive group much more regularly and effectively.

First of all, designers have to learn about the perceptual differences and needs of those who will use what they create. Sadly, very little useful information of this kind is available. Many narrowly focused clinical studies have been conducted on many detailed aspects of perception in general and vision in particular. They are generally designed to provide highly reliable and precise information; and to accomplish this they are properly confined to very specific issues with a limited number of variables. They also tend to be undertaken in clinical settings, which yield results that are not necessarily ideal for designers. What we need to know is what works out there in the real world: not an understanding of visual acuity obtained from a relaxed and seated subject in a comfortable, well-lit room, but information about how a frustrated and confused subject worried about meeting an appointment while struggling with an overloaded shopping bag comprehends a critical message in a crowded and noisy environment.

All this is not to criticize hard-nosed clinical research, but simply to acknowledge that such research is designed with different goals in mind. The resource that we lack as designers is accumulated wisdom. The number of potential parameters affecting any real life situation is so great that obtaining clean clinical information is next to impossible. But what we can do—and do with relative economy—is obtain some less tidy information by conducting simple real-life tests in real-life situations. Such information might also help us focus on areas of concern that can then be the subject of much more controlled and detailed research.

I recently had the opportunity to do just that, in the one specific area of vision impairment, when my firm was asked to design a comprehensive wayfinding system for the new headquarters of The Lighthouse Inc., in New York. This task provided us with a unique opportunity to study a specific population whose special perceptual needs also could lead us to a better overall understanding of how *all* individuals perceive and process their environment.

The Lighthouse is the world's leading provider of services for individuals with vision disorders. Its clients range from those whose reduced vision is the natural consequence of aging, to those with severe loss of vision or with partial or total blindness resulting from disease or accident, to those who have been blind from birth.

Apart from the particular profile of its users, The Lighthouse offered us a special opportunity. Because it works with clients on a day-to-day basis to provide them assistance and training, we were able to set up a series of simple tests with the same users during their daily visits, helping us to determine what differing perceptual needs our design solution would have to meet.

To begin, we sought out the existing research literature and other work that would help us understand the task at hand. The Lighthouse itself provided a great deal of specific information on such issues as color and contrast for people with poor vision and on the details of its clients' various types of vision impairment. We found, however, very little information about other questions we needed to answer in order to design an effective system. For instance:

- How do users with little or no effective vision form cognitive images that enable them to find their way around?

- Are tactile maps a possible solution to the problem of general orientation? If so, what form should they take? What kind of, and how much, information should they contain?

- How do users read tactile information? What letterforms work best? How big should the letters be and how should they be spaced? What are the most effective locations for tactile information?

- What is the most effective kind of visual information for individuals with low vision? How big should letters be? Should they be all upper case, or is upper and lower case better? What letterforms are most easily understood?

- What about contrast and color? Light on dark, or dark on light? Is monochrome or color better?

- Will symbols help? What kind of symbols can be distinguished tactually? Can tactile and visual symbols be combined effectively?

- To what extent will a one-size-fits-all approach work, or are the needs of different user groups in certain areas so divergent that duplicate or redundant information systems are needed?

To unearth some answers to these issues, and to evolve a final design, we first set about designing the design process itself. The conventional approach would have been to find out what we could, extrapolate from that to fill in what we didn't know, use our intuition to develop a design solution, and then build it and hope for the best. Instead, we decided to build a set of approximate prototypes based on whatever information we could gather, test them with an appropriate group of users, then use that information to build another set, test those, and repeat the process until we felt confident we could design and build the final components to install in the completed building. Even when the system was complete we planned to return to evaluate it after users had become familiar with the system over a period of time. In this way, we hoped to begin establishing some common wisdom about what really works.

Figure 6.2
Testing for Letterform Preferences. Individuals with little or no effective vision helped identify the most readable style, size, contrast, and spacing to use on tactile signage.

Together with the staff of The Lighthouse, we first put together a series of tests. We typically used a group of six to eight individuals, each with a different type of vision disability or blindness relevant to the specific tests being conducted (figure 6.2). Working with each subject in the group for fifteen minutes to half an hour—with enough time between interviews to get organized and provide some buffer space—added up to a manageable day's work.

Altogether, we devised twelve different tests, some of which progressed through several iterations. Six of the tests were for individuals with impaired but useful vision.

- Preference for light or bold letterforms
- Preference for serif or sans serif letterforms

- Preference for all upper case, as opposed to upper and lower case, letterforms
- Size of letterforms for use on eye-level signs
- Acceptable degree of contrast between message and background
- Preference for light on dark or dark on light copy for messages

The other six tests were for users who had no effective vision.

- Preference for light or bold tactile letterforms
- Preference for serif, sans serif, or other letterforms for tactile messages
- Size of letterforms for use on tactile signs
- Intercharacter spacing for tactile letterforms
- Tactile map forms
- Effectiveness and potential form of tactile symbols

Although we could not always conduct tests as thoroughly or as comprehensively as we wished, the information we were able to obtain was invaluable for creating our wayfinding system at The Lighthouse. It led us to develop some unique design features, including special tactile maps, custom tactile typefaces, the placement of visual and tactile components on separate plaques, and a tactile "ledge" to make reading Braille and other tactile elements more comfortable. The finished building is the first in the world to be completely signed: visually, tactually, and audibly. We do not believe it is in any way the ultimate solution; we regard it, rather, as a laboratory for the ongoing evaluation of its many special features. The degree to which our various design components emerge as useful mainstream solutions remains to be seen.

This is not the place to document in detail all the extensive practical results and observations that emerged from our work. But, as a consequence of observing the test subjects and listening to the comments we encouraged them to make, we began to understand the ways in which each user's perceptual process was unique and affected the system we planned.

a TIMES ROMAN
HELVETICA BOLD
VAG RUNDSCHRIFT

b HAPTIC TO4
HAPTIC VT10

c S A 4 O M W
S A 4 O M W

Figure 6.3
Typefaces Tested for Tactile Signage. (a) Three standard typefaces. (b) Typeface designed for the Lighthouse; slightly bolder form (bottom line) was suitable for both tactile and visual signage. (c) Modifications to conventional letterforms (bottom row) helped tactile readers distinguish between similar characters.

One of the first series of tests we designed concerned the issue of suitable tactile letterforms. When we started this project, we were unable to find any information on this subject. Although we set out with the simple goal of discovering what letterforms would be most legible, we uncovered a wealth of invaluable information about other issues we were not even aware of when we began. By the time we finished, we had designed two custom typefaces to incorporate and make use of what we had learned.

We began by testing different letterforms (figure 6.3): a serif face (Times Roman), a conventional sans serif face (Helvetica Bold), and a geometrical engineering sans serif face (VAG Rundschrift). In this test, we measured how long it took subjects to read nine random characters of each alphabet tactually and asked them about their preferences. (Interestingly, on two occasions subjects preferred letterforms other than those they had read most quickly and with most apparent ease.) We also logged all pairs of characters they mistakenly transposed.

Of the typefaces we tested, the geometrical engineering face, VAG Rundschrift, was the best performer. In fact, two users managed to read it in half the time it took for them to read Times Roman. Six of the seven individuals tested also expressed a subjective preference for this face. Helvetica fared only marginally better than Times Roman. While this might seem inconsequential in the context of visual type, it took an average of about twenty to thirty seconds for each user to read a set of nine characters. Considering that the average message is much longer than that, the time it takes to read a tactile lettering message becomes critical.

In the letterforms test, the act of observing the users and discussing their progress with them provided us with the most valuable information. Instead of tracing the outline in a clear progression—for instance, following the curve of an *S*—users "kneaded" the character, often with more than one finger, as if it were dough. The typical running commentary might be: "What is this? Is it a *9*? No, it's got another bump down here; is it a *B*? But there's no flat bit; or an *8*? No, it seems to be open here; is it an *S*? Yes, that's it, it's an *S*." Then the reader would go on to the next character, intently going over and over that character until he or she had determined its identity. As part of this test, we also noted which characters tended to be confused with each other. The most prevalent mistakes—and they occurred quite frequently—included the following pairs: *MW, MN, OQ, VY, A4, I1, O0,* and *69*. Interestingly, several users confused the characters *MW* and *69* by transposing them vertically (that is, reading them upside down), leading us to believe that polarity is not as clear a perceptual issue tactually as it is visually. For a blind reader, up and down are relative to the orientation of the tip of the finger. In fact, Braille users sometimes read a book upside down, while it is facing away from them and propped on a cushion. At The Lighthouse this up-down reversal led us to install the stairwell Braille markers indicating floor levels upside down on the back of the handrails, which is right-side-up to the fingertips of Braille readers.

We were made aware of another important issue during the tactile-letterform test. Users who were blind from birth, or at least from early childhood, had such highly developed finger sensitivity that they raced through this test with a very high degree of accuracy. Interestingly, these were the same users who read Braille and therefore did not normally need to read tactile letters. The commentary about recognition of a tactile *S* quoted above, on the other hand, was typical of users who had lost their sight later in life. Although several of them were attempting to learn Braille, they often found it very difficult and, having a memory of visual letterforms, preferred the tactile letters. Some of them had lost their sight as a result of diabetes and had also experienced a loss of fingertip sensitivity, a typical consequence of this disease. It is often very difficult for those who have lost their sight after childhood to develop the tactile sensitivity and seventh sense to understand Braille, whereas those whose basic knowledge of written language comes through this medium from the beginning have far greater tactile fluency. Once again, we found much greater perceptual diversity than we might have imagined. The blind are not just a single group, but, like everyone else, are individuals with a wide spectrum of perceptual abilities and needs.

It was because of what we learned in these tests that I decided to develop some alphabets specifically tailored to the needs of tactile readers. We designed two separate alphabets, one for tactile reading only and one intended to be read both visually and tactually. The key difference between the two faces is something we discovered by testing: the ideal "weight" for tactile-only reading is a very thin profile, similar to the cross section of a Braille dot, or about 4 percent of the height of a half-inch character. This would have been too thin for the alphabet to be read visually; in the latter instance, we settled on a stroke thickness of 10 percent of the character height (figure 6.3b). We named the typefaces Haptic Light (intended for tactile reading) and Haptic Bold (intended for both tactile and visual reading).

The bottom row of characters in figure 6.3c illustrates some of the characteristics of Haptic compared to the more conventional letterforms shown in the upper row. Because tactile recognition of letterforms is so difficult, simple open forms work best. We made open shapes such as the *S* as open as possible. For characters readers often transposed, such as *A* and *4*, we used an open form for the numeral to distinguish it from the letter. In the case of the letter *O* and the numeral *0*, a short diagonal line was borrowed from computer display technology to distinguish the numeral (∅). The frequent vertical transposition of *M* and *W* was solved by listening to one subject's commentary: "Is this an *M* or a *W*? I don't know. It seems like an *M*, but it's got slanty sides. *W*s have slanty sides, *M*s have straight sides." We therefore used this differentiation to design these two characters, and, through ongoing testing, confirmed that most users felt comfortable with this convention.

Determining an appropriate size for tactile letters was another interesting issue. Through testing, we eventually settled on half-inch-high characters instead of five-eighths of an inch. Our subjects' preferences were evenly divided between the two sizes, but it was generally agreed that the smaller size was preferable because, in several instances where space was limited, it made the difference between having the information in the smaller size or not having it at all.

The tests of letter size led us to yet another important perceptual issue about tactile information. Whereas visual size is always relative (i.e., the image on the retina is constantly changing with the viewing distance, which can be adjusted by the user), tactile size is constant. As a consequence, a standard size for raised lettering should perhaps be established. It may also be advisable to have a standard typeface, for the same reason that Braille letters are always constant in both size and form.

Because we carried out our tests in realistic situations (e.g., by mounting letterform samples, like conventional signs, on vertical walls), we learned that tactile readers had difficulty positioning themselves to read the lettering. Because Braille is read with the pads of the fingertips, they had to hold the palm of the hand flat against the wall, a position they found both uncomfortable and conspicuous. In response, we developed a slanted *tactile ledge*, which presents Braille and raised lettering at a forty-five degree angle. Most blind users much preferred this solution. The only drawback is that because the plaque is no longer vertical, it more easily collects dust and dirt and could become unpleasant to touch if not properly cleaned.

Probably the most interesting part of our research involved tactile mapping. From the very beginning, tactile maps were considered a very important part of the program. We hoped they would assist us in solving the problem of providing users both general orientation within the building and helping them locate signs identifying specific rooms. In discussions with The Lighthouse staff, we decided that the maps should be both tactile and visual, so that sighted and blind users could use and discuss features of the map together when assisting one another to find their way around. For the same reason, we decided to locate the map so that the receptionists on each level could use the map to explain the layout of the building to visitors. In consultation with Mitchell/Giurgola-Architects—who incorporated many unique accessible architectural features into the new facility—we decided to integrate the map with the reception desk on each floor.

In our research we discovered and studied several types of tactile maps, but found none that bore directly on our task at The Lighthouse. Knowing that developing the maps would be a very complex task, we developed a series of repeated test cycles during which we created a prototype, tested it, revised it, tested it again, and so on. In this manner, we eventually progressed through six iterations before arriving at the final design. Our tests involved four alternative concepts for mapping space tactually (figure 6.4).

- A full spatial map—in essence a complete floor plan made dimensional
- A partial spatial map, which only delineated corridors and other major circulation spaces
- A route- and event-diagram—in essence, a diagram of the major routes on each floor and the "events" (doorways to rooms, stairways, and the like) that users would encounter when navigating this route
- A directional diagram that simply indicated what could be found in any direction from the user's present location

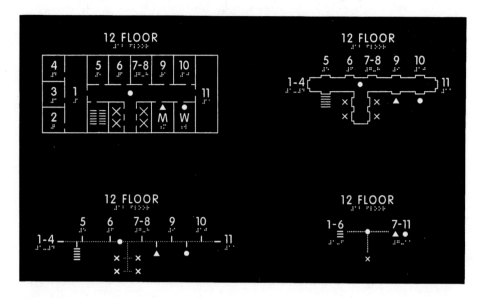

Figure 6.4
Four Alternative Concepts for Mapping Space Tactually. Top left: A full spatial map, in essence a complete floor plan made dimensional. Top right: A partial spatial map, delineating only corridors and other major circulation spaces. Bottom left: A route-and-event-diagram showing the major routes on each floor and the sequential "events" (doorways, stairways, etc.) users would encounter along the route. Bottom right: A directional diagram indicating simply what users could find in any direction from their present location.

These tests, like the tactile-lettering tests, provided us with a wealth of information. By observation, we discovered that our subjects used the same "kneading" process they employed for the lettering to read the map. The Braille readers surpassed others in both speed and accuracy, again, by a considerable margin. Subjects invariably began at the top left-hand corner and took from ten to twenty minutes to read the full spatial map. The partial spatial map took about half that time, and the route-and-event diagram about a third of the time. The directional diagram took a very short time to read but, because it contained so little information, was not considered appropriate for this project. It is important to realize here that, in many cases, this was the first experience subjects had had with tactile maps of any description; consequently, they probably read the maps much more slowly than they would have after training and practical experience.

Moreover, many blind individuals—particularly those who were congenitally blind—found the whole notion of a map very mystifying. Some congenitally blind users were particularly interested in the route-and-event diagram, which made us aware of a dramatic perceptual difference in the way sighted and congenitally blind individuals take in and interpret the environment around them. Sighted individuals can scan their surroundings and simultaneously become aware of the multiple possible structures and destinations within their purview; theirs is a complex and three-dimensional spatial understanding of the relationships of all of these things. The blind individual, on the other hand, experiences the environment sequentially, discovering first the door handle, then the door, then the frame, then the wall, then the wastebasket, then the chair, and so on. From these multiple experiences, he or she forms a cognitive image of interrelated "events," though what form this cognitive image takes is difficult for a sighted individual to conceive. I doubt that there is any clear interrelationship of objects that are not in the immediate vicinity of each other. The experience of Virgil, cited earlier, suggests that the image is almost certainly nothing like that of an individual who is, or at least once was, sighted. There are documented cases of individuals who have had their sight restored but could not distinguish between a sphere and a pyramid by sight, even though they were familiar with the objects by touch.

We had included "You-are-here" tactile arrows on all versions of the map. Observing the users' response to this feature was a revelation that led me to the notion of what I came to call *visual prejudice*. As a sighted person, I was so accustomed to the notion that I could randomly scan the map, locate the point on the map where I was standing, and begin to form a cognitive image of destinations and features in relationship to that location that it did not occur to me that blind individuals would not do the same thing. In fact, it took the average blind user ten minutes or so to find the arrow. When they did, they could not distinguish what it was.

When we explained it to them, they were even more mystified and could not easily, or sometimes at all, grasp the concept of their relationship to the spot on the map. Once again, unless blind individuals had lost their sight later in life and had a clear memory of using maps, they appeared to have a very difficult time creating any kind of cognitive image based on the map's information. In fact, some of the users translated the information on the map, when they began to understand it, into sequential instructions: "O.K., so if I'm here, then I need to turn left, go past this door, then past this other door, then turn right down this corridor, and the classroom is at the end, on the left." It was for this reason that we developed the route-and-event diagram—which effectively provides sequential information—as an alternative to the full spatial map.

In developing the full spatial map, we started by indicating doors with a diagonal line, like the half-open door seen on building plans. Users found this extremely confusing. In one instance, the subject could only satisfactorily explain the meaning to herself by reinterpreting it as "a line leading you toward the doorway." Other issues became evident as well; for example, the need to adequately separate tactile components and to select symbols carefully so that they could be easily distinguished from one another by touch. On the basis of this feedback, we proceeded to prepare the next sets of test maps, which evolved through six iterations before we designed the maps finally installed (figure 6.5).

In the succeeding tests, we continued to develop and test new features. We simplified doors into openings in the line representing the walls. To indicate the "you are here" location, we created a "super tactile pip" that could be easily located by "scanning" the map with the hand. We thickened the wall lines to distinguish them better from tactile letters. Discovering that cane users counted doors as a key part of their sequential wayfinding , we indicated doors to inaccessible spaces such as mechanical rooms as a shallow recess in the wall.

The tests showed no clear preference for either the full spatial map or the route-and-event diagram. Ultimately, The Lighthouse decided to install the full spatial map, because it contained information about the configu-

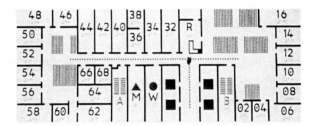

Figure 6.5
Detail of the Full Spatial Map. This final version incorporated simplified door openings, thicker wall lines, and a "super tactile pip" to indicate the "you are here" location.

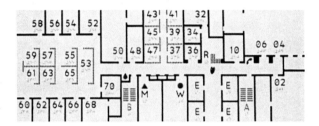

Figure 6.6
The Final Full Spatial Map. This installed version contained information about the configuration of the rooms and could be used effectively by both blind and sighted users.

ration of rooms useful to, especially, staff members and frequent visitors. The full spatial map also had the advantage of being an effective visual map that could be used by both blind and sighted users, which was not the case with the route-and-event diagram. Nevertheless, at our suggestion, a route-and-event diagram was installed on one floor so that we could gather, over time, some user feedback to evaluate and compare the forms (figures 6.6 and 6.7).

At an early stage of developing the maps we realized that symbols could act as a kind of tactile shorthand to reduce the time it took users to recognize certain commonly used designations, such as bathrooms and stairwells. We soon discovered, however, that tactile symbols had to be very carefully selected. Many users, for example, could not easily distinguish between a tactile square and a triangle; several of them described both

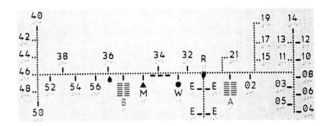

Figure 6.7
Final Version of the Route-and-Event Diagram. This diagram was installed on one floor in order to gather user feedback for evaluation and comparison with the full spatial map.

shapes as "bumps with sharp bits." They could, however, easily distinguish them from a circle, a "smooth bump." Again, visual prejudice was at work here. Sighted readers can so easily distinguish between different shapes that they find it hard to believe blind readers cannot do so too. An easy way to discover this for yourself, if you are sighted, is to try to read some tactile symbols. To be an effective test, it should be arranged so that you don't see the symbols first; it's surprising how easy recognition becomes when you know what they are beforehand.

Among many visual tests we conducted were studies to see what, if any, preference users had for messages presented as light symbols on dark backgrounds or vice versa. Here there was, as anticipated, a unanimous preference for the former, for two likely reasons. First, because there is considerably more area of background than message, the amount of glare is much reduced with a dark background. Second, out-of-focus or diffused light spreads into any adjacent dark space. Thus, a light message on a dark background makes the message appear bolder, whereas a dark message on a light background appears lighter.

We were also interested in identifying an acceptable degree of contrast between a message and its background. We tested the same message in white on black, white on 85-percent gray, white on 70-percent gray, and white on 55-percent gray. We expected that a reasonably high contrast—say, 70 percent—would be acceptable to most people, but we were mistaken: everyone we tested not only preferred the strongest contrast possible but was vehement about it. Observing several individuals struggling to read even the white-on-black sample from just a few inches away gave us a vivid understanding of why contrast is so important for anyone with any kind of clouded or obscured vision—for example, a cataract, a not-infrequent part of the natural aging process. Consequently, we cannot stress too strongly the importance of contrast as a key factor in legibility. Unfortunately, we did not have the opportunity to test color contrast, which is probably of considerable value for its aesthetic potential as well as its ability to provide contrast between message and field.

At an early stage of the project, The Lighthouse staff decided to investigate using audible "signs" to provide environmental information to those with no effective vision. Two potential solutions were available: a push-and-play system, which speaks to the user when a room-identification plaque is touched, or a spoken message transmitted by infrared light beams in or near a door, which can be picked up with a hand-held receiver. The infrared system was chosen because it allows the user to "scan" the environment with the hand-held device for any potential destinations and then determine the precise direction of the desired destination. This system, in effect, gives the blind user some of a sighted user's ability to scan the environment. In our final design solution, we made use of the underside of the "tactile ledge" to house the infrared LED transmitters and to angle them in a way that provides the most effective directional signal.

As we explored all of these aspects of differing individual perception, an interesting philosophical issue arose. When should designers adopt a one-size-fits-all solution and when should they consider separate and, in some cases, redundant systems? We discovered at The Lighthouse that the needs of sighted and blind users demand very different solutions with regard to letterforms. In addition, the separate needs of congenitally and adventitiously blind users required us to include both raised lettering and Braille. While the conventional solution would have assumed a one-size-fits-all scenario, we believed that in this situation "one size fits nobody" and that separating visual and tactile information on the plaques identifying room functions was the most helpful response. Furthermore, we decided that it

Figure 6.8
Talking Signs. The room-identification plaques installed combined audible, visual, and tactile components useful to blind, deaf, and sighted visitors.

was appropriate to incorporate some degree of redundancy—in the form of audible components or talking signs—into each of the room plaques (figure 6.8). In addition to giving blind users the option of choosing either the tactile or auditory system, the two systems permit users with hearing impairments to take advantage of the tactile components and users who lack fingertip sensitivity (such as diabetics) to utilize the talking signs.

With the tactile maps, however, we decided that a one-size-fits-all approach was most appropriate, so that blind and sighted users could simultaneously read and discuss the information displayed on them. A sighted user could, for instance, place a blind user's fingers on the correct part of the map, the tactile equivalent of pointing. Although this is not necessary for room signs, it is important that the visual, raised lettering, Braille, and auditory messages be consistent with each other so that verbal discussions of the messages—including directions one individual gives to another—are not confusing.

In thinking about the implications of this project, readers should remember that our objective was to undertake specific research, with actual users, and with a specific goal in mind—gathering information to create a way-finding system for The Lighthouse. Consequently, the tests we designed and the conclusions we drew from them focused specifically on that end. We expected to gain, and did in fact gain, some general understanding of the direction in which designers of information systems should be heading, as well as some insights into specific issues that might be important in the design of similar projects. Nonetheless, it is important to caution readers that we were able to survey only a relatively small sample of users and, although the results were invaluable to our work, care should be taken not to inappropriately extrapolate from these results and conclusions or attempt to apply them universally.

Nonetheless, the results of our testing of the maps and typefaces alone convinced us of the extraordinary value of the design process we had developed. By simple testing and observation, we not only gathered a wealth of information that had previously been unavailable, but we also became aware of some of the practical implications of individual perceptual differences. Most importantly, we began to understand how easy it is to disenfranchise individuals simply by not perceiving and correctly interpreting the most basic facts about their needs.

As designers, we need to be conscious of, accept, and embrace the notion of unique perceptual abilities and respond generously to the needs it implies. Although this notion is entirely analogous to multiculturalism, it is more difficult to defend, because it operates on a much more individual level. But it is important to defend it, because the consequences of ignorance, avoidance, and exclusion are serious. It is tragic when dyslexic children are made to feel stupid, defective, and inferior just because we are uncomfortable with the idea of allowing our "standards" of performance to be bent enough to include them. It is tragic when the prevailing attitude avoids or ignores the fact that aging persons with failing eyesight may have needs we can respond to with more effective lighting; larger, higher-contrast print; or larger and clearer controls on their VCRs and washing machines.

Because we blithely assume ourselves to be the standard or norm, we often tend to think of the differences between others and ourselves as aberrations of normality, rather than accepting others as just a different kind of normal. They become "them," different from and no longer the concern of "us." In more extreme cases, we see them as "disabled," incapable of playing an active part in our culture. At best, we tend to tolerate them, when what they require, and deserve, is active inclusion.

It is time to realize that, precisely because we are all so different, there are no "them" and "us." We are all us. There is as much reason to embrace and celebrate our perceptual differences as our cultural and ethnic distinctions. If that embrace is expansive and generous enough, we can all be a part of one truly common humanity.

References

Oliver W Sacks. 1985. *The Man Who Mistook His Wife For A Hat And Other Clinical Tales.* New York: Summit Books.

Oliver W Sacks. 1995. *An Anthropologist on Mars: Seven Paradoxical Tales.* New York: Alfred A. Knopf.

7 Information Design in Informal Settings: Museums and Other Public Spaces

C. G. Screven

The psychology of human learning, attention, and behavior—as well as recent findings in how the brain learns—provide an array of empirical data and principles with important implications for the design of signage, thematic exhibitions, and self-directed learning in public environments. Perhaps the most challenging application is communicating knowledge, ideas, and concepts in public spaces like museums, zoos, science centers, botanical gardens, and shopping malls. Messages delivered in such settings require the voluntary cooperation of potential "receivers" while they are surrounded by distractions and choices. Visitors do not have to pay attention but are free to attend, ignore, or distort the messages being communicated. In such situations, it is immensely important to design information systems that not only reflect the needs and characteristics of audiences but also attract and hold their attention.

Since the late 1960s interest in studying the behavior and learning that takes place in informal settings—museums, neighborhoods, recreational centers, and so forth—has grown steadily. While much of this work has focused on measuring visitor behavior and factual learning in museum-type environments and recreational areas, current efforts are searching for ways to anchor museum learning to underlying principles and theories of learning, instruction, and motivational processes; memory; perception; thinking; and social factors.[1]

Communicating new ideas to the unguided public in quasi-educational settings like museums presents many obstacles—visitors' uncertainties about what to see and how to get there, a poor knowledge base for exhibit content, negative attitudes and pervasive misconceptions, wide variations in thinking styles, physical and psychological fatigue, social and visual distractions, the lack of tangible goals, and the pressures of time.[2] Information design, therefore, must be responsive to all these factors, as well as to underlying biological and cognitive processes.

Unless unguided viewers are already knowledgeable about the exhibit topic, the interpretive materials must connect the unfamiliar with the familiar and suggest useful things the viewer can do with the information. Unfortunately, few of those who plan and design exhibit content give serious attention to developing effective interpretive materials (as reflected by such arguments as *"Rembrandt speaks for himself," "Explanatory materials distract viewers from experiencing the objects,"* and *"Visitors don't want labels"*). Thus, little effort or money is budgeted for pretesting interpretive (explanatory) text, graphics, and formats to determine whether they are meaningful to targeted audiences. So visitors are often on their own to make sense of what they see. Even exhibits designed for easy interpretation may still—given viewers' limited time, fatigue, and other distractions—discourage the selective attention and effort needed for learning.

In the 1920s and 1930s, and again more recently, various researchers studied visitor behavior and learning, investigating such questions as: How do people behave and move about in exhibit spaces? What do they learn? Do they learn what the exhibitors aimed to convey? Do they learn other things? Even though freely moving visitors who were the subjects of these studies did learn some useful information (Shettel 1968; Screven 1969), the results were generally disappointing. While their movement patterns mostly followed the physical layout of exhibit galleries and areas, visitors of most ages and background absorbed little or nothing of the exhibits' intended messages (E. Robinson 1928; Melton 1933, 1935; Lakota 1976), except when displays were modified to improve viewer attention and exhibit communication (Miles 1987; P. Robinson 1960; Shettel 1968;

Screven 1969). As the average viewing time at individual displays was only 10 to 25 seconds, this result should not surprise us. Visitors stopped at some exhibits, often looking at random, then went on, making few comments and not examining materials. "Hands-on" and "interactive" exhibits elicited more active attention, but, again, it was mostly random and centered on trivial elements unconnected with the substantive content of the exhibit. In general, before and after testing showed that visitors knew little more about their subjects after viewing exhibits than they had before. Sometimes, in fact, they interpreted exhibit content as support for misconceptions the displays were designed to correct! Such findings may reflect inadequate exhibit objectives, invalid measures of learning, or exhibitors' inexperience at meeting visitors' needs.

Perhaps viewers would do better, researchers speculated, if they were more motivated to learn. As early as the 1950s and 1960s, several studies examined how rewards affect the motivation of the general public (Nedzel 1952; Shettel et al. 1968; Screven 1969). Shettel offered to donate money to a charity if visitors would carefully study an exhibit's content. Screven gave rewards (sometimes cash) to visitors themselves in exchange for correctly answering a few basic questions about an exhibit's content. Both reported that visitors who worked for rewards indeed spent more time than usual looking at the exhibits but that the majority of them still did not grasp the intended messages—as measured by post-tests devised by the exhibits' curators. Some researchers suggested that the poor results were misleading, because the tests reflected too narrow a view of what visitors were supposed to learn; useful learning may have taken place, they argued, but the tests did not measure whether, for example, the presentation increased visitors' interest in the topic, gave them personally useful information, or added to their self-esteem. Subsequent work indicated that visitors did indeed learn other things, although they were often counterproductive; for example, they "learned" that science is boring, that modern art is a scam, and so on. Some visitors could not paraphrase the ideas presented or even follow exhibit instructions.

Of course, not all visitors show such poor learning. People generally gain useful information from an exhibit when they are already somewhat knowledgeable about its subject. Background and familiarity often enable them to link unfamiliar information with existing knowledge, resulting in a rewarding educational experience. But for those lacking such background, exhibit content may not be of much value.

One might argue that what an exhibition communicates has more to do with visitors' entering attitudes, moods, and preconceptions than with its content and design. Personal beliefs and other baggage often play important roles in how messages are perceived and processed, what visitors tell their friends, and so on (Borun 1992). But the impact of public displays is more complex than that. Ultimately, a display's ability to convey new knowledge and understanding is shaped by the interface between visitor dispositions and preconceptions and the exhibit's content, delivery media, and format. If so, being informed about this interface is essential to designers hoping to communicate effectively with their publics.

Encouraging steps toward improving this communication have been taken in recent years. Museums appear to be shifting toward visitor-centered approaches, in which target audiences play an equal part with staff members in developing planning protocols (Screven 1993, 1999). In contrast to top-down planning by experts, visitor-centered (bottom-up) approaches focus on behavioral, motivational, and learning variables and how they influence users' responses to an exhibit's media, message design, and interactive elements.[3]

In this paper I address visitor-centered approaches and exhibit features, focusing on methods that improve a display's ability to deliver useful information and ideas to freely moving, voluntary, leisure-oriented people in public environments. The applications of these approaches, however, go beyond museums and include the planning and design of directional signage, wayfinding, trade shows, malls, job-retraining programs, brochures, guidebooks, and software documentation. The main tasks in all of these areas are essentially the same—to affect people's actions, attitudes, preconceptions, and/or comprehension. Their purpose is to encourage self-directed people to focus on and retain messages in which they may or may not be interested initially.

The Public as an Editor of Information Design

The complexity of human behavior and learning in open settings makes it difficult to predict—without advance evidence about a given audience—how a design will affect behavior and learning. The same display, sign, headline, or placement can have different effects in different settings for different users or with different messages. Information designs need to be pretested in real settings with real people early in planning—the earlier the better. In recent years, exhibit evaluators have developed cost-effective methods of pretesting to identify and adjust features that could adversely affect attention, behavior, and/or communication. These procedures allow them to observe and test the effect of specific graphics, text formats, interactive displays, and placement on their human "receivers," and then make adjustments. This approach (called *formative evaluation*) is a practical tool for detecting and correcting behavioral and communication problems before an exhibit is installed (Griggs and Manning 1983, Miles et al. 1988). The approach is not the same as testing late-stage prototype text and graphics for communication effectiveness, reliability, or human factors; until recently, the use of formative evaluation during each stage of exhibit design was rare. Evaluation, when it occurred, often employed overly complex materials that were tested too late in the design process to effectively spot and modify problem elements.

The operative term here is *evaluation*. Most planners, graphics designers, and communication specialists are familiar with socioeconomic surveys that provide data on the demographic attributes of visitors (e.g., age, income, education) and their visitation habits and attitudes. While these surveys can be very useful, knowledge of the effect of other attributes—such as, among those mentioned earlier, fatigue, distractedness, preconceptions, motivation—have more direct relevance to early decisions about exhibit elements and formats.

The post-1970s research literature describes four kinds and stages of visitor evaluation: front-end evaluation, formative evaluation, summative evaluation, and remedial evaluation. All four types go beyond the familiar visitor survey and broaden the meaning of the term *visitor research*.[4] The first two types are described in the following brief sections.

Front-end Evaluation

This form of testing identifies an audience's entering knowledge, biases, attitudes, and preconceptions about prospective exhibit topics *before* actual exhibit design begins. It also examines the time constraints, perceptual sets, curiosity levels, thinking styles, and other activities or characteristics likely to affect visitors' responses and ability to learn from a given design. Finally, it looks for the particular elements likely to make an exhibit rewarding to specific groups of visitors. Designers can then carefully analyze prospective messages and goals and establish exhibit priorities that take these viewer characteristics into account. Such information can also guide choice of language and text formats and help designers avoid easily misconstrued presentations that could distort visitors' processing of exhibit information.

Formative Evaluation

In this type of evaluation, used during exhibit development, investigators observe and pretest visitors' behavior, attention, and learning with mock-up panels containing sample layouts and labels, and formats; they then make the needed adjustments in formats and strategies *during* planning and design.[5] This process includes measuring how visitors react to and/or are motivated (or "turned off") by specific features and how well they comprehend the mocked-up messages: the interpretations of artifacts through illustrations, texts, placement of elements, and instructions. Problems that emerge at this early stage can then be addressed by rewrites and format adjustments.[6]

The same tools can be employed to improve already-installed exhibits and graphics that are functioning poorly and to fine-tune newly installed exhibits, a process called *remedial evaluation* (Bitgood and Shettel 1994, Screven 1990a: 53–59).

Communication in Museums

Communications with unguided museum or zoo visitors cannot usefully be related to one-way communication models, such as Shannon and Weaver's: source → transmitter → channel → receiver → destination (McQuail and Windahl 1993: 17). Two-way "feedback" models are better, because they incorporate the role of successive message-altering feedback (Shannon and Weaver 1949, Knez and Wright 1970). Yet these too are unsuitable for the dynamic and interdependent nature of most communication situations, including those between people and displays in a public environment (Miles 1986). Instead of discussing formal communication models in detail, therefore, we summarize some of the primary components of the communication process that apply to exhibits, signs, posters, and so on as they are used in museums, malls, and parks aimed at unguided leisure visitors.[7]

Figure 7.1 illustrates some of the specific aspects of these components in the museum context. Six primary components appear to be involved.

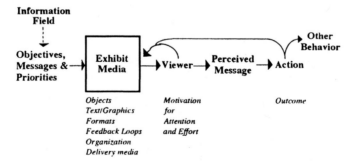

Figure 7.1
Elements of Communication in Interpretive Exhibits

- The *information field*. All the information within an immediate environment.

- The *message* or *messages* to be derived from the information field. These are the objectives of the communication—that is, the knowledge, concepts, behavior, and feelings developers want viewers to receive, in accordance with the priorities for these messages established for particular audiences and resources.

- The *exhibit* or *display*. The objects, paintings, plants, animals, or other content that are the message-related resources of the information field.

- *Delivery media*. Channels through which messages are delivered (text, film, graphics, figures, sound, docents, format, layout, interactive components).[8]

- *Perceived message*. The message as received by the viewer (Ashcraft 1989).

- *Viewer action* (if any). Viewer behaviors at the exhibit (ranging from selective to random), including time spent at the exhibit, involvement level, play, and tasks performed.

The exchange between viewer attention and observation and an exhibit's content form a loop that ultimately determines what message, if any, the visitor receives. The message is imbedded in the larger information field that—given planning, organization, and evaluation—should enable viewers to receive and process the elements and relationships that comprise the message.

Visitors identify, encode, organize, reorganize, interpret, and perhaps act on exhibit information through their attention, perception, memory, and cognitive processes. Though these are complex interactive systems, recent views indicate that the brain's learning system is more than just a complex system. Within the physical structure of the brain, learning is not a "hard-wired" interactive system like a linear computer but a process constantly changing and adapting to incoming information (Kaufman 1993, Gell-Mann 1994). If so, changes taking place during learning are nonlinear, self-organizing systems that take in and interpret information non-sequentially, constantly identifying, classifying, interpreting, and adjusting rules and cognitive maps (schemas) in accordance with actual experience. In other words, learning and communication involve ongoing changes in the rules making up our cognitive maps of the world as they adapt to new information from the environment. How we detect and change these rules also reflects biological programming that, from birth through adolescence, determines the incremental development of capabilities for attending and thinking in successive stages (Lowery 1989, 1990).

But the message received may or may not be the intended message. It may be distorted, or it may be an entirely different message. Any exhibition (or mall, park, zoo, highway sign, poster, lobby art) contains a great deal of information. Theoretically, designers create and organize that information so as to channel viewers' attention to features that create the story or message (e.g., they may focus attention on the textures and colors of pottery rather than on its shape, cultural provenance, history, etc.).

Motivating features or *elements* associated with the exhibition environment (e.g., lighting, text legibility, crowding, sight lines, terminology, visual overload) facilitate or inhibit information processing, because they affect the time viewers spend and their effort, psychological fatigue, selective focus, and enjoyment (if any). An exhibit's organization, relevance, clarity, and attractiveness and viewers' perceptions of its potential value are also motivational influences, in that they affect viewer attention, allocation of time, level of effort, and, ultimately, learning.

Museums as Learning Environments

People can learn little, if anything, if they do not pay attention. Even when they do attend, most visitors view objects, paintings, texts, signs, animals, exotic plants, and computers without benefit of someone or something to direct their attention to the salient points and explain what they are seeing. If and how visitors interpret an exhibit depends on its content; the effectiveness of its labels, graphics, and interactive elements; the knowledge, attitudes, and preconceptions they bring with them; and the motivational variables (fatigue, confusion, stimulus overload, etc.) that affect time spent, level of involvement, and focus (Csikszentmihalyi 1990; Csikszentmihalyi and Hermanson 1995; Hooper- Greenhill 1992, 1994; Miles 1987; Screven 1969, 1993).

In informal settings, viewers pay attention on their own terms and at their own pace. Decisions to attend or not to attend to a display reflect a host of personal and social agendas that interact with exhibit content and other features. A few of the factors that can influence viewers to focus on a display include:

- How quickly they can relate display content to their familiar, everyday world

- Whether they can find answers to common questions raised by display content (*How did they make that? What's that painting worth?*)

- Whether the exhibit's information has a personal use or value for them. (*Where do I start? That will be fun to tell Jane. That helps me remember where I parked the car.*)

- Is the "action" to be taken at a display well matched with their knowledge or skills? (*Could I understand this if I try?*)

- Does the display's message connect to their immediate personal agenda? (*This may help me deal with my crabgrass! Maybe I could be like her! I'd like to do my hair like that! My brother will be impressed when I tell him this! I wonder if I could use this for tomorrow's class?*)

While there is still much to be learned about communication under informal conditions, knowledge of the factors that play important roles in what unguided people do at an exhibition are emerging: what they read or attend to, how they move through exhibit spaces (Melton 1933), how much time they spend at a display or how long they remain in an exhibit hall (Shettel et al. 1968, Lakota 1976), what exhibit halls they choose (Lakota 1976), and what they like and don't like about exhibit displays (Griggs 1990). These findings include the following:[9]

- The majority of museum visitors explore museums and zoos on their own, voluntarily, on their own time and on their own terms, usually in groups of two or three.

▪ Because attention is self-directed, an exhibit's content, organization, and presentation must (a) provide positive reasons for paying attention to them by creating personal connections, supplying sharable information, and presenting challenging tasks; and (b) minimize such negative reasons for avoiding exhibits as impersonal tone, passive formats, unfamiliar terminology, information overload, and confusing presentations.

▪ Attention varies from passive (casual) to active involvement; in the latter, visitors compare things, ask questions, look for connections, and so on. Better learning occurs with active attention.

▪ The more time visitors expect an exhibit or text to require, the less likely they are to attend to it without compelling reasons for doing so (e.g., personal interest, an exciting challenge, expectations of success, an immediate use for the information, or opportunities for participation).

▪ Initially, many visitors without significant background in an exhibit's subject find its visual, social, emotional, action, and sensory aspects (objects, colors, shapes, movement, buttons, touch, smell, texture) more interesting and more fun than abstract information in text form. When written materials are necessary to understand an exhibit, they must be not only informative but also readily understood, enjoyable, succinct, and, if possible, contain information viewers can share with others.

These characteristics, among others, form the context in which communication systems, graphics, and exhibits function. Both the positive and negative impressions that viewers take away with them depend, in part, on the extent to which information and delivery formats address these characteristics. In turn, they affect whether visitors come back, bring friends, and encourage others to visit (or not to visit) a museum.

Visitor Attention

One of the most important factors influencing whether or not communication occurs is how exhibit design affects viewers' observation behavior (attention); that is, whether they notice relevant objects, relationships, textures, and features that may have personal meaning for them. A critical issue is the quality of observation—active or passive, focused or scattered. Museum research on attention often uses objective measures of (1) the frequency of approaches to a display (*attraction power*), (2) time spent in front of a display (*holding time*), and (3) the ratio of time spent to the time required to take in the message (*holding power*) (Shettel et al. 1968; Shettel 1973; Screven 1986). But these gross measures of attention say little, by themselves, about what visitors are actually paying attention to, what information is encoded and later recalled, or how it is interpreted or related to existing knowledge. In other words, they say little about the quality of attention.

Perception researchers Gibson and Gibson (1952) emphasize that while objects are rich in information, making contact with this information requires *selective attention*, which design features like organization, media, and presentation modes can facilitate or inhibit. Obviously, overcoming whatever misconceptions or biases visitors bring to a topic requires them to pay attention to certain aspects of the exhibit. Designs therefore need to be pretested and adjusted during the planning stage to improve the possibility that they encourage, not discourage, selective attention. Research by Barnard and Loomis (1994) has confirmed that the more time people spend attending to something, the more they recall about it. In addition, recall and recognition of visual information decline as the number of items on display increases, whereas combining audio labels with visual modes enhances visual learning and produces better recall than either method used alone.[10]

Dazzling graphics, participatory components, and scholarly accuracy are not as important as the ability to connect exhibit experiences (especially initial experiences) to visitors' worlds or to suggest that exhibit content has personal value for them. While mindless activities at razzle-dazzle displays are often amusing, this kind of fun is usually transient and is likely to diffuse attention rather than focus it. Only selective attention can lead to meaningful connections. When it does, learning activities and their outcomes are likely to sustain the learning activity, which will generally be *more* fun and more sustainable than the ephemeral enjoyment of casual attention.

The Role of Attention in Learning

The basic communication (learning) process involves "rules" for encoding and processing information (Gell-Mann 1994). These rules are themselves complex adaptive processes influenced by the self-organizing cognitive maps that result from previous experience and from the viewer's ability to

- Detect patterns in the stream of incoming information,
- Interpret (classify, organize, connect) these patterns, and
- Act on these interpretations.

Obviously, attention plays a crucial role in all three steps. As used here, therefore, the term *attention* (and *attending to*) includes the various processes involved in detecting, interpreting, and acting on existing schemas and new incoming information. I use the word *communication* to describe the overall impact of these processes on cognitive schemas (maps, rules) and on actions. Communication can break down or be distorted at any of the three stages: detecting patterns requires active, focused attention; interpreting information requires matching existing schemas with new information, symbols, and rules for classifying, organizing, and integrating new information; and taking action requires a set of tasks and goals that test and apply new information and schemas to the real world.

Attention varies in how long it is sustained, how efficiently it scans exhibit content, and how well it separates meaningful from peripheral data and focuses on interrelationships among information elements. To understand conceptual messages, the viewer's attention must last long enough to detect the information and relationships that comprise such messages, be selective enough to bring key information into focus so it can be encoded, and be active enough to engage cognitive schemas and adaptations.

People's processing of a conceptual exhibit message is improved by engaging them in activities that place them in direct, conscious contact with the interrelationships that make up the concept. Some types of attention are more efficient than others at facilitating this process, and certain kinds of experience are more likely than others to be encoded and recalled. Over half the memories visitors reported six months after a museum visit involved objects or things; 23 percent involved specific episodes (e.g., doing things, using masks, and writing in comment books); and 15 percent were about feelings aroused by the exhibit (McManus 1993).

Three aspects of attention that underlie how information is processed will be considered below: the information field, perceptual filters, and exhibit efficiency.

Information Field

Figure 7.2 illustrates the relations among the information field, the information elements that make up a given message, the elements that make

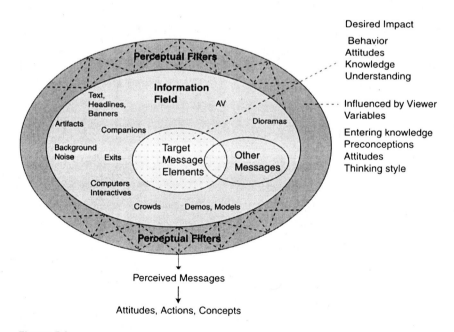

Figure 7.2
Information Field, Perceptual Filters, and Messages (©1998, all rights reserved, Screven & Associates)

up other, potentially competing messages, and the perceptual filters that
may distort incoming information. We can envision an exhibition as consisting of a field of many information elements (large gray oval), only
some of which are essential for conveying the intended messages (center
oval). Nontargeted messages (small overlapping oval) share some elements
with the target messages and some with various irrelevant elements
(crowds, companions, etc.). Information passes through various perceptual
filters (outer ring) that may reorganize, distort, inhibit, or in other ways
modify perception of the target message, thus affecting the viewer's cognitive schemas, attitudes, and actions. The degree of distortion reflects how
well (or poorly) message elements are organized, as well as how efficiently
a given format delivers information (e.g., through feedback loops, leading
questions, appropriate vocabulary, graphics, etc.).

Perceptual Filters

A visitor's prior knowledge, attitudes, preconceptions, and beliefs about a
given topic may influence the degree and kinds of distortion that can
occur. As visitors vary widely in these respects, the challenge for designers
is to minimize such distortions. The fact that some design features operating in public environments affect most viewers' attention and behavior in
the same way makes this task easier. Table 7.1 lists some common viewer
predispositions. Two studies report on visitor likes and dislikes of specific
exhibit features (Alt and Shaw 1984, Griggs 1990). They found that visitors
strongly liked exhibits that "come to life," make their points quickly, help
them learn, and use familiar things and experiences to explain something.
They strongly disliked exhibits and text that do not give enough information, do not relate to the real world, are confusing, or lack personal
connections. Surprisingly, the study indicated that visitors were neutral
toward participatory displays and toward exhibits' artistic or aesthetic
features.[11]

Visitors with limited knowledge of a topic, or those whose learning
styles predispose them to resist "big-picture" interpretations of information,

Table 7.1
Common visitor dispositions in museums

Linear disposition	Visitor resists moving through the exhibit as arranged; efforts to direct visitor movement needed (e.g., *"Obtain the most from this exhibit: follow the orange line!"*)
Exploratory disposition	Exploration of informal and novel spaces may include attention to exhibit content and meaning but also to places to eat, random play, and other features unrelated to planners' educational goals.
Visual orientation	Visual media (objects, movement, graphics, film, colors, etc.) readily gain visitor's attention; movement and living things generally more attractive than static, inanimate objects.
Action orientation	Visitor predisposed to touch and manipulate exhibits and take part in activities involving control, goal achievement, competition, and challenge to skills.
Social orientation	Visitors, usually in groups of two or three, like to talk, perform, and share social context that may directly or indirectly compete with exhibit activities. Single visitors are less frequent.
Time orientation	Average museum visit lasts one to two hours, is limited by physical and psychological fatigue, hunger, other commitments, parking meters, etc. Visitor may anticipate becoming tired and explore exhibits before this happens. Decisions to approach exhibits, read text, etc., depend on time visitor expects to spend. Time expectations increase with cluttered, visually complex, inefficient, and unfriendly formats.

are likely to resist conceptually oriented materials unless they are given good reasons for paying careful attention to them. One such good reason is the potential relevance of the information to achieving a personally important goal. Interest in the exhibit topic per se may not be enough.

Exhibit Efficiency

The time and effort it takes to process a display's content are affected by a number of factors, including personal circumstances (children, time limitations, hunger, fatigue, attitudes, etc.), and the viewer's interest (incentives) in seeking out and learning something new from the displays. However, the time it takes to examine exhibit content is not based solely on personal and motivational interests; it is also affected by the physical design of layouts, organization of content, formats, labels, lighting, terminology, and media, as well as the content itself. The ways exhibit components are chosen, prepared, formatted, arranged, and organized affect how easy or hard it is to find and utilize their information and, thus, the time viewers must spend to receive important messages.

We will refer to the average time it takes viewers to find and process message-related exhibit information as *design efficiency*. Efficient exhibit designs conserve the time and effort needed for viewers to find, respond to, and understand, messages. The greater the design efficiency, the greater is the potential for viewers to absorb the content within a given time. Conversely, inefficient designs require viewers to spend more time and effort to process the same information, increasing the chances that they will quit before learning the exhibit message. If it takes viewers longer than they are willing to spend to learn or experience something new from a display or exhibit, designers need to either increase its efficiency through improvements to its physical design or provide incentives for spending the additional time needed. A few of the physical attributes that reduce an exhibit's efficiency are

- Label texts that are hard to read or find: tiny type and designer fonts; poor contrast, lighting, and placement; unfamiliar vocabulary; "see through" labels on glass.

- Long, poorly spaced paragraphs: lack of "chunking" and white space.

- Ambiguous and abstract headings: titles or labels that do not refer to the actual objects or other features on display or to interests viewers may bring to the exhibit.

- Information overload and visual clutter, which scatter attention and increase fatigue.

- Labels and graphics disconnected from exhibit content.

- A low ratio of needed to unneeded information.

- Lack of information-free spaces: "cognitive rest areas" that separate thematic areas and help visitors absorb what they have seen. This lack may increase psychological fatigue and viewers' ability to process data.

- Carelessly designed interactive formats, questions, graphics, or colors that focus on trivial, secondary, or inappropriate exhibit elements.

The design efficiency of thematic exhibitions is especially important. Many members of the general public have limited exposure to the concepts underlying the themes of popular exhibitions, so special effort is needed to encourage visitors to increase effort and holding time. In addition to careful front-end audience evaluations of potential formats, pretesting of delivery media, layouts, and other physical features with targeted audiences should be used to ensure that the exhibit's central concepts are as time-efficient and motivationally engaging as is possible within practical limits. Factors contributing to the low design efficiency of thematic exhibitions are often easily corrected by reducing information density, removing distracting visuals, improving thematic orientation at entrances, removing or relocating secondary and nonessential information, topics, and media, and so on. Although some large-scale thematic exhibitions attract much public interest, the process of sorting out the wheat from the chaff of their displays too often consumes more time than visitors can practically devote to it.

The nature of the incentive needed to induce viewers to spend more time depends not only on the benefits they expect to receive for their effort but also on the potential "costs" (e.g., lost time, stressful effort, fatigue, a possible parking ticket, missing another exhibit, or a delayed lunch). For simple messages, attention usually can be sustained for a short time by the naturally rewarding consequences that accompany attending to the exhibit (e.g., satisfying curiosity, sensory-motor involvement, sharing the experience with a companion, or responding to a child's question). Sustained attention to complex messages demand more time and may require stronger incentives—perhaps access to another activity that is de-

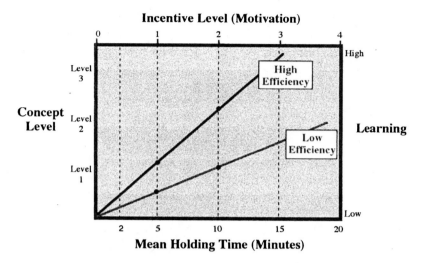

Figure 7.3

Theoretical Model for Interrelations Between Design Efficiency, Viewer Motivation, and Learning (© 1998, all rights reserved, Screven & Associates)

pendent on knowing information in the display; a concrete goal achieved by carefully attending to display content (e.g., take-home prizes as rewards for demonstrating knowledge of key exhibit information). In short, visitors' holding time usually can be increased when viewers are aware that objects, data, relationships, ideas, or other exhibit information has some application to their social, emotional, or utilitarian lives.

Figure 7.3 illustrates the relationships among efficiency, message complexity, viewer motivation, and learning. The gray line represents the rate of learning we would expect for an inefficient exhibit design, while the black line assumes a more efficient design and, hence, better learning. The two learning curves for three levels of concept complexity are shown on the left-hand vertical axis, and the horizontal axis represents the average time viewers are likely to remain engaged with exhibit content. The slopes of the two curves reflect different rates of learning based on the time visitors need to find and process relevant exhibit content under the two levels of design efficiency. Broken vertical lines indicate hypothetical times and degrees of effort that visitors would need in order to find and process (understand) the exhibit's message or messages; these levels of motivation represent the potential for understanding a concept of a given complexity at the two levels of design efficiency. As shown, when the incentive level increases, viewers devote more focused time and effort to the exhibit. With low-efficiency displays, they need higher levels of incentive to attain the time threshold for understanding a given message, and vice versa. Communication (i.e., understanding) is limited when either interest is not great enough or design efficiency is not high enough to motivate a viewer to spend the time necessary to receive a message of a given complexity.

When a conceptual message is not communicated because of excessive time requirements, several options are available to exhibit designers.

• Provide visitors with more incentives to spend extra time (dotted lines). This option is not practical when time needed exceeds practical limits.

• Improve the efficiency of delivery media and content to increase the rate (slope) of learning.

• Improve both options 1 and 2, or

• Divide the thematic message into several messages of lower complexity that allow them to be approached, processed, and rewarded separately.

Assuming an exhibit to have an incentive level of 1 and a low rate of learning because of an inefficient design (gray curve), the holding time would be five minutes. Given this low rate of learning, visitors would receive messages with a concept level of 0.3 (probably trivial). How might the four options above be applied to improve these results?

Option 1 Raise incentive level to 2, thus doubling holding time to ten minutes, which would enable the viewer to receive a message at a concept level of 1.0. Given the exhibit's low efficiency, communicating a level-2 concept would require a twenty-minute holding time and raising the incentive level to 4.0 (e.g., by adding a goal-directed task that requires the visitor to actively seek and use exhibit or label information).

Option 2 Keep incentives at level 1.0 but improve design efficiency: by reorganizing layout; adding leading questions to attract and focus attention; making key information easier to find; improving the match between interpretive media and forms and the teaching, motivational, and audience needs they are supposed to serve; relocating or layering secondary and technical information for the minority of visitors who need it; and reducing or eliminating visual clutter that serves no measurable function. Such adjustments should enable visitors to process information faster, which should increase the rate of the learning curve (i.e., slope of the black curve).

Option 3   Combine options 1 and 2 by improving both efficiency and holding power (motivation) to enable delivery of concept level-2 messages (up from level 1) over the same period of visitor's time (ten minutes).

Option 4   Break up the primary thematic message into several messages of lower complexity that require lower levels of motivation and so can be approached and processed independently. Some, more complex themes might require more than one visit for viewers to understand them thoroughly.

Mindful versus Mindless Attention

Because so much routine daily behavior, including social behavior, occurs with minimal conscious effort, the gross measures of holding time and holding power described earlier probably reflect variations in the level of conscious involvement but tell us little about how the time spent facilitates reception of intended messages. Levels of attention range from focused and active to casual and unsystematic. Some researchers have referred to this continuum as *mindful* at one end and *mindless* at the other (Langer 1989; Moscardo 1992; Carlson 1993; Grünig 1979, 1980; Screven 1990b) and have used *involvement* to refer to generally the same phenomena.[12] In this paper, both *involvement* and *mindful attention* are used to describe systematic selective attention, in contrast to casual, random attention.

In the midst of an array of information elements in public displays, the identifying feature of mindful attention is its *selectivity*; that is, the viewer focuses on some elements while ignoring others. The level of attention may range from highly focused and active to casual and unsystematic (Grünig 1979; Langer et al. 1978; Saloman 1983; Screven 1990a). The importance of the mindful–mindless (or involvement) concept is the evidence that higher involvement levels may facilitate transfer to long-term memory and enhance the quality of "observing" behavior and thus the communication of conceptual messages (Ashcraft 1989; Langer 1989; Moscardo 1992; Moscardo and Pearce 1986; Saloman and Globerson 1987). If so, the practical issue for conveying priority conceptual messages is how to design interpretive content and formats that generate and sustain mindful attention and discourage casual attention.

In mindful modes, the scanning of the information field is systematic and is characterized by the following kinds of behavior:

- Making comparisons

- Raising questions (*How is the object made? Why is it there? Why is the eye in the middle of the forehead? Why are some bodies painted purple?*)

- Looking for interdependent relationships (*Predators of deer improve deer populations.*)

- Making connections to personal knowledge or experience

- Noting contradictions (*If whales live in water, why aren't they fish?*)

- Searching for particular information or categories of information

- Looking back and forth between text and reference objects; carrying out actions

- Pointing out features to companions

- Moving closer for a better view, lifting hinged labels to read text beneath them

Sometimes such mindfulness is encouraged with text or graphics that employ challenging questions or puzzles that focus attention on important display elements.[13]

Mindless Attention ("casual attention")—at the other end of the continuum—is scattered more or less randomly over a variety of items without apparent purpose or direction until something "catches the eye." It is thus analogous to window shopping. Several researchers use the term *mindless* because attention appears automatic, lacking in much, if any, conscious involvement (Langer 1989, Moscardo and Pearce 1986). Viewers' attention to objects or text is brief and erratic. Moderate levels of casual attention often center on sensory/motor activity, or on social agendas, or on novelty or movement, rather than on topics or messages. Visitors show little if any deliberate or systematic attention, frequently looking away from exhibits and being easily distracted. Conversation with companions has little or no relationship to the exhibit, and questions are trivial and disconnected.

In addition to the need to enhance quality of learning—when they are giving priority to a specific conceptual outcome—designers are faced with the practical question of how to generate and sustain mindful attention and inhibit or discourage casual attention. Two processes are fundamental to this issue: *learning* and *motivation*.

Learning

As described above, the degree to which attention is scattered, selective, mindful or mindless, and sustainable is affected by attitudes and pre-conceptions (perceptual filters), entering knowledge, display content, exhibit efficiency, and such motivational factors as challenge, enjoyment, and goal-directed activities that accompany attention to the exhibit. All contribute to whatever learning may or may not take place and, ultimately, to what is communicated. So, what *is* learning?

Learning is not something we can observe directly. It must be inferred from what people do under given conditions. Thus, the impact of information design on learning can only be evaluated in terms of what persons are *supposed* to do when they receive a given message. Researchers measure the learning impact of exhibit content and formats (interactive formats, labels and graphics, entrance headlines, signs, brochures, interpretive multimedia, etc.) indirectly, in terms of viewer behaviors. But the task is more complicated than that. For example, the effectiveness of a typing program for improving typing skill cannot be measured simply by counting a person's typing errors before and after training, because a reduction in errors could reflect changes in at least five factors: (a) fatigue, (b) distractions, (c) hunger, (d) amount of practice, or (e) training. Only *d* and *e* would reflect actual learning. Errors from *a* would decline after rest; errors from *b* would decrease when distractions are removed; and errors from *c* would disappear after the subject eats a meal. Only *d* and *e* would reflect learning, because changes in the person's typing skill would persist over time.

While behavioral measures vary, four frequently used approaches to evaluating exhibit learning employ

- *Observation*: Of visitors' use of exhibit instructions, exhibit materials, wayfinding cues, etc.

- *Objective tests*: Multiple-choice questions, sorting and matching tasks, discrimination tasks, fill in questions

- *Behavioral indices*: Can visitor paraphrase a display's message, list key points, identify key message from a list, recall key-message elements, identify implications, describe connections, engage in spontaneous activity that reflects understanding of the message? Borun et al (1996, 1997) propose a three-point rating scale of behaviors that reflect level of learning.[14] These levels are

Level 1 Can give one-word statements/answers but makes few associations with appropriate content; remarks about content but misses the point

Level 2 Can give multiple-word answers that connect to exhibit's main point; connects display's content to life experiences (not concepts)

Level 3 Can give multiple-word answers; connects content to concepts behind exhibit; connects concepts to life experiences

- *Naturalistic observation*: Data obtained from visitors in open-ended conversation, semi-structured interviews, video/audio tapings, etc. These records—of attitudes, feelings, perceptions, misconceptions, and so on—

are transcribed and categorized according to how well they reflect learning outcomes (Wolf 1980).

In terms of motivation and learning, design details can have different effects and serve different purposes. Some features (e.g., moving elements) attract attention but may not hold it—a motivational issue. Interactive components may increase the quality of attention but not of communication—another motivational issue. Visitors may understand a conceptual label or graphic if asked to read it but may not read it without being asked to do so. Some messages require high attraction, such as billboards and television advertising, but do not require sustained attention. Getting viewers to paraphrase the main point of a conceptual display not only requires high attraction but also formats that induce them to focus and sustain their attention.

Thinking Styles

Different people learn, or prefer to receive, organize, and implement information in different ways. Some prefer lectures or reading, working with peers, using learning games, discussing the pros and cons of a question, studying independently, doing concrete tasks, and so on. Sternberg (1988, 1991, 1994) calls these preferences for seeking, organizing, and using information *thinking styles. Learning styles* (Meyers and McCaulley 1985) and cognitive styles (Witkin 1990) are other terms for this process.[15]

Sternberg's categories are built around the metaphor of U.S. branches of government.

- *Legislative style.* Prefers planning, problem solving, and so forth

- *Executive style.* Likes to implement, follow established rules, and so on

- *Judicial style.* Prefers judging others, evaluating existing ideas

- Sternberg also describes four subcategories of thinking styles found within each of the overall styles

- *Monarchic.* Prefers focusing on one need or goal at a time; ignores obstacles

- *Hierarchical.* Prefers to work with multiple goals with different assigned priorities

- *Oligarchic.* Works with multiple goals but no priorities. (Thus, goals often are not met.)

- *Anarchic.* Avoids rules, guidelines, and regulations; resists authority; employs random approaches and insight rather than working within existing frameworks for solutions

There are no right or wrong styles. Each has advantages and disadvantages, depending on the context, the task undertaken, and what is required to perform it. In educational settings like classrooms and museums, students' or museum visitors' different thinking styles mean that they are likely to process the same message differently, or, when free to do so, will approach learning it along different paths. Some teachers (and students) are most comfortable with global approaches that involve abstract understanding of broad issues, preferring to leave details to others. These teachers (and designers, artists) work best in the world of ideas. But others prefer to work on concrete tasks, detail work, and precise data. Some studies (e.g., Sternberg 1994) have demonstrated that differences in students' classroom performance reflect the degree of match between the thinking styles of the teacher and individual students. Teachers in the study taught through lectures and textbook assignments and evaluated student learning with objective exams. Students who preferred this style of pedagogy got better grades than those who did not. When the teacher shifted his or her style toward use of a variety of resources for examining and explaining the pros and cons of conceptual problems, formerly "poor" students started doing better and some formerly "good" students did worse.

In a related study, Vance and Schroeder (1992) gave the Meyers-Briggs Type Indicator (MBTI; Meyers and McCaulley 1985) to four hundred randomly selected adult visitors to a rain forest exhibition at the Milwaukee Public Museum. Visitors' scores were based on MBTI indices for (a) *sensing-type* learners, who prefer lack of ambiguity and concrete, practical uses of things and devices; and (b) *intuitive-type* learners, who prefer creative problem solving, self- learning, and relationships rather than details or practical uses. The exhibit labels used differed in their appeal to sensing-type learners (e.g., "All living things are made up of cells") or to intuitive-type learners (e.g., "How are you like the tamarin and the morning glory?"). Intuitive learners performed better, both in terms of stops made and time spent, when intuitive labels were in place; sensing learners stopped more often and spent more time at exhibits when sensing labels were used.

In summary, educational materials, formats, and strategies affect behavior and learning in both formal and informal environments. Their effectiveness, however, depends on the conditions under which learning takes place and on their match with the needs and predispositions—including dominant thinking styles—of targeted audiences.

Motivation

The term *motivation* is often employed by exhibit planners during exhibit and graphics planning—but with limited understanding. The usual approach to motivating unguided visitors is to use appealing exhibit titles, signs, or visual media that engage them in action. But, too often, these approaches do little more than generate a mindless manipulation of hands-on activities with flip labels, games, and computers. The idea seems to be that if you can get visitors fiddling, flipping, stroking, gawking, pressing and—in the process—expose them to some message-related information, then the real message lurking beneath all this activity will seep through. Motivating visitors, at least in museums, is seen as something you do to make exhibits enough "fun" to attract and hold their attention for a short period, then let the logically organized and documented dioramas, paintings, objects, aesthetics, texts, and graphics do the rest (Bearman 1995). In reality, little meaningful interpretation takes place in these "fun" formats without the presence of educators or docents to provide direct interpretations.

Measuring motivation's impact on learning centers around the time people spend pursuing actions (approaching an exhibit, spending time in front of it, etc.) that can place them, potentially, in contact with exhibit content. Most measures of motivation do not, however, measure what visitors have learned, only whether they have come into contact with some of the content. Popular instruments of motivational impact measure

- *Attraction*: The response of a passing visitor who stops at a display for two seconds or less and looks in its general direction

- *Holding time*: Time spent looking at one or more segments of the display

- *Holding power*: The ratio of holding time to the minimum time required for targeted viewers to pay attention to the main elements of the intended message

- *Frequency*: Of appropriate use of display materials and spaces; for example, viewer proceeds in proper sequence, uses audio device, looks at display objects described in label or under flip label, and so on

- *Involvement scale*: Rating (on three-point scale) of the level of focused or systematic attention to message-related display content

- *Affective response scales*: Independent rating of adjective-pairs, affective rankings, interview remarks, frequency of positive or negative emotional reactions to display (e.g., laughter, grimaces, body language)

Because of their leisure orientation, most visitors, young and old, are looking for ways of spending time that will result in enjoyable value-added experiences. This applies to the instrumental (goal-directed) activities of humans and of most other living organisms (Ferster and Culbertson 1982, Banyard and Hayes 1994). We can distinguish two aspects of motivational factors:

- *Reinforcers and punishers*. Technically, these terms refer to experiences or events that increase or decrease the frequency (strength) of the behavior that precedes them.

- *Contingencies*: Dependent relationships between specific behaviors and their immediate consequences, such as when a reinforcer or a punisher is associated with a prior behavior or achievement—for example, the pleasure gained from solving a puzzle results from giving mindful attention to it over time.

Reinforcers and Punishers

Several assumptions underlie the practice of applying motivational concepts to communication in informal settings.

▪ The information field (e.g., exhibit) contains the content needed to make teaching points or generate other desired messages.

▪ Mindful attention to displays is *more* reinforcing than mindless attention.

▪ Redundancy, confusion, poor lighting, stimulus overload, useless information, user failure, and other aversive factors and experiences are minimized *or* countered by such reinforcing experiences as pattern resolution, progress toward a goal, useful information, and social recognition.

Using everyday words like *reward*, *fun*, and *enjoyment* can be misleading, because they imply meanings different from those of the carefully defined term *reinforcer* (see definition above). Technically, *rewards* are called *positive reinforcers*, because they are *presented* rather than removed after a given behavior or response occurs, whereas some reinforcers strengthen behavior when they are *removed*—because their removal reduces or eliminates aversive stimuli like pain, failure, boredom, confusion, and so forth.

Because aversive stimuli weaken (i.e., reduce the frequency of) associated behaviors when they are presented (e.g., drinking wine that produces a headache, ignoring a whining child, studying a boring textbook), they are called *punishers*. Therefore, behavior that reduces, removes, or avoids aversive stimuli is strengthened, just as taking an aspirin for a headache, giving in to a whining child, or leaving a boring display results in strengthening these escape behaviors. Actions to reduce or escape from punishers strengthen these actions and are called *negative reinforcers*, to distinguish them from positive reinforcers. Thus, the same stimulus (e.g., a headache) both strengthens escape or avoidance behavior (taking the aspirin) and weakens behavior that ignores the problem. This is why visitors learn to ignore or avoid text they find confusing, poorly lighted, boring, useless, or hard to read; their avoidance is expressed as inattention, distractibility, departure from the area, and similar responses. Mindless attention and low involvement may therefore simply reflect escape or avoidance behavior resulting from poor exhibit planning and design. The sort of front-end and formative evaluations described earlier (p. 136) can uncover and minimize such potentially negative features of exhibit components. Taking defensive action may be prudent, as escape/avoidance learning at one display can generalize and transfer to other exhibit topics and ideas—even to the museum itself!

The visitor's level of mindful attention reflects the impact of concurrent sources of positive and negative reinforcers—for example, positive reinforcers associated with mindfulness competing with negative reinforcers and punishers related to time and effort, or positive reinforcers from casual, sensory/motor or social activities reinforcing casual and random attention. Except among the very young, casual attention and random guessing produce only short-lived positive reinforcement that is manifested as frequent changes in direction and focus (e.g., the frantic activity seen in science centers). In contrast, goal-centered activity reinforces and sustains mindful attention, because progress toward goals is fun and is not possible without mindfulness.

We can distinguish two kinds of positive reinforcers: *intrinsic* and *external*.

Intrinsic reinforcers are natural parts of many human activities, including freely exploring an open environment, meeting challenges, having conversations, and so forth. Table 7.2 lists some specific activities and events that are rich sources of intrinsic positive reinforcers that encourage mindful activities in the absence of external benefits. Such reinforcers shape and sustain many aspects of play, work, and learning in our everyday world. They also shape learning, because they are contingent on mindful attention, not on mindless attention. The considerable time and effort people

Table 7.2

Examples of intrinsic (natural) positive reinforcers

Day dreaming	Receiving counter-intuitive information
Watching people	Vigorous activity
Exploring a new environment, novel events	Experiencing achievement
Playing	Sharing information and activities
Pursuing goals	Completing a defined task
Predicting an event	Social recognition
A memorable experience	Acquiring (or improving) a skill
Discovering useful new information	Discovering new connections
Making something work	Measuring self against a standard; competing with others
Solving a challenging problem	Receiving feedback, evidence of progress

give, without external rewards, to sports, music, climbing mountains, hobbies, chess, research, crossword puzzles, and other nonwork activities reflect the pervasive influence of these natural incentives (Csikszentmihalyi 1975, 1990). A taxonomy of intrinsic reward may be found in Malone and Lepper (1987). Underlying this taxonomy is the brain architecture described earlier, which detects, interprets, and adapts information into continuously emerging, self-organizing schemas that encourage (reinforce) change (Gell-Mann 1994).

Given the diversity in visitor backgrounds, interests, and goals, attempts to effectively motivate the majority of visitors in open settings may seem bound to fail. Fortunately, this diversity reflects not differences in the underlying reinforcers themselves but only different *methods* that people use to meet their individual needs, obtain enjoyable consequences, and avoid negative ones. As table 7.2 demonstrates, the desires to meet challenges successfully; gain self-esteem, social approval, or power; and reduce fear and anxiety are common to most people and underlie the diversity of positive and negative consequences that shape individual behavior and personality (Csikszentmihalyi 1975, 1990; Malone 1981).

External reinforcers do not directly result from the learner's activities and are often symbols of achievement and access to opportunities (money, privilege, lapel pins, vouchers, shop discounts, etc.). They are under the control of someone or something outside the self. Because taking in complex concepts and giving up long-held misconceptions require time-consuming, focused attention, exhibit designers may have to combine external incentives with intrinsic reinforcers to increase the time and effort expended by novice visitors (Screven 1993: 8–9). Visitors already familiar with a display topic can often link new information with existing knowledge, which is usually more reinforcing than learning something entirely new. There may therefore be little need for extra incentives or external reinforcers to attract and sustain the mindful attention of such visitors.

Whether intrinsic or external, viewers must perceive the consequences of paying attention to have personal value. The greater this value, the more time and effort they are likely to give to a display.

The Role of Contingencies in Shaping Attention

A contingency is a one-way, dependent relationship between a given behavior (A) and its consequence (b); that is, behavior A must occur *before* event b (a reinforcer) can occur. Behavior A need not produce event b every time, but event b must be correlated with A in accordance with some rule (e.g., average number of responses or a predictable passage of time). For example, a student whose homework assignment is to learn to solve a quadratic equation may be offered one hour of television viewing (b) for solving the equation (behavior A). Here, television time (b) is made contingent on the product of the student's efforts (A)—not on the time spent. Figure 7.4 illustrates contingencies between exhibit information, attention modes, and the common behavioral consequences of focused and unfocused modes of attention.

Similar contingencies between behavior and its consequences are integral parts of the learning that takes place in natural environments; these natural consequences generally favor focused attention, not casual or random

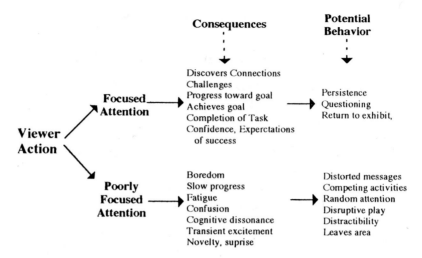

Figure 7.4
Action, Attention, Mode, and Consequences (©1998, all rights reserved, Screven & Associates)

attention. There are many examples of how people are changed by the natural consequences of their behavior, including museum experiences.[16] To quote Csikszentmihalyi: "The absence of conventional incentives does not imply an absence of rewards. Clearly, people are motivated to pursue activities because they derive some satisfaction from them, and this satisfaction itself acts as a reward" (1975: 13).

The quality of outcomes varies widely. But in one way or another, both desirable and undesirable behaviors, skills, interests, knowledge, and attitudes are shaped by *natural contingencies* operating within the environment. Consider, for example, how

• Gravity shapes what we learn about bouncing balls.

• Sensory and physiological structures mold how we see and how we learn (to jump, dance, play ball, talk, socialize, etc.).

• The daily actions and reactions of others develop the way we relate to and communicate with each other.

- Composing music is supported by the enjoyment of the composing experience.

- Jazz improvisation and sustained practice are influenced by unexpected and exciting musical phrases or rhythms.

Everyday activities like these "provide little worlds of their own which are intrinsically enjoyable" (Csikszentmihalyi 1975: 14). A closer look at how natural contingencies shape what we learn and how we feel in our everyday work and play can provide designers with blueprints for creating contingencies to bring about attention and learning in our contrived educational environments, as well as in our everyday natural environments. Think about the contingencies at work as a young child plays with a rubber ball.

- Throwing or rolling the ball encourages active, focused attention to the ball's movements.

- The ball's movements focus and sustain the child's attention over time.

- The different ways the ball moves encourage the child to process different ways of throwing or bouncing the ball that produce different effects.

The child's growing ability to predict (and control) the ball is a contingent natural reinforcer that encourages and sustains the repeated practice that leads to increased ability and success, and to more practice, more success, and so on.

The point is that in museums, zoos, parks, aquariums as well as in classrooms and shopping malls, natural and contrived contingencies generate behavioral chains that, in fact, shape attention, attitudes, and learning. The principles that affect attention and learning in all these settings are essentially the same as those applied in learning to predict and control the ball: people scan the information in their surrounding environment and discover new patterns and uses, which reinforce further exploration, and so on. Thus, the fun associated with these activities supports the same kinds of attention that lead to understanding the messages in museum exhibits.

Mixing Entertainment with Education

In recent years, numerous museums in the North America, Europe, and Australia, recognizing the importance of entertainment, have made efforts to, combine entertainment with education without compromising substantive educational messages. The Natural History Museum in London has done so successfully in many exhibitions that have stimulated other museums sensitive to the needs of their publics. In many cases, however, efforts to add "fun" to educational exhibits have come at the expense of educational content, probably because, in part, of exhibit planners' pervasive misconceptions about the conditions and costs of making exhibits both educationally productive and enjoyable.

Yet, as Cikzsentmihalyi (1990) and Gardner (1991), among others, have shown, there is hard evidence that viewer enjoyment need not impede education. For example, experimental studies of what makes computer games fun identified design features that not only sustained focused attention but also facilitated learning, including self-directed learning (Malone 1981). Perhaps the most common reason for the failure of viewers to learn much from participatory and entertaining displays is that their entertaining qualities are available to viewers *whether or not* they carefully attend to or understand the display messages (figure 7.4). If such amusement is available with little mindful attention or understanding of key messages, it should not surprise us to learn that viewers do not pay close attention and, therefore, often understand little about a display's content. Judging by the thousands of ineffective applications of flip labels and computers found in public areas, many designers apparently have not grasped the importance of making the "fun" aspects of educational displays contingent on understanding or using the information they contain. Many participatory exhibits suffer from the same problem—visitors can operate them without paying attention to or understanding the point of their exhibit messages.

What visitors learn depends on the interplay between the specific exhibit elements they focus on and how they interpret them. This issue is well

illustrated by popularity of participatory displays, whose components—
buttons, flip labels, mechanical or electronic controls, bicycles to pedal,
or wheels to turn—are presumed to provide the necessary focus. Yet,
although such displays attract and engage visitors, that engagement may
or may not add to viewers' awareness of relationships and other attributes
needed to understand the message but may simply reflect the intrinsic
enjoyment of the activities (Langer et al. 1978, Borun 1992).

We can distinguish two contrasting participatory situations that differ according to whether or not visitors can use exhibit experiences to
choose among several ideas and actions, answer questions about a display, make predictions, and so on. Figure 7.5 illustrates these different
situations.

On the left (passive participation), visitors press, lift, flip, turn, and
manipulate but do not have to make choices—they may activate a demonstration, roll a marble down an incline, turn a wheel exposing data

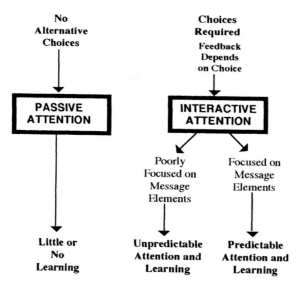

Figure 7.5

Passive versus Interactive Participation (©1998, all rights reserved, Screven & Associates)

to match with birds, or press a button that lights up a text panel. Such participation is one-way. The visitor may observe an effect or read an explanation or definition, but the feedback is the same for all responses. In passive participation, novice visitors can do little or nothing with the information; nor can they make decisions about it that would help encode and transfer it to long-term memory.[17]

By contrast, in interactive participation (on the right), visitors can choose between two or more actions that each yield a different result. As long as they do not simply guess the answers, what they see or read depends on their own interpretation of the information, which in turn determines the action they choose to take—hence the term *interactive*. For them to learn really well, visitors' prior information, logic, principles, and personal experiences—which form a basis for their interpretations and actions—must engage the higher cognitive processes *before* (or simultaneous with) making a choice. A well-designed leading question with, for example, a choice of three answers, can encourage visitors to seek solutions from a display if its information appears relevant and accessible; under these conditions, it is more fun to find solutions by themselves than to guess or be given the answer by lifting a panel or pressing a button. In such an exhibit, therefore, many visitors seek out display information before making their choices.

While feedback about incorrect choices can encourage visitors to continue their efforts, it should not provide a direct answer; whenever possible, the answer should come from exhibit content.

To sum up, *what* is learned from participatory situations depends on what viewers attend *to*, how they interpret this, and what they *do* with the information.

Goals

Providing visitors with an achievable, tangible goal accomplishes several things: (*a*) it can initiate focused attention to unfamiliar information, even when the topic appears uninteresting; and (*b*) it can help them integrate new information with existing knowledge, attitudes, and dispositions.

Successful use of a tangible goal depends on a viewer's ability to act on or apply message-based information to achieve the goal, especially if the actions depend on the proper use of the information. Application of information is an overt action that requires *both* information and action. For example, practicing the piano, taking a class, seeing a doctor, or listening to a traffic report are intermediate actions (goals) that must precede performing for a group, obtaining a degree, overcoming a medical problem, or avoiding traffic snarls.

Many everyday personal goals stimulate us to seek and use information that may help us attain them—even "boring" information that could not otherwise compete with more intrinsically interesting activities. Even for accomplishing rather trivial tasks, having a goal can sometimes be very effective. So why is having a goal effective?

A tangible goal has the advantage of having a clear beginning, a middle, and a definable end. Commitment to a goal initiates a chain of actions such as information seeking, organizing, and selective (focused) attending—reading, observing, interpreting, planning, comparing, asking, connecting, trying out, experimenting, and so on. Information sources can include almost anything—peers, teachers, encyclopedias, CDs, television programs, books, magazines—even public exhibits. A goal creates a framework, a "stage setting" in which its various activities generate intrinsically enjoyable feedback that sustains the effort and time spent reaching the goal.

Human beings are biologically predisposed to look for patterns and explore the novel and unknown. Initiating and sustaining pattern-seeking behavior usually requires a clearly defined goal that seems potentially achievable. In early childhood, sensory exploration of unfamiliar objects is dominant—through feel, touch, sound, smell and other sensory properties. After objects have become familiar (i.e., predictable), exploration of other characteristics and objects is more likely. In later human development, goals are more complex but still provide the motivation and context in which searches for information and patterns are initiated and sustained.

Because a prerequisite to learning anything new is paying attention to information, goal-based activities must put viewers into contact with message-related information that, without a goal, might be abandoned too soon. Interestingly, the goal itself is probably less important than the fact that there *is* a goal. As long as required tasks have an acceptable time frame and are suited to users' abilities and thinking styles, almost any goal—even an arbitrary one—might help, although goals that incorporate target messages are preferable for educational purposes. Many kinds of goals are applicable to most museum audiences and exhibit conditions; for example,

- Earning an achievement symbol (lapel tag, token, "diploma," reprint, poster, souvenir, etc.)
- Gaining access to working models (of a habitat, a power plant's load controls, space capsule, etc.) that allow users to control or execute an operation
- Receiving a ticket to a behind-the-scenes tour or a seat in an IMAX theater
- Earning an opportunity to participate in a second task, game, goal, and so on
- Solving a mystery
- Receiving verbal compliments, positive feedback, or evidence of progress
- Obtaining closure for an activity (completing a puzzle, finishing a paper, attaining a score)

A goal need not involve an external prize as long as it is specific and definable. (But, as stated earlier, complex messages consume extra time that may require external rewards.) Four of the above goals do not involve take-home items but are specific enough to be definable. While many of the intrinsic reinforcers that normally accompany learning and problem solving help sustain goal-directed activity (table 7.2), they are often not as effective for initiating the activity as more tangible goals—especially if visitors are not yet aware that gathering information is itself a rewarding experience. Because a definable goal can initiate a chain of goal-directed activity, it provides the opportunity for novice visitors to discover the intrinsically rewarding properties of learning. For some visitors, in fact, gathering and using information may become more rewarding than the goal itself.

Because new messages may not at first be integrated with existing knowledge, attitudes, and dispositions, they may have only a minor impact on existing cognitive schemas (Csikszentmihalyi 1975, 1990; Langer 1989; Moscardo and Pearce 1986). Over time, however, goal-directed activity that stimulates action, decisions, and the application of information increases involvement and facilitates the transfer of new information to, and integration with, existing schemas.

Goal-Centered Strategies

A goal-centered exhibition strategy might be described as follows: A visitor selects a definable goal (e.g., solving a puzzle) that requires understanding and using certain exhibit information. Progress toward the goal is contingent on focused attention to those aspects of exhibit information that constitute a targeted message or messages. If sustained, a process of searching for and applying exhibit information that is challenging and relevant to a visible goal (puzzle, poster, or other product) should facilitate learning and transfer of messages to long-term memory and/or lead to changes in cognitive schemas.

Although not all exhibits need goal-centered systems to generate mindful attention and learning, such designs *are* needed when an exhibition's content contains many topics, layers and branches of concepts, models, demos, and facts that novice visitors cannot absorb in a single visit—as is the case for thematic exhibitions. Even well-organized and logically presented high-density exhibits can produce information and sensory overload in visitors; the resultant psychological fatigue and cognitive dissonance

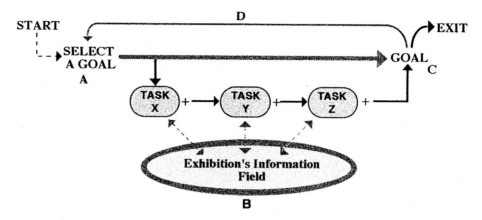

Figure 7.6
Goal-centered Sequence (©1998, all rights reserved, Screven & Associates)

may then invite inattention, distraction, and other escape behaviors. Such exhibitions become something like three-dimensional encyclopedias containing too many possible messages, topics, layers of interpretation, and implications for the general public to absorb. Goal-centered designs can overcome or at least reduce these aversive factors by encouraging visitors to navigate within a smaller information field centered around goal-related topic elements.

Figures 7.6 and 7.7 illustrate two facets of goal-centered exhibits in terms of a hypothetical goal-centered activity in a thematic exhibition.

In figure 7.6 a goal-centered sequence is initiated when a visitor or visitor group selects a goal (A) and becomes aware of one or more intermediate tasks (X, Y, Z) that require them to use exhibit information (B) to advance toward their goal (C). The specific task(s) focuses visitors' attention on appropriate topics and content within the larger exhibition field and helps them avoid irrelevant information. Subtopics and levels within the thematic exhibition are also reduced to manageable proportions suited to different goals, topics, ages, entry levels, interests, time frames, and learning styles. Visitors selectively engage in collecting and applying information to specific narrower aspects of the larger concepts, processes,

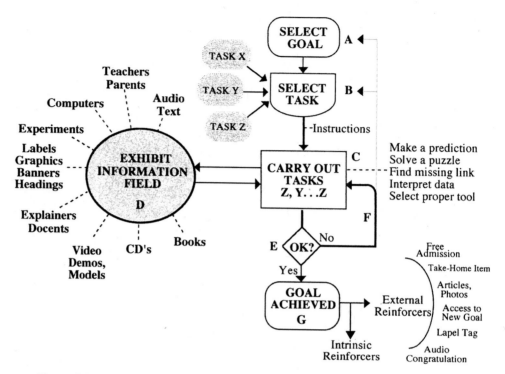

Figure 7.7
Goal-centered Communication Model (©1998, all rights reserved, Screven & Associates)

and questions addressed by the exhibition. At another time, or during other visits, visitors can pursue another goal through the same exhibition on another topic, at another level, for another outcome (D). They may also return to A to select another more appropriate goal or exit the exhibit area entirely.

A more detailed schematic of the six primary components of a goal-centered system is shown in figure 7.7. Visitors or small groups

- Select a goal from a range of choices at entry point A.

- At B, choose the task or tasks to be completed or mastered to attain the selected goal.

▪ At C, carry out the selected task(s) X, Y, Z, using exhibit content (D) and/or other information sources needed to do so. (Tasks consist of one or more actions, such as solving a mystery, interpreting data, completing a puzzle, sorting information, matching art styles, or identifying an emotion expressed by a sculpture.)

▪ On completing the task(s), go to stage E to demonstrate or test themselves on their understanding or mastery of the message or messages; if unsuccessful, return to C via return-loop F to review the exhibit and the chosen task.

▪ Continue via C and F until their understanding of message(s) has been successfully demonstrated. They may also return to B or to A to select a different task or goal or to exit the exhibit area entirely.

▪ If and when performance at E is satisfactory, proceed to G, where success is acknowledged and attainment of goal is confirmed with some form of intrinsic and/or external reinforcer.

Exhibit designers must be careful to slant goals and associated tasks in a way that makes it likely that visitors who pay mindful attention will in fact succeed; that is, designers need to organize, format, and code exhibit materials for easy navigation, providing frequent evidence of progress and suggestions (not answers) during stages C, D, and E. In other words, goal-centered designs should be as efficient as possible. In the author's experience, some visitors initially move too quickly, without making thoughtful use of exhibit content. Interviews have suggested that visitors often assume that they can be successful without paying attention to exhibit content (see Example 2 below). After one or two returns through the F loop, however, most find it quicker and more rewarding to use exhibit content than to ignore it! When necessary, docents or exhibit texts should encourage visitors to change goals or tasks to those better matched with their age, ability, or available time. Most visitors adjust quickly, learning to make better choices of goals or tasks and more systematic use of exhibit content.

Although more research is needed, the author's experience has shown that the following tasks can be critical to designing a successful goal-centered framework:

- Developing clear and measurable objectives for each task and message component (label, map, sign, chart, interactive film, etc.) to motivate visitors—preferably before detailed planning or mock-up testing.

- Developing goals and subgoals for intermediate tasks and pretesting them with target visitor(s) to ensure that they can be completed within a reasonable time frame.

- Selecting goals that pretested target visitors perceive as having personal value. The higher this value, the more time and effort they can be expected to spend pursuing a goal. Visitors' perception of this value depends on their expectations of what a goal will do for them in terms of (1) social importance (sharability, recognition); (2) personal significance (practical uses, cognitive compatibility); (3) support for existing attitudes, beliefs, and values; and (4) financial advantage (e.g., free admissions, store discounts).

- Pretesting and observing visitors attempting each prospective task (C) and adjusting tasks to be sure that they connect clearly to the target message(s).

- Evaluating feedback and correctional loops (E and F) for their effectiveness in helping visitors use information, recognize connections, reduce misconceptions, and so on.

- Regularly observing how visitors search for and use exhibit information at D and adjusting media, formats, and content as needed.

As figure 7.7 suggests, information sources (D) may include computer stations, various kinds of interactive displays, quick-time videos, audio recordings, and other media that deliver information, feedback, and reinforcement efficiently and help viewers separate relevant from irrelevant content. (For details, see Bateman 1990; Bitgood and Loomis 1993; Hooper-Greenhill 1992, 1994; and Screven 1990a, 1992: 198–201.)

The following features and formats appear to improve exhibit efficiency.

- *Leading questions*, which focus attention on relevant message elements of the exhibit (e.g., texture, color, categories, relationships, misconceptions)

- *Animated and simulated processes* that help visualize complex processes (e.g., blood-vessel action, interconnections among components of natural habitats)

- *Directive text and graphics* that provide clues by pointing out key information elements, suggesting search strategies, and encouraging group collaboration

- *Matching and sorting tasks* that help visitors connect new concepts with existing knowledge

- *Information maps* to help visitors visually conceptualize categories of print information, functions, interconnections, and other print content (Horn et al. 1969; Horn 1976, 1998; Fields 1981; MacDonald-Ross and Waller 1976)

What About Failure?

A danger in any goal-directed activity is the potential negative effect of making mistakes. Frequent failures are aversive. They disrupt (punish) attention and may lead visitors to abandon an exhibit activity and acquire a generalized dislike of the topic, or even the museum. Visitors may increase their error rates and sense of failure if they guess the answers to the tasks (C), either don't consult or make careless use of information resources (D), or simply misunderstand the information provided. Because information resources are open-ended, visitors must decide for themselves what is relevant, what to ignore, how to interpret what they see or read, which formats and modes they find most helpful, and so on. Even at best, therefore, visitors' efforts to explore and apply new information will result in some errors, setbacks, misunderstandings, or confusion. During early stages, scattered and random attention, guessing, and other shortcuts that increase errors are common. At this point, too, prior misconceptions and limited knowledge, fatigue, and poor observation skills can contribute to high error rates.

But failures need not disrupt learning. Indeed, occasional errors and lack of success are a normal part of everyday life and usually do not prevent us from learning to ski, swim, climb mountains, cook, solve crossword puzzles, conduct research, or write plays. Errors can also make positive contributions—by providing feedback that helps overcome misunderstanding, improving mindfulness and discouraging carelessness, guessing, shortcutting, and other unproductive behavior. Though momentarily frustrating, the negative effects of errors are often counteracted by their help in shaping new skills and signaling progress. Probably the best antidote to failure is a system that assures frequent successes along with some failures—that is, one that gradually increases the ratio between success and failure. The following practices help increase visitor success:

▪ Alerting visitors to common misconceptions about the topic by adding "warning labels" that anticipate potential mistakes. When errors occur anyway, the display provides corrective feedback.

▪ When applying information to a task doesn't work, encouraging visitors (via feedback) to re-examine their interpretation or look for new approaches or new information.

▪ Suggesting that visitors share information and ideas to find common solutions.

▪ Adding encouraging remarks when a visitor makes an error; e.g.: *"You show lots of promise!—but you didn't look carefully enough."* or *"You can do it! Check again."* or *"I've made that mistake! Take another look."*

Examples of Goal-Centered Exhibits

There are, of course, many possible ways of using goals to facilitate attention and learning. The following examples conducted by the author and his students summarize several exhibit applications ranging across different topics, exhibit settings, and audiences. Each one utilized a goal-centered strategy to motivate unguided visitors to attend to and use exhibit content actively.[18] In some cases, only intrinsic reinforcers were employed; in others, intrinsic and external reinforcers were used.

Example 1.   Paleo-Indian Exhibit (circa 1978)

▪ *Developer's Objective*: To increase the frequency of mindful attention to adjacent interpretive text-and-graphics information and the visitor's ability to choose on the first try the Paleo-Indian projectile point from among the three different points illustrated on a multiple-flip label.

▪ *Procedure*: A mocked-up text-and-graphics label defined and illustrated the key properties of Paleo-Indian Clovis-points. This label was placed to the left of a three-choice flip question picturing Paleo, Archaic, and Woodland Indian projectile points; the lead question is shown in figure 7.8. The visitor's *goal* was to use the text-and-graphics information to distinguish between the Paleo-Indian point and the two other points.

▪ *Results*: The action intended was for visitors *first* to search the text-and-graphic information at left to find the "answer" and *then* to make their choice (i.e., lift the appropriate panel). After revisions during the formative stage, over 75 percent of the adult individuals and small groups tested did so; they mindfully examined the label, often several times, *before* making their choice. Guessing was minimal. Additional testing at this site and in other applications with similar materials showed that this result depended on: (*a*) a lead question that is unambivalent; (*b*) labels configured as single flippable units that clearly *look* flippable (figure 7.8); and (*c*) users recognizing that the information source (label) contains the information needed for quickly making a good choice. (For details on interactive graphics, see Screven 1992: 199–203.)

Example 2.   TVA Energy Center (Screven 1990b)

▪ *Developer's Objective*: To increase and sustain the time visitors spend in focused attention on surrounding information panels explaining TVA's methods of producing and controlling energy.

▪ *Procedure*: In the orientation area at the entrance to the exhibition two robots demonstrate the use of a special card for answering questions on a self-test computer; answering them correctly earns visitors a take-home lapel button from the exhibition's Energy Store as acknowledgment of

Figure 7.8
The Lead Question of an Exhibit Illustrating the Key Properties of Paleo-Indian Projectile Points. [photoslide]

their accomplishment. The card contains six cells (one for each topic), all of which need to be stamped to obtain the lapel button. The visitor's goal is to earn a lapel button by answering three multiple-choice questions testing their knowledge or understanding of the conceptual messages of the exhibits in each of six sequentially arranged rooms: orientation, hydropower, fossil-fuel generation, nuclear power, power controls, and solar energy. When the card is first inserted into a self-test computer, the message on the screen reminds visitors (1) that each question must be answered before going on to the next one; (2) that if they make more than one error they will be out of the game and receive the card back; and (3) that a careful study of the surrounding exhibits will help them win. Visitors who make a second error see an encouraging screen message, which varies from room to room, urging them to look at the exhibits more carefully. Here is one example:

SORRY, YOU JUST MADE SECOND ERROR, SO YOU'RE OUT OF THE GAME! YOU SHOW A LOT OF PROMISE. DID YOU STUDY EXHIBITS CAREFULLY? LOOK AT THEM AGAIN AND GOOD LUCK NEXT TIME!

Visitors can freely replay the self-test game, move on to the next room without answering questions and return later, and collaborate with companions. (As all visitors receive a card, they can collaborate in answering the questions and viewing the exhibit messages.)

▪ *Results*: Most visitors over eight-years-old persisted until their cards were filled. The number of visitors who tested themselves without visiting the displays varied. After their initial effort, about 30 percent of the adult visitors (5 percent of the teenagers) began using the display information to help them answer the questions. However, the majority of visitors (including teens) eventually engaged in mindful interaction with the exhibits until all six card cells were stamped (Screven 1990b: 120–21).

Example 3:   Picasso Museum (Screven and Giraudy 1991)

▪ *Developer's Objective*: To overcome misconceptions about how simple it would be to paint and draw like Picasso, and to increase viewers' respect for the artistic talent involved in creating the simple balances in his painting *The Green Fawn*.

▪ *Procedure*: Four five-by-six-inch versions of Picasso's *The Green Fawn* were mounted on four parallel slanted panels. One was Picasso's own; the others were identical to the original except that several minor elements had been rearranged. Each print was mounted on the outside of a hinged flip label under a headline readable from fifteen feet away:

Which Do You Like Best? (Is Yours the Same as Picasso's?)

The display stood on a stand a in long narrow hall visitors used to approach the gallery where the painting itself was on exhibition. Each of the panels could be lifted to provide visitors with feedback about their choices. The *visitors' goal*, as defined by the headline, was to compare the different versions and choose among them according to their own personal taste, continuing to examine and compare the remaining choices until they found Picasso's. The effectiveness of the display was evaluated by (*a*) the quality of visitor involvement in the display (comparing/studying choices before making each choice); (*b*) the time spent in the gallery where the painting itself hung; and (*c*) the time spent in the gallery looking at four other, unaltered fawn paintings by Picasso. Baseline times for b and c were also obtained prior to installing the flip display.

▪ *Results*: Over 80 percent of gallery visitors became actively engaged with the display, often working together in small groups. Most people (more than 75 percent) spent a median of six minutes discussing details of the four versions and making their choices before finding Picasso's version. A large majority (more than 90 percent) examined all four choices before lifting any of the panels for feedback. We observed little random guessing, even though less than a third of the 130 visitors observed selected Picasso's painting on their first try. Another third made two choices before finding Picasso's version. Most visitors spent at least thirty seconds discussing a version after choosing it. A sample of the visitors who had used the display were tracked in the gallery and observed to spend significantly more time—compared with earlier baseline observations—looking at each of the five unaltered Picasso fawn paintings in the gallery.

Example 4. Rain Forest Exhibition (circa 1988)

▪ *Developer's Objective*: To communicate to family groups messages about the interconnections of life forms in certain habitats, using information from three widely separated displays of a rain forest exhibition at the Milwaukee Public Museum. The *visitor's goal* was to earn a "golf-certificate" at the exit.

▪ *Procedure*: At entry, a life-size cardboard golfer invited visitors to earn the certificate by answering three questions about each of three rain forest habitats. Visitors picked up a question booklet to use at three habitat exhibits identified by the numbers 1, 2, and 3, which were easy to see from a distance. Each target display contained information that answered questions focusing on objects, relationships, and texts related to the teaching objectives for each display. To receive the golf certificate at the exit, visitors took a three-item self-test based on the three teaching objectives. Correctly answering all three questions for all three exhibits earned visitors a certificate. If they made errors, they were offered a new booklet and invited to return to the displays a second time.

▪ *Results*: Most participants (n = 110) were family groups. Tracking visitors revealed a high 2.2 rating on the involvement scale (described earlier under "Motivation"), as well as systematic attention to display content, active intragroup discussions, sharing answers, pointing, and so forth. Over 65 percent of participants visited all three target displays; the median time spent by groups at each display was 4.2 minutes. Most participants (more than 65 percent) took the self-tests, and over 70 percent earned a certificate on their first or second try.

Example 5.   Advance Organizer for Woodlands Exhibition (circa 1996)

▪ *Objective*: To design an exhibit to serve as an advance organizer at the entry to a woodlands exhibition on how forest succession and interdependent ecological processes create forest diversity and, eventually, old forests of specific tree species. Front-end studies, however, showed that visitors (*a*) believed that, although trees get bigger and older, the same species are present at all stages of a forest's life; (*b*) could not recognize tree species by sight; (*c*) were unfamiliar with the common names of most trees; and (*d*) had little interest in the topic of forest succession. Because of visitor misconceptions and a low level of interest, the exhibit message was simplified to promote awareness that forest species change over time.

▪ *Procedure*: Overcoming visitor resistance to spending time at entry to the forest was approached by providing a goal-directed activity—a domino game using pictures of tree species instead of dots to reinforce the message. Starting and ending points were established by attaching one domino (an aspen) at the beginning of the game board and another (a sugar maple) at the end. The task was to "bridge the gap" by placing the remaining dominoes in proper sequence between them. The game had only one correct solution and was simple to execute and easy to understand. Designers tested a mock-up picturing a Wisconsin forest scene with the title

WHAT'S WRONG WITH THIS PICTURE?

along with a statement: "These trees grow in Wisconsin, but they DON'T grow side-by-side like this. As woodlands become older, certain trees follow others." Another panel read:

PLAY SUCCESSION DOMINOES!

- Place tree dominoes in right order to
- Connect the aspen trees to the maple trees.
- (Remember: these changes take hundreds of years.)

- *Results.* Most visitors caught on quickly and showed high levels of involvement and sustained focused attention. After playing the game, visitors questioned about how a forest changes over time said—in contrast to those in a pretest—that tree species change according to the age of the forest. They all acknowledged that this was new information for them.

In all these examples, visitors found gathering, interpreting, and applying information more rewarding than simply guessing. They maintained their attention long enough for the majority of them to (*a*) attain a goal, and (*b*) receive (i.e., comprehend) exhibit messages. Only three of the examples relied on external incentives.

Using today's technologies, exhibit designers can create a wide range of formats and modes that give visitors control over information delivery, pacing, style of presentation, and the consequences that follow their interactions with the exhibit. These modes include, among others, such so-called "doing" technologies as games, interactive books and labels, animations, CDs, multimedia computer programs, and information sharing. Debate will continue over the best ways and best technologies for advancing self-directed learning both inside and outside public settings. Regardless of which emerging information technologies we ultimately adopt for facilitating communication, they will have to provide methods of managing contingencies, eliciting user involvement, and presenting genuinely meaningful choices.

Some Final Words

Designers of exhibit media and delivery strategies for communicating information in public environments face a variety of obstacles. Delivering simple messages and images for relatively limited purposes—as in advertising, wayfinding, and leisure entertainment—is relatively easy. But communicating more complex educational and cultural messages (i.e., ideas) to self-directed people in public spaces is much more difficult. On the one hand, we need entertaining features to gain and sustain the public's voluntary attention and effort. On the other hand, viewers' attention must be focused and selective if they are to grasp complex and generally unfamiliar target messages. Communication designers often err on the side of providing features that entertain and visually please audiences, in the hope that messages will be understood because they are associated with appealing features. Although designers often concentrate on visuals and aesthetics, at other times they hope to attract viewers by focusing clearly on valuable content. But too often both approaches impair the audience's ability to receive or understand the message. Increasingly, however, some planners and designers are seeking to ensure that the fun of their exhibits is contingent on users actually receiving (understanding) the message.

In the course of this chapter we have examined some of the psychological and other considerations that can help communication systems to simultaneously entertain and convey information. We have argued that we can adapt our knowledge of human curiosity, the challenge of problem solving, game strategies, and goal-centered tasks—as well as of emerging scientific understandings of how the brain learns—to the task of connecting mindful attention with the enjoyable consequences of using exhibit content. In the future we can expect to see goal-centered strategies and "brain compatible" games for delivering complex information, not only in museums and similar facilities but also in leisure playgrounds, shopping areas, Web pages, multimedia studios, and, even, schools. Blueprints for adapting such strategies to information systems hide many dangers, but the kind of front-end and formative evaluation described earlier should help planners and designers avoid the most serious·obstacles to effective informal communication in public environments.

From an economic standpoint, competition for the discretionary time of audiences will probably ensure more effective communications in all the settings we have touched upon. Information designers will have to learn to link meaningful communication with entertainment and natural learning processes without sacrificing either gate receipts or educational outcomes. Over time, competition may advance the design of self-directed learning habitats until learning and cultural enlightenment—as well as fun—become by-products of all natural biological, cognitive, and social processes.

Notes

1. Summaries relating museum learning to these underlying principles and theories can be found in Schauble and Glazer (1996), Choi and Hannafin (1995), Gagné (1974), Keller (1983), Reigeluth (1983), Resnick (1989), Screven (1969), and Banyard and Hayes (1994).

2. For information on the effect of these factors, see Alt and Griggs (1989), Dierking and Falk (1994), Griggs (1990), Hood (1993), Hooper-Greenhill (1994), McManus (1989, 1991, 1994), Miles (1986), Miles and Zavala (1994), and Screven (1986).

3. Representative museums that have made major commitments to visitor-centered design include the London Natural History Museum, New York Hall of Science, Denver Art Museum, Denver Museum of Natural History, Phoenix Desert Botanical Garden, Cincinnati Museum of Natural History, National Museum of Natural History (Smithsonian Institution), Minnesota History Museum, Indianapolis Museum of Science, Quebec's Museum of Civilization, and the Powerhouse Museum in Sydney, Australia.

4. For reviews of these types of evaluation, see Bitgood and Shettel (1994), Hooper-Greenhill (1994), Miles et al. (1988), and Screven (1990). For the overall evaluation process, see Bitgood and Loomis (1993), Miles et al. (1988, chaps. 1 and 16), and Screven (1990). For introductory information on the front-end assessment of visitor knowledge, attitudes, misconceptions, and other characteristics, see Hood (1992, 1993) and Shettel (1990).

5. For description of the use of mock-ups and prototypes, see Loomis (1987, chap. 6) and Screven (1990a, 1993).

6. Research has shown that if key features found to be effective during formative evaluations (contrast, colors, fonts, placement, format) are faithfully incorporated into the

final installed exhibit, visitor responses will be similar to those obtained during formative testing (Griggs and Manning 1983).

7. For subsequent improvements and variations in this communications model and on communication theory and practice, see Hooper-Greenhill (1994: 37–53) and McQuail and Windahl (1993).

8. In the classical communication model, exhibit objects are regarded as media channels through which messages are "delivered." In museums, malls, and zoos, they are seen as simply another type of delivery media that conveys messages similar to those delivered by other means. In this chapter, however, exhibit objects are parts of the information field that viewers may attend to along with other information.

9. Based on Screven 1986, 1990a.

10. For introductory summaries on semantic memory, procedural memory, episodic memory, feelings, and encoding processes operating in informal environments, see Barnard and Loomis (1994); Bitgood and Shettel (1994), Kinch (1994), Hooper-Greenhill (1995), and McManus (1993).

11. What seemed more important to visitors was whether or not participatory features and aesthetic appeal helped them understand exhibit concepts.

12. However, *involvement* sometimes also refers to visitors' general level of activity, independent of the focus of attention, because both focused and unfocused behavior may show higher levels of activity. High activity at participatory exhibits may or may not be *selective*; for example, visitors often energetically interact with computer tasks while paying little attention to the intended messages (Moscardo 1992).

13. For example, a challenging question posed in a layered label draws attention to certain display features. If visitors are then selectively attentive to these features prior to seeking feedback in the label's next layer, they are using the exhibit interactively in a mindful mode and their interpretation of the feedback they receive will depend on the particular features they have paid attention to.

14. This rating scale is not the same as the three-point scale used to measure involvement (Screven 1990a).

15. The Meyers-Briggs scale (Meyers and McCaulley 1985) is an intuitive measure of learning styles. More behavioral and systematic methods of assessing differences in thinking styles have been developed (Sternberg 1994, Renzulli and Smith 1978). These include a self-report rating measure (*Thinking Style Inventory*), a *Thinking Style Questionnaire for Teachers*, which measures seven styles, and a task-based preference scale in which students are given a situation and asked to choose their preferred approach. (E.g., "When I'm studying literature, I prefer to (a) follow the teacher's advice ..., (b) make up my own story with..., and so on.")

16. Many examples of natural incentives can be found in publications by Carlson (1993), Csikszentmihalyi (1975, 1983, 1989, 1990), Csikszentmihalyi and Hermanson (1995), Deci (1985), Gardner (1991), Lepper (1980), Malone (1981), Moscardo and Pearce (1986), Perry (1992), and Screven (1969, 1986, 1990b, 1992).

17. This does not mean that passive participation cannot result in learning when visitors' pre-existing interest in a topic stimulates them to pay careful attention to an exhibit. Novice viewers unfamiliar with the subject, however, are likely to ignore passive information or—at best—pay it only casual attention.

18. Various models have been proposed. A model offered by Perry (1989, 1992) utilizes intrinsically motivating, goal-centered activities to sustain attention and facilitate exhibit learning. Borun et al. (1996) and Czikszentmihalyi and Hermanson (1995) offer other examples and research data on visitors and families involved in goal-centered tasks in museums.

References

Alt, M. B., and K. M. Shaw. 1984. Characteristics of ideal museum exhibits. *British Journal of Psychology* 75: 25–36.

Ashcraft, M. H. 1989. *Human Memory and Cognition*. Boston: Scott Foresman.

Banyard, P., and Hayes, N. 1994. *Psychology: Theory and Application*. London: Chapman & Hall.

Barnard, W., and Loomis, R. 1994. The museum exhibit as a visual learning medium. Visitor Behavior 9 (2): 14–17.

Bateman, W. L. 1990. *Open to Question: The Art of Teaching and Learning by Inquiry*. San Francisco: Jossey-Bass.

Bearman, D., ed. 1995. *Hands-on: Hypermedia and Interactivity in Museums*. Pittsburgh: Archives and Museum Informatics.

Bitgood, S., and Loomis, R. 1993. Introduction to environmental design and evaluation in museums. *Environment and Behavior* 25 (6): 683–697.

Bitgood, S., and Shettel, H. 1994. The classification of exhibit evaluation: A rationale for remedial evaluation. *Visitor Behavior* 9 (4): 4–15.

Borun, M. 1992. Naive knowledge and the design of science museums. *Curator* 36: 201–219.

Borun, M.; Chambers, M.; and Cleghorn, A. 1996. Families are learning in science museums. *Curator* 39: 123–138.

Borun, M.; Chambers, M.; Dritsas, J.; and Johnson, J. 1997. Enhancing family learning through exhibits. *Curator* 40 (4): 279–295.

Carlson, S. P. 1993. Cognitive model for learning in educationally oriented recreation facilities. Ph.D. dissertation. East Lansing: Michigan State University.

Choi, J., and Hannafin, M. 1995. Situated cognition and learning environments: Roles, structures, and implications for design. *Educational Technology Research and Development* 43 (2): 53–59.

Csikszentmihalyi, M. 1975. *Beyond Boredom and Anxiety: The Experience of Play in Work and Games.* San Francisco: Jossey-Bass.

Csikszentmihalyi, M. 1989. Optimal experience in work and leisure. *Journal of Personality and Social Psychology* 56 (5): 815–822.

Csikszentmihalyi, M. 1990. *Flow: The Psychology of Optimal Experience.* New York: Harper & Row.

Csikszentmihalyi, M., and Hermanson, K. 1995. Intrinsic motivation in museums: What makes visitors want to learn? *Museum News* 74 (3): 34–37, 59–61.

Deci, E. L. 1985. *Intrinsic Motivation and Self-determination in Human Behavior.* New York: Plenum Press.

Dierking, I., and Falk, J. 1994. Family behavior and learning in informal science settings: A review of the research. *Science Education* 78 (1): 57–72.

Ferster, C. B., and Culbertson, S. A. 1982. *Behavior Principles*, 3rd ed. Englewood Cliffs, N.J.: Prentice-Hall.

Fields, A. 1981. Information mapping ten years on: A survey. *PLET* 18 (3): 155–161.

Gagné, R., and Briggs, L. 1974, *Principles of Instructional Design.* New York: Holt, Rinehart & Winston.

Gardner, H. 1991. *The Unschooled Mind: How Children Think and How Schools Should Teach.* New York: Basic Books.

Gell-Mann, Murray. 1994. *The Quark and the Jaguar.* New York: W. H. Freeman.

Gibson, J. J., and Gibson, E. J. 1955. Perceptual learning: Differentiation or enrichment? *Psychological Review* 62: 32–41.

Griggs, S. A. 1990. Perceptions of traditional and new style exhibitions at the Natural History Museum, London. *ILVS (International Laboratory for Visitor Studies) Review: A Journal of Visitor Behavior* 1 (1): 78–90.

Griggs, S., and Manning, J. 1983. The predictive validity of formative evaluations of exhibits. *Museum Studies Journal* 1 (2): 31–41.

Grünig, J. E. 1979. Time budgets, level of involvement and the use of mass media. Journalism Quarterly 56: 248–61.

Grünig, J. E. 1980. Communication of science to nonscientists. In *Progress in Communication Sciences*, B. Dervin and M. Voigt , eds. Norwood, N.J.: Ablex Publishers.

Hood, M. G. 1992. Audience research helps museums make informed decisions. In *Visitor Studies: Theory, Research, and Practice*, vol. 4, A. Benefield, S. Bitgood, and H. Shettel, eds., pp. 38–55. Jacksonville, Ala.: Center for Social Design.

Hood, M. G. 1993. After 70 years of audience research, What have we learned? Who comes to museums, and Who does not, and Why? In *Visitor Studies: Theory, Research, and Practice*, vol. 5, D. Thompson, A. Benefield, S. Bitgood, H. Shettl, and R. Williams., eds., pp. 16–28. Jacksonville, Ala.: Center for Social Design.

Hooper-Greenhill, E. 1992. *Museums and the Shaping of Knowledge*. London: Routledge.

Hooper-Greenhill, E. 1994. *Museums and Their Visitors*. London: Routledge.

Hooper-Greenhill, E. 1995. *Museum, Media, Message*. London: Routledge.

Horn, R. E. 1976. *How to Write Information Mapping*. Lexington, Mass.: Information Resources.

Horn, R. E. 1998. *Visual Language*. Bainbridge, WA: MacVU, Inc.

Kaufman, S. 1993. *The Origins of Order—Self-Organization and Selection in Evolution*. New York: Oxford University Press.

Keller, J. M. 1983. Motivational design of instruction. In *Instructional Design Theories and Models: An Overview of Their Current Status*, C. E. Reigeluth, ed., pp. 383–434. Hillsdale, N.J.: Lawrence Erlbaum.

Kinch, W. 1994. Text comprehension, memory, and learning. *American Psychologist* 49 (4): 294–303.

Knez, E. I., and Wright, A. G. 1970. The museum as a communication system: An assessment of Cameron's viewpoint. *Curator* 13 (3): 204–212.

Lakota, R. 1976. *The National Museum of Natural History as a Behavioral Environment. Part II: Summary and Conclusions*. Special Report. Washington, D.C.: Office of Museum Programs.

Langer, E. J. 1989. Minding matters: The consequences of mindlessness/mindfulness. In *Advances in Experimental Social Psychology*, J. Berkowitz, ed., pp. 50–89. New York: Academic Press.

Langer, E. J.; Black, A.; and Chanowitz, B. 1978. The mindlessness of ostensibly thoughtful action: The role of interaction. *Journal of Personality and Social Psychology* 6 (6): 635–642.

Loomis, Ross. 1987. *Museum Visitor Evaluation: New Tool for Museum Management.* Nashville: American Association for State and Local History.

Lowery, Lawrence. 1989. *Thinking and Learning.* Grove, Calif.: Midwest Publications.

Lowery, Lawrence. 1990. *The Biological Basis for Thinking and Learning.* Berkeley: Lawrence Hall of Science, University of California.

MacDonald-Ross, M., and Waller, R. 1976. The transformer. *Penrose Annual* 69: 141–152.

McManus, P. 1989. Oh yes, they do: How museum visitors read labels and interact with exhibit texts. *Curator* 32: 174–189.

McManus, P. 1991. Making sense of exhibits. In *Museum Languages: Objects and Texts*, G. Kavanaugh, ed., pp. 35–46. Leicester, Eng.: Leicester University Press.

McManus, P. 1993. Memories as indicators of the impact of museum visits. *Museum Management and Curatorship* 12: 367–380.

McManus, P. 1994. Families in museums. In *Towards the Museum of the Future: New European Perspectives*, R. Miles and L. Zavala, eds., pp. 81–97. London: Routledge.

McQuail, D., and Windal, S. 1993. *Communication Models.* London: Longman.

Malone, T. W. 1981. Toward a theory of intrinsically motivated instruction. *Cognitive Science* 4: 333–369.

Malone, T. W., and Lepper, M. R. 1987. Making learning fun: A taxonomy of intrinsic motivations for learning. In *Aptitude, Learning, and Instruction: Vol. 3. Connotative and Affective Process Analyses*, R. E. Snow and M. J. Farr, eds., pp. 223–253. Hillsdale, N. J.: Lawrence Erlbaum.

Melton, A. 1933. Some behavioral characteristics of museum visitors. *Psychological Bulletin* 30: 720–721.

Melton, A. 1935, 1988. *Problems of Installation in Museums of Art.* Washington, D.C.: American Association of Museums.

Meyers, I. B., and McCaulley, M. H. 1985. *Manual: A Guide to the Development and Use of the Meyers-Briggs Type Indicator.* Palo Alto: Consulting Psychologists Press.

Miles, R. S. 1986. Museum audiences. *International Journal of Museum Management and Curatorship* 5: 73–80.

Miles, R. S. 1987. Museums and the communication of science. In *Communicating Science to the Public*, D. Evered and M. O'Conner, eds., pp. 114–22. New York: John Wiley.

Miles, R. S.; Alt, M. B.; Gosling, D. C.; Lewis, B. N.; and Tout, A. F. 1988. *The Design of Educational Exhibits*, 2nd ed. London: Unwin Hyman.

Miles, R. S., and Zavala, L., eds. 1994. *Towards the Museum of the Future: New European Perspectives*. London: Routledge.

Moscardo, G. M. 1992. A Mindfulness/Mindlessness Model of the Museum Visitor Experience. Ph.D. dissertation. Cooktown: University of North Queensland, Australia.

Moscardo, G. M., and Pearce, P. L. 1986. Visitor centers and environmental interpretation: An exploration of the relationship among visitor enjoyment, understanding, and mindfulness. *Journal of Environmental Psychology* 6: 89–109.

Nedzel. L. 1952. The Motivation and Education of the General Public Through Museum Experiences. Ph.D. dissertation. Chicago: University of Chicago.

Perry, D. L. 1989. The creation and verification of a development model for the design of a museum exhibit. Ann Arbor: University Microfilms (90–12186)

Perry, D. L. 1992. What research says … Designing exhibits that motivate? *ASTC (Association for Science-Technology Centers) Newsletter* 20 (1): 9–10, 12.

Reigeluth, C. E., ed. 1983. *Instructional Design Theories and Models: An Overview of Their Current Status*. Hillsdale, N.J.: Lawrence Erlbaum.

Renzulli, J. S., and Smith, L. H. 1978. *Learning Styles Inventory*. Mansfield Center, Conn.: Creative Learning Press.

Resnick, L. N. 1989. *Knowing, Learning, and Instruction: Essays in Honor of Robert Glaser*. Hillsdale, N.J.: Lawrence Erlbaum.

Robinson, E. S. 1928. *The Behavior of the Museum Visitor*. American Association of Museums Monograph, n.s., no. 5. Washington, D.C.: AAM.

Robinson, P. V. 1960. An Experimental Study of Exhibit Arrangement and Viewing Method to Determine Their Effect Upon Learning of Factual Material. Ph.D. dissertation. Los Angeles: University of California.

Saloman, G. 1983. The differential investment of mental effort in learning from different sources. *Educational Psychologist* 18 (1): 42–50.

Saloman, G., and Globerson, T. 1987. Skill may not be enough: The role of mindfulness in learning and transfer. *International Journal of Educational Research* 11: 623–27.

Schauble, L., and Glaser, R., eds. 1996. *Innovations in Learning: New Environments for Education.* Hillsdale, N.J.: Lawrence Erlbaum.

Screven, C. G. 1969. The museum as a responsive learning environment. *Museum News* 47 (10): 7–10.

Screven, C. G. 1986. Exhibitions and information centers. *Curator* 29: 109–38.

Screven, C. G. 1990a. Uses of evaluation before, during, and after exhibit design. *ILVS Review: A Journal of Visitor Behavior* 1 (2): 33–66.

Screven, C. G. 1990b. A "self-test" computer system for motivating voluntary learning from exhibitions. *ILVS Review: A Journal of Visitor Behavior* 1 (2): 120–21.

Screven, C. G. 1992. Motivating visitors to read labels. *ILVS Review: A Journal of Visitor Behavior* 2 (2): 183–211. (Reprinted in *Text in the Exhibition Medium*, Andrée Blais, ed., pp. 96–132. Québec: Societé des Museés Québecois.)

Screven, C. G. 1993. *Behavioral Research and Environmental Graphic Design.* Special Bulletin. Cambridge, Mass.: Society for Environmental Graphic Design (SEGD).

Screven, C. G., ed. 1999. *Visitor Studies: Bibliography and Abstracts,* 4th ed. Chicago: Screven & Associates (1700 East 56th St., Suite 1203, Chicago 60637).

Screven, C. G., and Giraudy, D. 1991. The Musée Picasso–Antibes Project. *ILVS Review: A Journal of Visitor Behavior* 2 (1): 116–117.

Shannon, Claude, and Weaver, Warren. 1949. *The Mathematical Theory of Information.* Urbana: University of Illinois Press.

Shettel, H. 1973. Exhibits: Art form or educational medium? *Museum News* 52: 32–41.

Shettel, H. 1990. Front-end evaluation. *ILVS Review: A Journal of Visitor Behavior* 2 (2): 275–80.

Shettel, H.; Butcher, M.; Cotton, T.; Northrop, J.; and Slough, D. S. 1968. *Strategies for Determining Exhibit Effectiveness.* Report No. AIR E95–4/68–FR. Washington, D.C.: American Institutes for Research.

Sternberg, R. J. 1988. Mental self government: A theory of intellectual styles and their development. *Human Development* 31: 197–224.

Sternberg, R. J. 1991. *Thinking Styles Inventory.* Tallahassee, Fla.: Star Mountain Projects.

Sternberg, R. J. 1994. Thinking styles: Theory and assessment at the interface between intelligence and personality. In *Personality and Intelligence*, R. J. Sternberg and P. Ruzgis, eds., pp. 169–87. Cambridge: Cambridge University Press.

Uzzell, D., ed. 1989. *Heritage Interpretation: vol. 2. The Visitor Experience*. London: Belhaven Press.

Vance, C., and Schroeder, D. 1992. Matching visitor learning style with exhibit type. In *Visitor Studies: Theory, Research, and Practice*, vol. 4, A. Benefield, S. Bitgood, and H. Shettel eds., pp. 185–200. Jacksonville, Ala.: Center for Social Design.

Witkin, H. A. 1990. *Cognitive Styles in Personal and Cultural Adaptation*. The 1977 Heinz Werner Lectures. Worcester, Mass.: Clark University Press.

Wolf, R. 1980. A naturalistic view of evaluation. *Museum News* 58 (1): 39–46.

8 *Visualization for Thinking, Planning, and Problem Solving*

Yvonne M. Hansen

Vision can no longer be employed simply to support verbal and conceptual meanings: Its potential as a cognitive power in its own right must be exploited.
—Kepes 1965: v

The pace of change continues—swift, unpredictable, and chaotic—and affects us all. Though we long for simplicity and certainty, complexity, disorder, and unpredictability are our daily lot. The time has come to accept that today's problems cannot be solved with yesterday's cause-and-effect thinking, outdated formulas, or antiquated and inefficient approaches that lock struggling minds in boxes. Complexity isn't what it used to be. It's more—and different.

Complex problems are made up of many interrelated elements. They demand innovative approaches—flexible processes that reveal relationships among parts—that require us to look at problems from new and varied points of view merely to understand them, much less to solve them. Problems are situated in specific contexts and their parts interact continuously at many levels and across shifting boundaries.

The problem solvers and innovators in many organizations are groups, individuals who bring to discussion of any issue a wide spectrum of opinions. When they meet to explore messy, nonroutine problems that are often subtly connected to each other, they generate huge volumes of facts, ideas, and opinions. This plethora of information cannot be recalled or managed with such traditional, words-only methods as notes on legal pads, computer printouts, flip charts, and audio recordings. Confusion and conflict can result as group members propose their various solutions.

However, if a problem is first defined as a whole in context, the group is more likely to achieve clarity and agreement and less likely to shoot down the remedies and solutions proposed by individual members. *Graphic modeling*, a method combining simple graphic notation and words in visual arrangements, can often define an issue and its context more completely than words alone. Drawing graphic models or diagrams provides a visual, nonlinear, whole-systems approach to problem solving, planning, innovation, diagnosis, and envisioning the future.

In this paper I address the diverse sources of information, the inadequacy of verbal language to clearly convey complex matters, the need to understand and express dynamic complexity, and the rationale for using a graphical language. I suggest that simple, graphic shapes, the building blocks of a graphical language, play an instrumental role in cognition, visual thinking, and the communication of complex, dynamically changing realities. I describe in particular Graphic Tools®, a graphical language for facilitating understanding of problem complexity, and present an array of applications for using it effectively.

Information Acquisition and Display

Intelligence does not operate in verbal abstractions alone.... Visual thinking is not a delayed system; information is conveyed directly. The greatest power of visual language lies in its immediacy, its spontaneous evidence. Visually, you see content and form simultaneously. They must be dealt with as one single force delivering information the same way.
—Dondis 1973: 106

Information comes to us from three general sources:

- External—the observable world; what is seen and perceived; printed texts, verbal accounts, media presentations, and so forth

- Internal—one's own images, ideas, visualizations, and perceptions
- Combined external and internal sources informing the cognitions and perceptions that give rise to new combinations of knowledge and information

Words, the most common form of communication, are powerful enough when uttered in the right tone at the right time to move people to great deeds. As important as words are, however, what people remember is the gist of a message; words play only a supporting role. The notion that ideas and words occur simultaneously in the mind, and that thought without words doesn't exist, is questioned, if not refuted, by the oft-heard phrase, "I can't find the right words"; that is, an idea exists in some form apart from words. The idea-word connection is further disproven by the fact that when professional translators strive to interpret the meaning of a text or speech, they may not transmit it as precisely as when they translate it word for word.

It is important for information designers to be fully aware of internal thinking processes and mental models, for they influence communication processes and content as ideas take shape. Our thoughts progress through several unevenly paced phases from less defined to more defined, evolving in fits and starts. Initially, an idea may be vague and "fuzzy"—impossible to conceptualize clearly. Then, at the preverbal phase, it can be expressed graphically without verbal labels. At this stage, Graphic Tools, which employ six simple shapes, work well to make the evolution of the thought—from nebulous to conceptual—visible on paper. Along the way, although words may be useful in fleshing out details of the thought, verbal descriptions can narrow emerging concepts too quickly and impede their full development. An individual's recognition of these mental stages is related to the ability to introspect, to throw light into the shadows of the mind and even sweep away a cobweb or two.

There are a surprising number of graphical languages and notation systems, as well as verbal languages that contain graphical and nonverbal elements. Although the philosopher Leibnitz dreamed in the early eighteenth century of a future universal symbolism of pictorial images recognizable by speakers of all languages, it was Charles K. Bliss who in 1949 devised Semantography, a language of basic symbols now in international use (Dreyfuss 1972). Another system, ISOTYPE, was devised by Otto Neurath; the acronym stands for International System of TYpographic Picture Education. Neurath's pictographs show what an observer actually sees rather than an abstract symbol such as a word or a number associated with some object or person. In the United States, for example, the abstract symbols for paper currency and coins are, respectively, the dollar sign (an upper-case S with two vertical parallel strokes through the center) and the cents sign (a lower-case c with a vertical stroke in the center). A pictograph for coins, on the other hand, might be a drawing of a stack of coins with ridged edges and a president's profile on the face of the top coin.

International travel signage too is graphical information, the purpose of which is to allow viewers to grasp meanings immediately. Throughout human history, motivated by a recognition of changing needs and assisted by the technologies of their eras, professionals and specialists in fields as diverse as music, choreography, chemistry, geometry, statistics, geography, cartography, and geology developed nonverbal symbols. Current examples are found in all kinds of systems design, including programming (Venn diagrams, object-oriented flow charts), project management (P.E.R.T.), and organizational development (organization charts, visioning strategies, mission statements, etc.), as well as in process and production engineering, architecture and drafting, interior design, maritime communications (signal flags), and nonverbal signage.

As we have seen, a number of arguments refute the belief that words are the only and primary means of communicating information and that our thoughts and ideas are formed first as words and sentences. Moreover, words can be highly ambiguous. An example of the ambiguity of words is found in this headline of unknown origin: "Stud tires out." While a resident of the northern states will understand that there is a new law forbidding the use of studded tires, a westerner knows that somewhere a cowboy-type is growing weary.

Graphic exploration and communication begin very early in life. During preverbal development, children communicate with sounds, gestures, and images. Using pencils, crayons, and paints, they draw rounded shapes, scribbles, zigzags, and other nonverbal expressions to express thoughts their limited vocabulary has no words for. Even in the early school years, children continue to express ideas by drawing lines, shapes, and curlicues that their teachers and parents label as "art"—and therefore irrelevant to the communication of concepts, facts, and ideas. Sadly, children are usually told to stop "drawing" and put away their crayons and paper when it is time for reading class. What to the child is nonverbal communication is "art" to adults. To Rudolf Arnheim, professor emeritus of the psychology of art at Harvard, this process of nonverbal communication is *visual reasoning* (1969).

Graphics of all kinds are visible everywhere; they invade our every moment, attempt to attract our attention, inform us, entice us to act. Whereas once text was king and the only tool (except mathematics) available for computer displays, the new easier-to-use computers now abound in icons, symbols, and graphic metaphors (e.g., the screen as a desktop) that encourage visual thinking. Graphics, which earlier made only occasional appearances on the Internet, are now constantly visible on the World Wide Web.

Edward Tufte (1989) investigated computer screen displays and urged makers to simplify them for ease of use and better absorption of information. Steve Jobs and Steve Wozniack, the conceptualizers of the Macintosh, with its desktop metaphor and elegant use of icons, placed functional graphics at our fingertips, while the software developed soon afterward made the design of graphical information an essential feature. Before then, graphics—compared to words—were generally perceived as less-effective, after-the-fact conveyors of ideas, mere extras and decorative add-ons. Now the elegance and importance of iconic simplicity is increasingly recognized, accepted, and applied.

Pattern: Phenomena Made Visible

Our sense of pattern is an extremely important part of all intellectual activity, and the externalization and representation of pattern in visual communication is ... at the core of many advances.
—Sless 1981: 148

A multitude of environmental events perceived as chaos, heard as noise, and read as information overload are continuously present to us, clamoring for our attention. More information is out there than the mind can manage and use productively, because it comes to us in a linear mode, word by word, and is thus difficult to synthesize into new, meaningful arrangements. Words are not the only means to convey information, to inform us, to give inner form to something. In fact, words can impede understanding, because they are often inadequate to deal with the experience of information overload, not to mention chaos, disorder, and randomness. Words and phrases that represent concepts and ideas can, however, be displayed and stored graphically, in "mind maps." Somehow, our brains know that there is something of value in what we consciously perceive as randomness and disorder. It can render phenomena, relationships, and ideas visible, allowing patterns to emerge from apparent disorder and become detectable, and available, to our senses and intellect.

In the Austin laboratory of the University of Texas Center for Non-linear Dynamics, its director, Harry Swinney, introduced melted crayons into a spinning tank of water to simulate the behavior of the jet stream as it meets mountain ranges. He thus made an invisible phenomenon visible for the purpose of detecting patterns. In another experiment, Swinney used tiny plastic beads in a tank of water to form a miniature red spot showing how Jupiter's atmosphere arranges itself to create the Great Red Spot, a whirlpool storm. Swinney is a leader in the search for "universal patterns in seemingly random behavior ... referred to as the study of

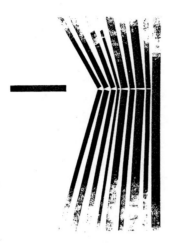

Figure 8.1
A Visual Representation of the Idea "Pushing Forward" (from: Stankowski 1991).

chaos" (Stanley 1996). His work demonstrates that phenomena must be made visible, not just verbalized, to produce the detectable, observable patterns in which we discern meaning.

Making invisible phenomena visible is also the work of Anton Stankowski, who devoted a book to showing how invisible processes can be made visible (1991). He developed a series of studies showing how ideas might be visually represented. In the example shown in figure 8.1 he used black lines to convey the notion of a force (horizontal line) acting on objects (a group of more-or-less vertical lines of various widths). The vertical lines are solid black where the push will occur and diffused black at their peripheries. This abstraction—an *arbitrary graphic*—demonstrates how a concept—in this case, pushing forward—can be conveyed clearly without showing any recognizable objects, such as an arrow aimed toward a sheaf of straw.

Information Overload

Information overload is a stressful condition, perhaps because we don't know how to organize and categorize the wealth of verbal information we receive. It is time-consuming and frustrating to access, reflect on, and store information and ideas in ways that will let us easily retrieve and apply them to everyday problems. The task of managing the proliferation of information and the accompanying complexity is daunting. Yet, addictively, we reach out for more, hoping to discover a secret key hidden somewhere—or in plain sight but unrecognized—that will bring instant relief. There is no secret key, but help is available if we are willing to think in a different mode and use our total mental capacity.

On the *Learning Organization Digest (LO Digest)*, an Internet site for dialogues about organizations as systems and how they learn and change, recognition of the wealth of good information available to us is a common thread of discussion. So too are laments about managing and storing it. Subscribers comment appreciatively on "the breadth of the *LO Digest's* coverage and the degree of enthusiastic involvement of its participants," but say they have trouble finding time to save, classify, and store each of the three or four digests—ranging in size from twenty to thirty megabytes —that are posted daily.

Subscribers to the *Digest* make frequent reference to graphics as aids in all manner of applications. Alan Scharf of Creative Leap International describes how he creates various sorts of models—"physical, analog, symbolic, graphical, schematic, descriptive and pictorial"—to use in overheads, flip charts, and handouts (*LOD* 5/96). He goes on to say that with graphics the "solution space can be suddenly expanded beyond its apparent physical reality (a physical paradigm shift)." In situations where many pages of explanatory text would otherwise be required, graphics can help us communicate complex matters visually and simply.

Reference is often made in the *Digest* to Sun Microsystems's World Wide Web site, "Distributed Objects for Business," which points out that competitive advantage is achieved by increasing the ability to learn fast and think in fundamentally new ways, especially systemically. The statement alludes to Peter Senge's book, *The Fifth Discipline* (1991), which he illustrates with his original systems graphics (as shown in figure 8.2). Senge says that "the essence of the discipline of systems thinking lies in a shift

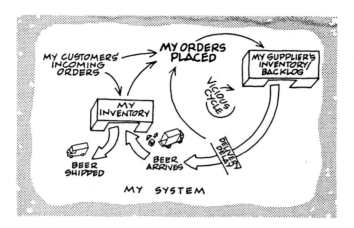

Figure 8.2

"My System," a Graphic Representation of the interrelationships and processes involved in being a beer distributor (From Senge 1991).

of mind: seeing interrelationships rather than linear cause-effect chains, and seeing processes of change rather than snapshots" (1991: 73). The moderator of *LO Digest* and Senge's business partner, Richard Karash, adds that "examining our business entities, activities, and processes from an object-oriented approach can be more effective in capturing and sharing knowledge" (LO6818). An *object-oriented approach* means, quite simply, a graphic approach.

The computer systems developer and organizational consultant David Taylor makes extensive use of rectangles, circles, lines, and arrows in the model-building process. He applies modeling to "convergent engineering ... [that] offers a new opportunity to create more flexible, adaptive business systems by combining business and software engineering into a single, integrated discipline" (1995: 3). In figure 8.3, part *a* illustrates a basic systems diagram showing relationships among system entities; part *b* shows a specific system, "Dylan Distributors," and identifies the internal entities, external entities, and the places where they interface. Thus business and software engineering, previously separate disciplines, are integrated. The verbal and the visual are united.

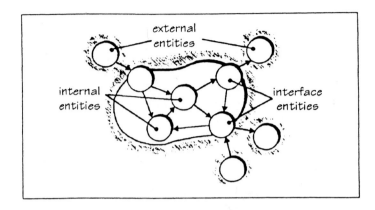

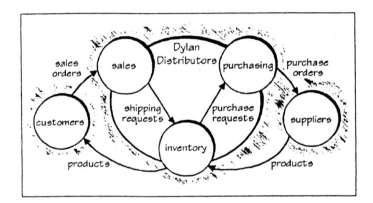

Figure 8.3
Two Systems Models by David Taylor (1995): (a) A basic systems model; (b) a model of a specific system.

Managing complexity, disorder, and information overload requires serious rethinking and escape from the verbal box that traps the mind in traditional linear, sequential thought processes. Re-entering a visual world to conceptualize a complex state of affairs holistically and systemically—after relinquishing that world in childhood—calls for an integrative, synthesizing dynamic. In a graphical model, data and ideas and even invisible processes (as Stankowski has shown) can communicate the structure of complexity.

Graphics have the capacity to transform our understanding of an issue and, to some extent, free us from the narrowness of words, labels, and classification systems. According to Arnheim (1969), perceiving and thinking are "indivisibly intertwined" in a "union of perception and thought." The mind can sense an underlying order within apparent chaos by detecting emerging patterns, noting the repetition of an entity or concept, and forming a category of something that has not yet been labeled. The effect of a label is to eliminate and exclude whatever doesn't fit, shut down creativity, and induce us to apply without hesitation the same solution that worked with the last problem labeled the same way. We are in too much of a hurry to take action instead of leisurely and curiously scanning the environment, with conscious awareness of the search, to see what's out there. Patterns, the recurrence of graphic, visible arrangements, are everywhere in the natural and manufactured world—in wallpaper borders, Oriental rugs, trees, ocean waves, and, sand dunes. Repetitions are constantly before us, sometimes in variations so subtle they might easily be dismissed as irrelevant.

Identifying, detecting, and tracking linear trends means that an entity has been labeled, has a name, and can probably be quantified. Patterns, however, are different in nature from trends. Perceiving an emerging pattern is like gazing at clouds, not knowing exactly what you're looking for and imagining that you see an object. Or it's like seeing your initials on a license plate, forgetting about it, then seeing them again, and yet again. You don't look for what you see, but you do note the repetition and perceive a pattern emerging. Think of it this way: First, you note an anomaly, perhaps more than one; then you see the anomaly again; it is not exactly the same but very similar, and you call it a coincidence. The third occurrence, however, indicates that a pattern of some kind is emerging from what you initially perceived as a disordered field. If your mind is focused on searching for a continuing trend, however, you will discount the pattern, excluding it as a nonconforming element.

The three stages of observation above enable you to perceive a pattern you might otherwise not see. Similarly, using graphics to construct sketches or models of entities and processes can help us perceive recurrent elements and detect patterns. The diagram or model is capable of showing the "big picture"; or, by "zooming in," it can focus on a part of the whole while we remain fully aware of what is being excluded.

Exploratory Graphics

The diagram can present at a glance what a verbal description can only present in a sequence of statements. It is the ideal mode for describing relations between things.
—Albarn and Smith 1977: 69

The advantage of using graphics along with words and phrases is being able to see relationships and structure among the data that are obscured in a text-only situation. Detecting patterns, which are visual phenomena, in a field of text is virtually impossible. In addition, reading and analyzing page upon page of text requires a powerful memory and the ability to absorb, store, categorize, and retrieve information. However, when information is presented in graphic form and concepts are given shape, relationships among the various elements are easier to see. And, as the graphic representation is further enriched with visual information, long-term memory is triggered and even more information and perceptions can be added, enabling viewers and oneself to detect new patterns, processes, and other phenomena.

In addition to enhancing the capacity to perceive patterns in situations of confusion, complexity, disorder, or chaos, a graphical approach encourages us to think visually. Wherever information is continuously generated, graphically based information design can help us, as individuals and groups, bring coherence and order to our external and professional worlds as well as to the internal worlds of our imagination.

Moreover, it is not only external sources of information that must be managed. There is also the continuous flow of our own stream of thoughts, the ideas and connections that come to us at odd times, which must be noted, written down, or sketched out before they are lost. We already do this, of course. Who has not jotted down ideas on torn corners of envelopes? We are all napkin scribblers when struck by an exciting, brilliant flash that we want to remember or communicate to someone else. These expressions are intuitive and informal. Until now, however, there has been no formalized language for capturing these creative flashes or synthesizing our exploratory thoughts. Adding images to words somehow alters how we perceive an object or idea. Graphical displays and idea sketches often trigger those precious ah-ha experiences that bring about shifts in perspective. When we see an issue in a new light, the mind perceives in it different qualities and becomes open to innovation and, frequently, a paradigm shift. Simple graphic shapes have the capacity to represent preverbal cognitions and give them concrete form. Even computer-assisted, outside-the-box approaches fail to tap into the mind's capacity to perceive the external world with insight and knowledge gained by thinking visually.

Until now, conceptual graphics, images, and other visual devices have been relegated to a low status. In the world of information they have usually been used to support texts or illustrate numerical data in charts and graphs displaying, for example, demographic information. Yet graphics are no less a representational language than are words: they too convey meaning, can concretize abstractions or derive abstract principles from the concrete. They can add a visual perspective to verbal descriptions and reveal connections not apparent when only words are used. Patterns, too, become, discernible.

Need for a Simple Graphical Language

Discussing reality as consisting of "messes," Russell Ackoff says that a problem is an abstraction that comes from analyzing a mess. In answer to the query "Then what is a mess?" he replies, "That's the significant thing: a mess is a system of problems" (1981: 19). Frequently, subscribers to the *Learning Organization Digest* refer to "seeing" systems, new aspects of systems, and archetypes. In response to the question "What is Systems Thinking?" one contributor wrote, "I find when I comprehend an archetype, I re-live past experiences that apply and interpret the memory using the new understanding.... It's like replaying a video. I see the scenes ... I recreate the scene with new dialog, new information" (*LOD*).

Subscriber Durward Humes, a specialist in meeting management, discussed modeling and wrote that, given the challenge of a complex business environment, "class models, object message models are important because they all help us collect, organize, verify complex, often conflicting bodies of knowledge" Referring to his own process, Humes says, "During the primary Conceptual Modeling Phase, we build a domain model, an event/use case model ... [which] forms the Conceptual Model ... which addresses the classes and their interconnectivity." (*LOD* 5/7/96).

Jac Vennix, another person who posts on the *LO Digest* site, writes: When working with contributions from individuals or a group, in reflecting, facilitating mode, we use causal loop diagrams (and system dynamics flow diagrams) to facilitate strategic discussions in management teams. They are great to prevent miscommunication and to 'integrate' the various viewpoints (mental models) of participants. Because of this integration process both consensus and commitment on a strategic issue can be obtained far more easily than with ordinary group discussions. (*LOD* 5/96)

The need to understand complexity and apparent disorder makes it vital to extend our ability to think visually and systemically and to envision ("see") systems as whole entities. Thinking systemically enables us to disregard details and cause-and-effect connections briefly and reach for the larger whole. People are already using graphic displays in a variety of ways and for diverse purposes. However, they are not doing so in an organized fashion, because until now there hasn't been a graphical language that is easy to learn and use. As Anonymous has said—and this is a key idea— "everything is a part of something larger." Showing both the part and the larger whole is vital, and it can't be done by writing words on a flip chart. It may not even be thought—because strictly linear approaches nip whole-systems thinking in the bud.

One of my own clients, a design team leader, explained that "the experience [of graphic facilitation with Graphic Tools] provided a different

way of looking at the problem. It allowed me to diagram the problem."
There is much to be learned about thinking visually and systemically; and
the more we perceive disorder in the external world, the greater is our
need for multiple languages and for ways of communicating and expressing abstract ideas. The diagram in its many forms is, as Keith Albarn and
Jenny Mial Smith, point out, "the instrument of thought."

> The diagram is evidence of an idea being structured—it is not *the idea* but a model
> of it, intended to clarify characteristics of features of that idea. It is a form of com-
> munication which increases the pace of development, or allows an idea to function
> and develop for the thinker while offering the possibility of transfer of an idea or
> triggering of notions; finally, through appropriate structuring, it may generate dif-
> ferent notions and states of mind in the viewer. (Albarn and Smith 1977: 7)

Thus, a graphic can provide a visual perspective on a verbal description
of a problem. It can expand the context in which the problem is understood, show how its parts are related to each other, and how they are
related to its environment and the external dynamics of that environment.

Obstacles and Resistance

Virtually any abstraction can be expressed graphically. We can give visible
form to ideas, concepts, and diverse complex matters—not only as a formal charts or graphs but also as idea sketches and exploratory jottings on
napkins set down as they emerge in rough form and begin to take shape
mentally. However, there are obstacles to the use of graphical displays, and
many people are resistant to this mode of communication, for a number
of reasons. Some believe, for example, that graphics, except for quantified
charts and graphs, are a form of art. Not being artists, they reason, we
have no business expressing ideas graphically and are certain to fail at it.
Others, having been chastised at school for drawing idea sketches during
reading or arithmetic class—as if such visual representations had nothing
to do with thinking—may be reluctant to try again. Yet others, perhaps
the majority, consider words and texts—the language of philosophers,
researchers, theorists, and poets—to be on a higher plane than graphics

and an intellectually privileged means of communication. But the predominant reason for avoiding the use of graphics may be that, until now, no, simple, easy-to-learn graphical language that is universally applicable to all subjects has been available. Although there are many nonverbal languages and notation systems that meet the needs of specific professionals, they cannot easily show content, process, and other abstractions—especially in small groups assembled for specific purposes and comprised of diverse intellects and experience.

Graphic Tools, which provide the mental and problem-solving aids needed to generate multiple levels of understanding, can help overcome this resistance. They can help us see the structure of an entity—no matter how nonroutine or messy—and move us beyond the belief that strangeness, disorder, and chaos are inevitably incomprehensible. Chaos is the label we put on things we believe we *cannot* understand; otherwise, given our analytic abilities, we would surely be able to comprehend them. Using Graphic Tools, however, enables us to perceive the essence of an issue and its structure early on, before it is beclouded by the effects of words and labels. Much of what appears to be inconceivable lies in its newness and unfamiliarity, and we encounter more and more new, unexpected, and nonroutine facts and ideas every day. Our typical linear, cause-and-effect thinking, as well as the inability to think visually, prevent us from perceiving wholes and processes and recognizing patterns. Cause-and-effect reasoning is time-bound and linear, whereas chaos can only be understood by observing phenomena with total openness, without labeling them. A graphical language can help us see them with a mentally alert mindset that is yet relaxed enough to detect subtly emerging patterns.

The Graphic Tools (GT)

Shapes are concepts and concepts are shapes.
—Rudolf Arnheim (1969)

The idea of creating a set of tools for graphical displays came to me from three sources: (1) the discovery that my own mind is able to conceptualize, capture, and convey information graphically; (2) curiosity about this phenomena; and (3) the work of Rudolf Arnheim, professor emeritus of the psychology of art at Harvard.

My involvement with the issue began in 1973, when I joined a federally funded program as a facilitator-in-training to help community-based teams design action plans and programs for substance-abuse problems. During the training, a curricular specialist spoke extensively to each team about the whole-systems approach to action planning. During meetings, I, as the facilitator, recorded the teams' ideas and discussions on a flip chart, using words and shapes. Seeing their work displayed in this way helped members integrate information and develop their plans. The action plans they devised were imminently feasible and were implemented appropriately in their home communities. I was interested to learn that my teams continued to work together long after other facilitators' teams had disbanded. In terms of group dynamics, graphic facilitation had a positive effect on the cohesiveness of my teams.

In graduate school I had the opportunity to investigate further the success of my teams, how my own mind worked, and what current theory and research said about the subject. I came to see, as David Weismann has pointed out, that

It appears psychologically sound to say that every shape—the circle, square, triangle, and every variant and combination—possesses its own inner structure. This structure, although an inexorable consequence of the visually perceivable qualities of the particular shape, is not visible. In our acts of visual perception we *intuit* the presence and operation of these concealed networks of forces; we do not see them. When we look at an "empty" square, for instance, we are made aware of more than just its apparent emptiness. (Weismann 1970: 102)

For my dissertation I wrote and field-tested a handbook, "How To Use Graphic Tools For Thinking, Planning and Problem Solving." Figure 8.4 illustrates the six Graphic Tools© I developed and shows various applications for each of them.

Each of the six GTs has a different shape: circle or curvoid, square with right angle, square with curved corners, triangle, line, point, and fuzz.

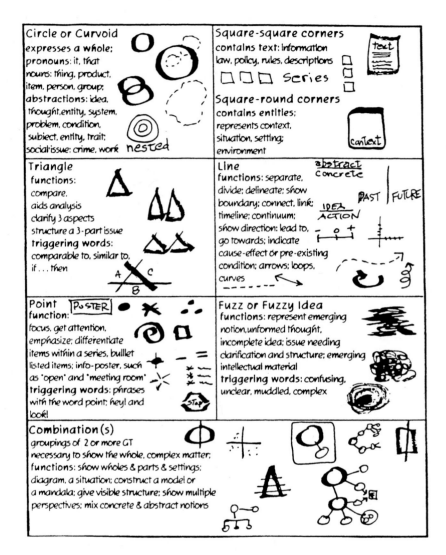

Circle or Curvoid
expresses a whole;
pronouns: it, that
nouns: thing, product,
item, person, group;
abstractions: idea,
thought, entity, system,
problem, condition,
subject, entity, trait;
social issue: crime, work   nested

Square-square corners
contains text: information
law, policy, rules, descriptions   Series

Square-round corners
contains entities;
represents context,
situation, setting;
environment

Triangle
functions:
compare,
aids analysis
clarify 3 aspects
structure a 3-part issue
triggering words:
comparable to, similar to,
if . . . then

Line
functions: separate,
divide; delineate; show
boundary; connect, link;
timeline; continuum;
show direction: lead to,
go towards; indicate
cause-effect or pre-existing
condition; arrows; loops,
curves

Point
function:
focus, get attention,
emphasize; differentiate
items within a series, bullet
listed items; info-poster, such
as "open" and "meeting room"
triggering words: phrases
with the word point; hey! and
look!

Fuzz or Fuzzy Idea
functions: represent emerging
notion, unformed thought,
incomplete idea; issue needing
clarification and structure; emerging
intellectual material
triggering words: confusing,
unclear, muddled, complex

Combination(s)
groupings of 2 or more GT
necessary to show the whole, complex matter;
functions: show wholes & parts & settings;
diagram, a situation; construct a model or
a mandala; give visible structure; show multiple
perspectives; mix concrete & abstract notions

Figure 8.4
The six Graphic Tools. The lower panel shows how two or more tools are combined to illustrate complex situations and ideas.

Each shape represents a different basic concept or function. Usually, GTs are used in combination to express an idea or concept. Just as words make up sentences, individual GTs used in combination convey more complex ideas, reveal relationships, and capture the formation of ideas and thoughts. The possible variations achievable by using different combinations are virtually infinite. The purpose of GT, and of most graphical languages, is to communicate to an audience nonverbally and immediately.

Circle or curvoid

- *Characteristics*: curvilinear edge with continuous or broken line; starts and ends at same point

- *Represents*: wholeness, an element, a system or subsystem, a concept, possibly something not yet clearly defined or labeled

- *Function*: Enclose an area; set a boundary; locate elements as internal, external, or span a boundary

- *Application*: an element for constructing a diagram, display, or model

Square with right-angle corners

- *Characteristics*: rectangle or square with ninety-degree corners

- *Represents*: a container for information, facts, policy, legislation, and so on

- *Function*: contain text; describe a relationship between elements; is located between elements

- *Application*: an element to construct a diagram, a display, or a model

Square with round corners

- *Characteristics*: rectangle or square with rounded corners

- *Represents*: setting, situation, condition, location, environment, context

- *Functions*: contain or hold the element, system, concept, or unknown in a place (temporarily or permanently); indicate location

- *Application*: an element to construct a diagram, a display or a model

Triangle

- *Characteristics*: three sides that end at the three angles; three sides of equal length (an equilateral triangle); two sides of equal length (an isosceles triangle); a triangle created by three intersecting lines that extend beyond the angles

- *Represents*: three aspects of something

- *Functions*: as a point of departure for analysis, for thinking, comparing, and contrasting three aspects of an entity; an extended-sides triangle to provide structure for analysis, comparison, description

- *Applications*: an element to construct a diagram, a display, or a model; with addition of horizontal lines, indicates hierarchical nature of an entity; also shorthand for an organization chart

Line

- *Characteristics*: straight, horizontal, vertical, diagonal, curved, continuous, broken, loops, spirals, various thicknesses; two or more lines make an arrow

- *Represents*: connection, link, direction, boundary, separation

- *Functions*: connect entities, systems, and so on.; link; show feedback or feedforward path or loop; separate; divide; emphasize

- *Applications*: an element to construct a diagram, display, or model. Horizontal line: underline the category in a list of items; represent a continuum (quantities, degrees, etc.) or a time line. Vertical line: separate lists; separate major categories of items; strike a point in time on a horizontal timeline. Horizontal and vertical lines: timelines, continua, organization charts, matrices and grids, an axis, vertical plus horizontal lines that are the basis of a chart; indicate direction in space or time.

Point

- *Characteristics*: small, medium, large; simple, complex; ornate, decorative, textured; single or multiples; can be any of the previous GTs used singly or in combination; a sign or label enlarged and used with words considered a point

- *Represents*: a point in time

- *Functions*: focus, draw attention, make a point, emphasize; code similar items; a sign or a poster

- *Applications*: as bullet for each item in a series or a list; to call attention to one or more items of a series in text; as a sign or label when the point contains words (e.g., "stop," "meet here," etc.)

Fuzz

- *Characteristics*: dark, scribbled lines; a blur, blob, or blotch; dark core with shaded periphery

- *Represents*: unknown, unlabeled; emerging concept, idea, or notion; undeveloped or unexplored entity; obscure, indistinct, dim

- *Functions*: a mark for an unknown or emerging entity intended to be clarified

- *Applications*: to externalize an idea, issue, etc., not yet defined, with a mark or symbol while identifying aspects of an issue

Combinations

- *Characteristics*: two or more GTs

- *Represents*: Complex entities, many-parted problems; stages or phases; evolution; changing nature of an issue through time; multiple perspectives, differing points of view; different relationships; abstracted and simplified tangibles; concretized abstractions

- *Functions*: Describe complex wholes more completely by showing structure, connection, and relationships; clarify

- *Applications*: mind maps that show graphically how various ideas and concepts are related; diagrams; models; concept development; organization charts; graphic outliners, and organizers; function maps; project and planning schemes; mandalas; medicine wheels; decision trees; hierarchical diagrams; nested arrangements; idea sketches such as a business concept or entrepreneurial idea; represent visually structure, order, relationships of information or knowledge

The Palette

The palette is the surface on which a graphical display is drawn. Unlined paper, such as a sketch pad, a stack of bond or newsprint, a four- or five-feet-high sheet of newsprint ten feet or more long hung on the wall (for group work), or, of course, the ubiquitous napkin—all work well as tabulae rasae. Sketches using GT can be drawn free form on paper as ideas unfold or more systematically.

Graphic Models

The Graphic Tools constitute a visual language that can be used to construct a model or a diagram. The content of the model comes from the individual's or group's knowledge of the entity to be modeled. That content might include, for example, the factors influencing restructuring of a company, integration of two agencies or departments into one, an entrepreneur's vision of a business, or the components of a complex project. An example of a graphic model incorporating systems concepts is shown in figure 8.5.

Individuals who are visual thinkers might already have a general image of the entity in mind and can use GT to reproduce it, adding new pieces and refining details. Such people—because they can readily accept that a particular shape represents something or conveys a particular class of information (such as a concept)—will probably find it quite easy to learn a graphical representational language. Others may take some time to become accustomed to it. Although people who are verbal (i.e., use language fluently) can recall images from the past—a mother's face, the illustration in a much-loved children's book, or a schoolyard—they have a hard time imagining or visualizing something that hasn't existed before.

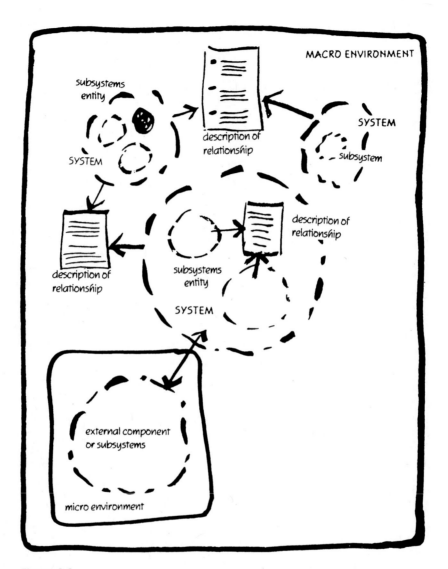

Figure 8.5
An Example of a Systems Model Using Graphic Tools.

During the meeting or meetings the model will unfold as the individuals or the group contribute information and ideas. A graphic, conceptual model, or a meta-model created with GT can indicate a total system, its context, operations, activities, information pathways, internal or external restraints or controls, and states (past, present, future, desired). As the model continues to develop and is enriched with visual and textual information, the group (or individual) will recall and better understand subtle aspects of the content seen earlier but not identified. Words and phrases suggesting ways to remedy flaws or add components will come to mind as group members continue to look at the model. And, because the graphic model is non-linear, such new or recalled information can be immediately added to the developing model. A particular model may look like the generic example in figure 8.5 or take on the dynamic look of graffiti, a work in process.

A model in progress is likely to be a series of approximations, each one incorporating more relevant information and evolving until the final form emerges. As the model develops and its structure is made visible, what was thought to be highly complex and disordered content somehow becomes manageable, and viewers' understanding deepens. New points of view are inspired by what has already been added to the diagram, and more of what is known is integrated into the model. New information is placed where it fits best, instead of being forced into tiny spaces between the lines, as in words-only, linear formats. With a visual model thus formed and available for continuous review, an individual, or a group, can clarify ideas and order knowledge. Strategies for action arise naturally from being able to see the whole—its structure, context, internal and external forces, connections among components, and so on. A group's productivity and cohesion are enhanced, and members feel satisfied by seeing before them the visible distillation of their ideas and efforts.

Using Graphic Tools in Groups

Drawings, paintings, and other similar devices serve not simply to translate finished thoughts into visible models, but are also an aid in the process of working out solutions.
—Arnheim (1969: 129)

A number of management theorists have studied the ways successful work groups produce good results. One study by Michael Doyle and David Straus (1982) emphasizes the roles that are essential for a productive meeting. Two of their functional roles—facilitator and recorder—are particularly relevant to our discussion. I have combined the two functions in *the graphic facilitator*, the person who draws information from members of the group, clarifies concepts and ideas, checks back continuously to ensure accuracy, provides feedback on the group process, and so on. This person functions just as other kinds of facilitator do, except for using Graphic Tools—along with key words—to record what members have to say about the problem. Wide sheets of paper six to twelve feet long (e.g., a roll of newsprint or bond paper) hung on a wall in two or three layers accommodate the wealth of information, impressions, thoughts, and experiences that group members generate. The large sheets probably minimize the possibility that group members will self-censor their participation. As one client said, "Seeing my ideas written on extra-large paper prompted my thinking to expand." Whether an individual or a group is building a model, large rolls of paper works best.

In meetings that do not use Graphic Tools or another system of nonlinear graphic facilitation, the comments or perceptions of group members that are expressed out of sequence can easily be lost. A graphic information-management and design process, however, can accommodate members' inputs whenever they come and place them on the model where they seem to fit best at the moment. It can also use graphical notation to integrate an array of diverse perspectives that enrich and expand the group's understanding of a problem.

It is important to begin notations for the model well to the right of the sheet, to allow for the addition of information that comes to mind out of sequence. Another helpful technique for recording ideas and information without knowing exactly where they belong is to use 3×5 index cards or Post-It Notes. For example, if the group has not yet determined the ultimate location of a particular entity or subsystem, writing it on a card or small note and sticking it tentatively where it seems to belong adds flexi-

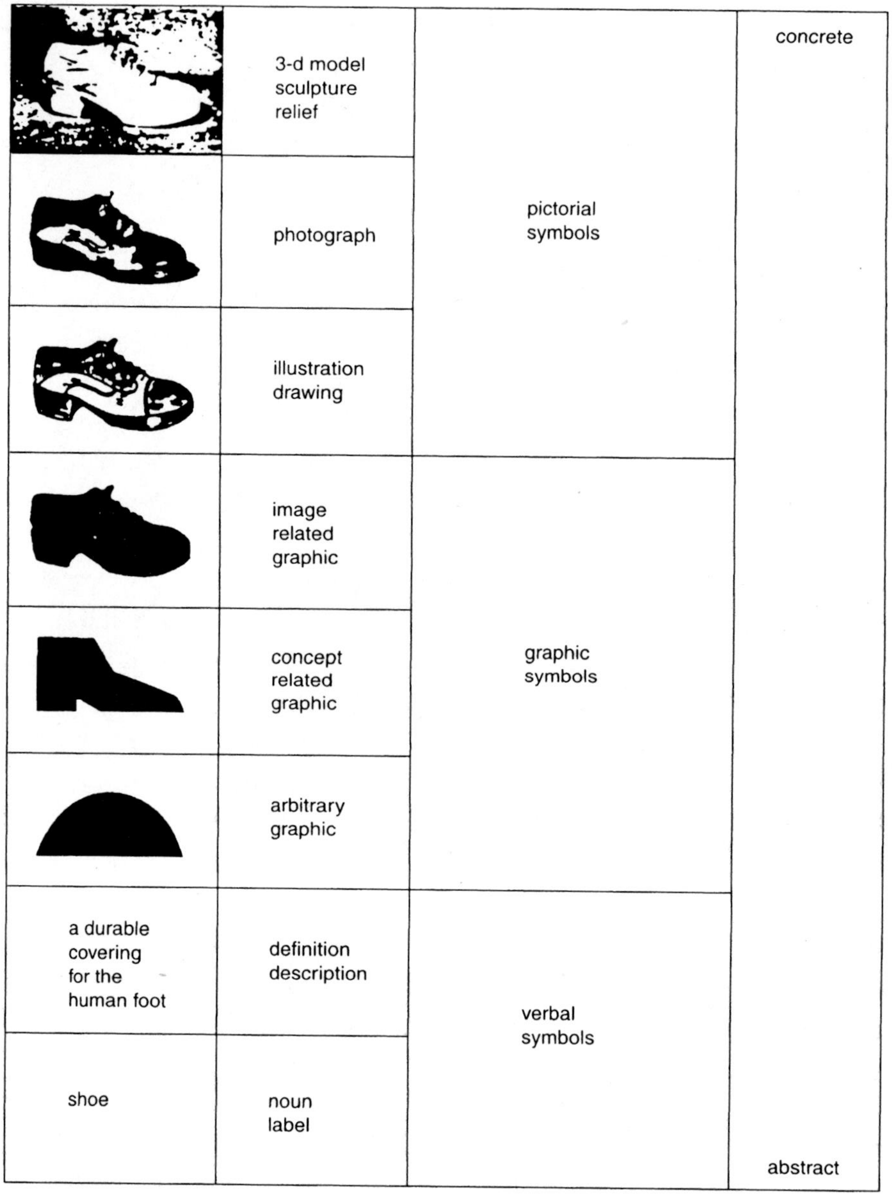

			concrete
	3-d model sculpture relief		
	photograph	pictorial symbols	
	illustration drawing		
	image related graphic		
	concept related graphic	graphic symbols	
	arbitrary graphic		
a durable covering for the human foot	definition description		
shoe	noun label	verbal symbols	
			abstract

Figure 8.6
Abstract and Concrete Ways to Represent Objects (from Wileman 1980).

bility to the model and prevents loss of the idea. In a graphic, nonlinear process of continuous insights, thinking sequentially is neither required nor desired. Ideas should flow freely, bouncing in any direction and landing on the model wherever the group thinks they belong. The graphic notation technique can be seen, in effect, as a form of visual brainstorming—or mental graffiti!

Summary and Conclusions

You can observe a lot by just watching.
—Yogi Berra

The obvious paradox of this paper is that in it I attempt to describe in words the essence of a graphical language and the techniques of creating visual displays that can serve a variety of purposes. Because we ordinarily think of words as describing concrete reality more accurately than visual symbols, the idea represented in figure 8.6, may surprise some readers. The chart ranks pictorial, graphic, and verbal symbols on a concrete-to-abstract scale (from top to bottom). It indicates that words are themselves abstract symbols. In fact, it shows that graphic images are really *less* abstract and *more* concrete than words.

My hope for this essay, therefore, is threefold: (1) to show that, while words are valuable tools, graphic information is also good information; (2) to introduce an easy-to-learn system of incorporating simple graphic shapes into thinking and planning processes; and (3), perhaps most important, to convince the reader that we need to end the separation between verbal and graphic ways of thinking.

Note

1. Graphic Tools is a registered trademark of Yvonne Hansen.

References

Ackoff, Russell L. 1981. The second industrial revolution. Paper presented at a seminar on the new age of systems thinking at San Jose State University School of Business.

Albarn, Keith, and Smith, Jenny Mial. 1977. *Diagram: The Instrument of Thought*. London: Thames and Hudson.

Alexander, Christopher. 1964. *A Pattern Language*. Cambridge: Harvard University Press.

Arnheim, Rudolf. 1969. *Visual Thinking*. Berkeley: University of California. Press.

Boulding, Kenneth E. 1969. *The Image*. Ann Arbor: University of Michigan Press.

Dondis, Donis A. 1973. *A Primer of Visual Literacy*. Cambridge: MIT Press.

Doyle, Michael, and Straus, David. 1982. *How To Make Meetings* Work—*The New Interaction Method*. New York: Jove Books.

Dreyfuss, Henry. 1972. *Symbol Sourcebook: An Authoritative Guide to International Graphic Symbols*. New York: McGraw-Hill.

Hansen, Yvonne M. 1989. A formative evaluation study: Development of a graphic handbook to promote visual thinking in adults. Unpubl. Ph.D. diss. Santa Barbara: The Fielding Institute.

Kepes, Gyorgy. 1965. Introduction. In *Education of Vision*, G. Kepes, ed. New York: George Brazillier.

Learning Organization Digest (LOD). (For information, send e-mail to *majordomo@world.std.com* with the message INFO LEARNING-ORG.)

Norman, Donald A. 1983. Some observations on mental models. In *Mental Models*, Dedre Gentner and Albert L. Stevens, eds. Hillsdale, N.J: Erlbaum Associates.

Senge, Peter M. 1991. *The Fifth Discipline: The Art and Practice of the Learning Organization*. New York: Doubleday.

Sless, David. 1981. *Learning and Visual Communication*. New York: John Wiley.

Stankowski, Anton. 1991. *Visual Presentation of Invisible Processes*. Teufen, Switzerland: Arthur Verlag.

Stanley, Dick. 1996. Finding order in the midst of chaos. *Austin American-Statesman*, June 9, B1: 4.

Taylor, David A. 1995. *Business Engineering with Object Technology*. New York: John Wiley.

Tufte, Edward R. 1989. *The Visual Display of Quantitative Information*. Cheshire, Conn.: Graphics Press.

Weismann, David L. 1970. *The Visual Arts as Human Experience*. Englewood Cliffs, N.J.: Prentice-Hall.

White, Jan. 1980. *Graphic Idea Notebook: Inventing Techniques for Designing Printed Pages*. New York: Watson-Guptill.

9 *Visual Design in Three Dimensions*

Hal Thwaites

In this chapter I describe a biocybernetic approach to information design that can be applied to such emerging high-density, three-dimensional visual communications media as three-dimensional high-definition television (3-D HTV), virtual reality (VR), virtual worlds, 3-D IMAX and SOLIDO films, and holography. The methodology of information design presented here was originated by Dr. Miroslav Malik (1976) and developed over a twenty-year period of research and teaching. It incorporates theories from the fields of neurocybernetics, artificial intelligence, and expert systems and embodies some of the first guidelines for developing three-dimensional systems software. I point to the inherent dangers of information overload, information-cascade break-up, and interruptions that are likely to occur if we simply transfer the information design practices of traditional media to 3-D design. In conclusion, I discuss 3-D information design practices we need to follow over the next decade.

From earliest times human artists have sought to capture the notion of space in two-dimensional images. The creators of the cave paintings at Lascaux and Altamira used a primitive method of portraying distance: they drew figures in different sizes, making the nearest animals larger and showing those in the distance as smaller. In one painting, the animal fleeing from the hunting scene is drawn over and over again in smaller and smaller versions to illustrate its increasing distance from the hunters. Sometimes dimensions of space are suggested by overlapping one figure over another. These techniques or spatial cues appear in the art of many civilizations—for example, the Sumerian, Egyptian, and Mayan—sometimes creating added spatial effects with different colors (for example, reserving black for backgrounds and gold for the foreground). Greek and Roman art reveals that artists had a vague notion of perspective, which they used not as a spatial cue in flat art but as an architectural tool for planning structures and for sculpting. In Chinese culture, a long continuum of tonal spatial cues expresses the space in a picture through different shades of ink or watercolors.

Thus our 1990s fascination with creating the third dimension in two-dimensional space is nothing new. It extends from the prehistory of painting, to the time of early stereoscopes, into the developing new realm of virtual reality (VR). The notion of 3-D has always implied more "real" or "lifelike" representations of the world, because human perceptions are oriented within the three-dimensional space that surrounds our bodies (Ungerleider and Mishkin 1982, De Jonge 1967). Today's efforts to heighten our mediated experiences by perfecting spatial-imaging systems continue an ancient quest.

In the 1990s 3-D is the current buzz-word, even though not all that's promoted as 3-D is actually *stereoscopic* in nature. Three-dimensional computer graphics abound on television; 3-D modeling is used in environmental design and is applied in many technical and scientific fields—such as the medical imaging techniques that give physicians a "more real" look inside the body. The concept of 3-D is even utilized in a theory of human memory (Pribram 1991). Three-dimensional models of human thinking are indeed ubiquitous. However, we should also regard them with a certain caution. The current 3-D media vogue could be just another temporary surge if, as has happened in the past, information design concepts are not applied to the software and content of three-dimensional artworks and productions.

The widespread acceptance and application of three-dimensional media technologies (3Dmt) in the mass media have always presented a challenge to researchers and producers. Whereas 3-D was first seen as a gimmick added to conventional media to thrill and excite the public, it has since been applied to create more accurate representations of reality. Many current 3-D technologies add critical information cues to actual images to form *meta-realities* that make visible phenomena or experiences we cannot perceive naturally. More recently, innovators in the field of *virtual reality* have learned to create artificial environments and worlds that may exist only in our imaginations.

Information Design

There is a substantial difference between the technological, psychophysiological, and semantic (content-related) factors that create 3-D media art pieces or programs and the factors that elicit viewers' perceptions of three dimensions. What sometimes amounts to a small, or negligible cue from the point of view of the author/producer (i.e., the cinematographer, artist, or holographer) may be the paramount reason why a piece delivers a high or low 3-D information impact to viewers, or fails to affect them at all. The scale of importance of 3-D cues from the viewpoint of artists or producers and viewers may, therefore, be entirely different; moreover, the specific technological requirements of each 3-D medium may result in yet a third hierarchy of importance. These differences necessitate an information design approach specifically geared to the 3-D visual technologies that produce media artworks.

Our information design approach was first developed for programming film and television programs and holographic shows in 1973, after a series of professional development seminars Dr. Malik gave at the Canadian Broadcasting Corporation in Montreal. It was subsequently published as a handbook, first in French (Malik 1976) and more recently in English (Malik and Thwaites 1993). The seminars were later given at various research and broadcasting centers in the United States, Europe, and Australia.

The approach defines *information design* as the organization of information to achieve preconceived goals; it uses principles and theories from biocybernetics and psychophysiology and combines them with the traditional protocols of communications-media production (Malik and Thwaites 1987). As a discipline, information design is a systemic approach that results in a framework (or skeleton) of the contents to be expressed through the particular 3-D medium. The systematization of the content is the *design*, which the author of the software brings into being through a creative process very similar to that employed by novelists, composers, filmmakers, videographers, or painters. Essentially, what we are describing here is artistic expression.

The design may be the output of the hardware and the accompanying program, in which case the software is really an extension of the machine. It may also result from the requirements of the environment (educational, military, industrial) and follow the strict discipline or procedures normal to those environments. Or it may be the creation of the user, which requires an information design that accommodates a high level of interactivity and is very user-friendly.

Information is defined as energy and as a process with catalytic characteristics. The emphasis should be on the process and on the catalytic characteristics rather than on energy, since information is not pure energy. It has a material core in the information source, the transmission conditions (technology), and the receiver (a biological entity), and it behaves during the process partially as physical matter and partially as a stress wave. Understanding information in this sense helps us see that the factor of time can be extremely important: stretching or condensing the process may completely change the semantics of the information (meaning/content), and different time scales (geological, biological, electronic) may have an immense influence on the information chain and its effect on the receiver. The notion of *trajectory* also requires us to think in terms of navigation or streaming, which in human terms is *hodology* (i.e., the study of spatial orientation within real or imagined virtual space).

Information Source	→	Transmission Conditions	→	Responding Receiver/s
3DTV, film hologram, VR		room, cinema theater, exhibit		individual, group, audiences

Figure 9.1
The Three-dimensional Information Chain in its Simplest Form.

Our research at the 3Dmt Center in Montreal has centered on this systems approach to three-dimensional media from a *biocybernetic* viewpoint. The field of biocybernetics focuses on how the human sensory system responds to and processes information and on the impact of information on the receiver/audience. Our principal concern is the individual, either the observer or the creator of the media program. The information process or *information chain* has, in its simplest form, three parts (as shown in figure 9.1): an information source, transmission conditions, and the receiver and his or her response.

Each part of the 3-D media event (the program itself, the space and conditions by which it is perceived, and the person(s) perceiving it) may contain pieces of the final message. If any part of the information chain is altered, the information itself is changed. The incoming information acts as a catalyst to other mental processes, which occur in the receiver's brain as a result of the processing and storage of earlier information and can thus affect the overall impact of the presentation. As 3-D media become more sophisticated and interactive, paying attention to the information chain and the information design of the software/hardware interfaces will become more important and have a major influence on their success (Malik and Thwaites 1990). The increased time and budgetary constraints often placed on 3-D media projects leave little room for costly experiments and wasted resources.

An information chain exists in a certain time and space, but the times in which information is produced and perceived have very different axes. People working in traditional media are very aware of production time (the time needed to plan, organize or structure, and produce certain segments of a complex of information), as well as of transmission time (the air time in television, screening time for film). The least-known time element is *perceptual time*. The intervals between biological information input and information perception are in the millisecond range. In the past, these tiny segments of time had little or no meaning. However, in the development of large successive complexes of information—particularly in three-dimensional media works (film, television programs, VR)—the audience's perceptual delays can cause a good deal of overlapping of information. While one piece of information is being processed, the brain cannot process new information of the same range or intensity. Even though short-term memory provides for a certain processing delay, a constant stream of incoming information results in more and more overlapping and less accurate processing.

Overlaps in information processing are the typical result of an *information complex*, also called an *information cascade*. There are two different kinds of information cascades. In one, receivers (people) are free to attend to and perceive each piece or part of the information complex one after another at their own pace (as at a gallery exhibit or when reading a book or newspaper). This is called a *horizontal* or *linear cascade*. Usually viewers have a great deal of freedom in both their individual speed of perception and in the order in which they attend to the pieces presented to them.

The second kind of information cascade, called a *vertical* or *structural cascade*, is typified by a fixed succession of pieces of information and a limited time in which to perceive them. These are the conditions in which a viewer is presented with the information in a film, television program, play, or concert). High degrees of overlapping are typical of vertical information cascades. Each piece of information (scene, shot, sequence) is perceived in a period called *perceptual time*, which varies across different people, cultural contexts, and historical periods. In the following sections, I outline how these differences affect information design practices for various 3-D media and discuss the considerations we need to take into account to produce successful information designs.

Three-dimensional Cinematography and Television

Three-dimensional film technology has been in use since its first demonstration at the Paris Exposition of 1890. In the present century, there were two brief periods of 3-D film boom—the first in 1953 and the second in 1982—before the recent development of technologies allowing us to experience 3-D movies that are very different from conventional films. Widespread public exposure to high-quality 3-D films occurs at the Disney theme parks—with films such as *Magic Journeys*, *Captain EO*, and *Muppet Vision 3D*—at special screenings, and at all recent international expositions.

In the summer of 1990, Science North, a museum outside Sudbury, Ontario, premiered a three-dimensional 70-millimeter film-and-laser adventure entitled *Shooting Star*. The film incorporates special in-theater laser effects that are synchronized with the 3-D scenes to create a unique viewing experience.

The Imax Corporation of Canada, the world leader in ultra-large screen, 3-D productions, uses IMAX® 3-D and the SOLIDO three-dimensional system with a domed screen (Naimark 1992). Their films are evidence of the meta-reality aspect of today's 3-D film experience, for they take us far beyond the reality of our physical world into totally new experiences. It is certain that 3-D film technology in its many forms will continue to be a prominent form of mass entertainment well into the next century.

Significant research on 3-D has also been undertaken in both conventional television and video-display technology (VDT) and in specialized applications (Smith 1989). Japanese researchers are developing several 3-D high-definition systems that may ultimately find their way into our homes. HDTV technology doubles the video scanning lines from approximately 525 to 1050-plus lines, greatly enhancing image definition. (For a comprehensive historical overview of three-dimensional film and video systems, see Lipton 1982.)

Three-dimensional cinema and television production use 3-D cues (convergence, retinal disparity, accommodation, and motion parallax), which are projected onto an essentially flat surface by manipulating the z-spatial (i.e., the third axis in a three-dimensional rectangular coordinate system). To perceive 3-D, viewers must overcome their very firm learned response to flat pictures, in which three-dimensional space is only imagined, that is, reprocessed from the cerebellum through the hypothalamic region of the brain to the parietal lobes. This processing is largely an interior process in which the 3-D cues in the picture are overlaid with our learned responses to conventional two-dimensional pictures. It is extremely important to co-ordinate the size of the picture very closely with the distance of the viewer from the screen. In these conditions, the increasing depth of the picture's z-axis will proportionally augment the impact of the spatial information, especially when it is enhanced by a three-dimensional sound system.

Visual Physiology

Physiological research (Ungerleider and Mishkin 1982; Leventhal 1988; Derrington 1988) points to the fact that signals from the retinal networks of the human eye are already highly processed by the time they reach the cerebellum region of the brain. This preprocessing takes place in the retina and in the lateral geniculate nucleus, where the exchange of signals leads to stereoscopic vision, which in turn produces a perception of distance within a two- or three-dimensional picture (Leventhal 1988, Searle 1984).

Electroencephalograph (EEG) analysis of activity from test subjects' visual cortex shows that the stereopsis (3-D) signal is not processed separately from other spatial cues of color, texture, pattern, motion, and shape but is interwoven into those signals as a part of an information matrix in the brain (Schiller et al. 1990). Within this matrix, three-dimensional pictorial space cues activate, at numerous points, larger or smaller indiscriminate neuron-circuit firings or stress waves (Jubak 1992); because these firings are indiscriminate, we perceive the impact of 3-D, in psychological terminology, as an *emotion*. Such cues cause rich and repeated feedback searches (identifiable within the EEG signal by Fourrier transform analysis) as the brain continuously struggles to recognize the various z-axes in the scene. This phenomenon is well known to cinematographers and TV cameramen who shoot 3-D as 3-D *overkill*, that is, overuse of z-axis shots. Because of some fault in the 3-D image design , or because of the editing, the viewer's brain "gives up" the notion of three-dimensional reality and perceives the 3-D images only in a sequential, semantic mode.

Electroencephalograph recording also shows that brightness, color, or shape co-act with the spatial stereopsis signal to produce the perception of three dimensions. Producers of 3-D have recognized for some time that reduced image brightness, for example, decreases the effectiveness of a 3-D image.

Picture Definition

The human eye, working in conjunction with the visual cortex of the brain, perceives an image not in the symmetrical fashion of the scanning lines of a TV image but according to certain preferences influenced by the contrast and visual densities of the image. The eye repeatedly scans an image in an asymmetrical fashion as the visual cortex of the brain influences eye movements to provide a complete series of visual signals of the image (Alkon 1992). If a two-dimensional picture has strong spatial characteristics (i.e., z-axis coordinates), the eye immediately spots them and scans this part of the picture more often. In this way the human visual system strives to make sense of the added information provided by distance cues, shapes, overlaps, and so on. The activity of the brain's visual cortex (as measured by EEG) increases when such details are present but decreases as the definition of the picture declines, as it does when a holographic image or conventional television or film image is viewed on a large screen.

Because 3-D pictures are rich in feedback responses from the visual cortex to the eye—they produce approximately three times as many responses as two-dimensional pictures do—we need to create a certain minimal level of definition to ensure that a three-dimensional picture is perceived as an effective *spatial transformation*. Viewers' ability to experience *transformational realism* (Pribram 1990) is always somewhat doubtful, because the picture attributes of conventional television work against the perception that what they are seeing in a 3-D image is indeed three-dimensional. The perception of realism is a process that grows out of cues such as texture, polish, and sharp edges (Nagata 1984), along with feedback from the visual and motor cortexes back to the eye. This results not only in muscular ocular motions and contractions but also in feedback from the retina to the columns of cells in the visual cortex that recognize the picture as "real" and three-dimensional. Therefore, an image of high definition, in both film and video media, is a significant factor affecting the viewer's sensation of realism (Nagata 1984, Kusaka 1990). Both HDTV and 70-millimeter film formats like Imax and Omnimax have the added definition and larger image size needed to make them effective three-dimensional tools for information design.

Image Size

The impact of visual information on the fovea of the human eye (the area of highest visual acuity) is greatest in a rectangle covering roughly 10 to 15 percent of the retina, an area approximately 6 mm^2 to 8 mm^2 wide in the typical viewing distances for a television screen. Seventy percent of the retinal input and most of the cortical feedback to the eye occurs within that area of the fovea (Malik and Thwaites 1990, Alkon 1992). Because cells in the area are so concentrated, the viewer rarely needs to moves his or her head or eye muscles to see an image from a different point of view.

Quite a different situation exists if the image is three-dimensional. In this case moving the eyes or changing the viewpoint is essential to spatial verification of the image. This is a one cause of fatigue for viewers of 3-D media. In anaglyph three-dimensional (NTSC) TV systems (which use red/green glasses) or lenticular three-dimensional TV systems, it is not easy for the user to visually fuse moving images with a large parallax. The wider picture area of three-dimensional HDTV (16:9 aspect ratio compared to 4:3 for NTSC television) will increase the fusional limits (dynamic range) of the stereoscopic picture (Nagata 1990, 1989).

In reality, what happens when we "see" in three dimensions is a cooperative mechanism of the peripheral vision area of the retina and the area of greatest acuity of fovea. This mechanism mostly channels feedback from the brain to the retinal area and does not enrich the incoming visual information, although in many cases it causes an increase in signal transmission within the brain (perceived as a stress wave or "emotional effect").

A similar situation occurs when a viewer is exposed to large or domed film screens (Imax, Omnimax, Solido), whose images occupy more than 30 percent of the retinal area. A large 3-D picture compels the eye to scan not only many z-axis coordinates but also the corresponding x and y coordinates and their connections with the z-axes. The apparent size and depth of a three-dimensional picture or screen therefore play an important role, not only for scanning the x-y coordinates in an image but also for combining them with the z coordinates (Ebenholtz 1992). Factors of particular importance to image size are movement of the pictorial elements, especially movements toward the pictorial frame. In these shots, the peripheral vision field can explore the image very successfully (Low 1984). The effectiveness of the large-screen stereoscopic cinematography formats of Imax, Omnimax, and Solido is largely due to the dynamic fashion in which they combine three-dimensional cues within areas scanned by the peripheral-vision—for example, through shots taken from aircraft, camera dollies, and cranes.

It is important when designing 3-D images to distinguish between signals from the fovea and signal transmissions to the brain from the area of peripheral vision. The fovea signal travels directly to the visual cortex of the brain. The peripheral retinal-vision signal, however, goes through the corpus calossum to both the visual cortex and the hypothalamus; in the latter it can cause specific neuron firings or stress waves that could start emotional reactions. Very often there is also a feedback connection with the vestibular mechanism, which can cause the viewer physical discomfort in the form of motion sickness, dizziness, fainting, or nausea. If the picture contains too many contradictory visual cues for optimal three-dimensional image perception, the viewer's conflicting emotional responses create a general inhibition of neuron functioning experienced as fatigue. This is quite a typical response to three-dimensional media productions (Malik and Thwaites 1990).

Three-dimensional Sound

Human spatial perception is not, of course, limited to one sensory channel but is a combined effect of cues gained through the perception of audio and visual information (Martens 1990). The use of a digital sound track and three-dimensional multiple sound sources can create a total viewing and listening experience.

The Imax Corporation opened a six-hundred-seat, 3-D-capable theater in New York City in November of 1994. In the spring of 1995 the company premiered new film, *Wings of Courage*, to initiate the theater's Personal Sound Environment (PSE) system. The PSE provides each member of the audience a special 3-D viewing headset, which includes liquid-crystal shutter glasses and stereo audio. The system precisely tailors spatial audio cues to each location within the 3-D Imax film space, creating a completely novel and very visceral effect. However, because spatial sound information is processed in the neocortex in different ways than other stimuli, it can easily conflict with other a sensory effects or cause a viewer information overload if it is not carefully incorporated into the overall 3-D information design.

Holography

The spectacular growth of holography, particularly display holography, is far beyond what Dennis Gabor imagined in 1948 when he sought to obtain sharper images in electron microscopy. Once its potential was recognized, researchers throughout the world began producing impressive three-dimensional visual images and artworks (Hariharan 1992). The last two decades have seen a variety of holographic applications, including the rainbow hologram, multicolor images, white-light holographic stereograms,

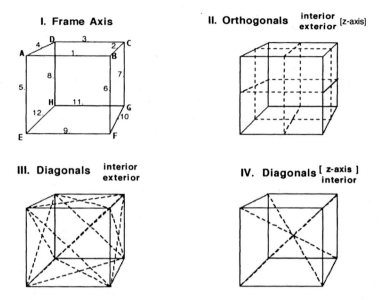

Figure 9.2
The Twenty-eight Axes of a Necker cube That Inscribe Holographic Space.

large format holograms (sizes up to 4 by 6 feet), computer-generated holograms, holographic video, and a proliferation of embossed holograms.

Holography's method of communication is radically different from that of 3-D media presented on a flat surface. Because there is no screen or frame effect, the absence of spatial cues other than those presented within the holographed scene or object makes a very strong information impact on the viewer. This medium is principally governed by the laws of scenography—the spatial organization and orchestration of an event or medium (Polièri 1971)—and is realized within the twenty-eight axes of a Necker cube (figure 9.2). Because the viewer is not seated in a fixed position, and is often able to move through the holographic space, many of the spatial cues laboriously created on a two-dimensional flat screen are unnecessary; the viewer experiences 3-D in a hodologic (i.e., way-finding, navigational) fashion among the separate spatial elements that create the image.

The creator of the image must acknowledge the special role of *negative space* (or black background) and use it functionally. The appearance and disappearance of the object in a holographic space is an integral part of the perception process (and not a "mistake" as in two-dimensional flat-screen media). The medium also presents viewers with the opportunity to interact with the image or three-dimensional object. Because of this unusual feature, the narrative continuum (story or plot) in a holographic space is less important than in other 3-D media and may well be an obstacle to interaction. Nor are realistic images and true colors necessary within the holographic space; in fact they sometimes decrease the spatial-information impact, whereas abstract images and artificial colors of high, precise spectral values can enhance it. Images and objects should flow easily into and out of the viewers' perceptual field, allowing them to immerse themselves in the holographic experience to create their own story and their own interactive relationships.

From a biocybernetic viewpoint, holographic spatial impact can be created instantly—and lost instantly. Information processing in the brain consists not of an information cascade (as in the other 3-D media) but of a series of unconnected information *domains* and information *details* that are important catalysts for memory retrieval. The fact that each of these domains can be stored in long-term memory separately makes a holographic narrative of little use.

What is the neurophysiological basis of the impact of holograms? Holography is a typical example of the use of projective geometry to create a moveable horizon in which the viewer's own eyes are a vanishing point, or camera. The most striking impact of a hologram comes from the fact that each time the viewer moves his or her eyes or head, the whole picture slightly changes its projective geometry (Pepper 1989). The picture starts to be "attached" to the viewer's eyes, a situation that demands a high level of perceptual participation and feedback from the viewer (moving, turning the head, etc.).

The consequences of such a perceptual reversal are astonishing. The image is no longer a carrier of the information impact but instead acts as a powerful catalyst. Because the spatial information of the image exists mostly in the viewer's mind, the pictorial representation can be strikingly simple but still have a significant visual impact. The brain no longer demands a fast succession of images or great richness of detail. The size of the image, however, is enormously important, especially when measured against the viewer's own (anthropomorphic) size.

Holography also has its limitations, although they are not related to three dimensionality. One troublesome problem is its wholeness: it is difficult to segment the picture, formally or semantically, into several smaller images. Even a simple story told by a succession of holograms may be somewhat lacking in structure and continuity. As a medium of information transmission, holography is more like the theater or architecture than it is like film and television. These considerations will become more important as we move toward real-time holographic video. At the present time, holograms of fairly complex scenes can be computed and motion sequences can be precomputed and stored on a hard-disc array of a supercomputer such as the Connection Machine at MIT. About three minutes of animation can then be played back at about six frames per second. Although the images are small, they are bright, have high resolution, and exhibit all the depth cues found in other holograms (St. Hilaire et al. 1990).

Stereoscopic Computer Graphics: Virtual Reality/Virtual Worlds

We can describe the environment of a virtual world as pure information that the user is able to see, hear, and touch (Bricken 1991). "The difference," as Bricken says, "is in the *design*."

At the present time, 3-D computer graphics and virtual reality can best be compared to the information impact and design of two-dimensional graphics or animated films. Viewers can perceive a computer-generated graphical image as an information symbol (or cascade of symbols) much more easily and quickly than they can perceive the images in realistic films, still photographs, and videos. Because they can also elicit faster and more numerous visual and spatial responses from viewers—more eye scans, more numerous and more extensive specific neural firings—these media can carry a higher density of information and deliver it faster. But, like other symbols, the information in stereoscopic computer graphics is processed, in large part, in the cerebellum, and viewers' retention of such symbols is often incomplete or deformed. The information should be delivered in short batches so as not to overtax the short-term memory capacity of approximately forty seconds and should provide for ample perceptual recovery time between segments. As the "space" of computer graphics systems can be interactive, viewers (users) should have enough time to verify or complete the spatial cues according to their individual perceptual ability.

Another advantage of VR is the ease with which viewers can move between scenes of the virtual worlds, and choose to program their own worlds and move through them—to whatever degree the software allows. It is too early to predict that every user of a VR system will artfully create his or her own software package or usage trajectories, but the concept is very promising.

Currently most virtual reality systems (and users) are limited to the processing and graphic-rendering power of the particular computer technology employed. Nonetheless, some simulator systems—like those used for *The Loch Ness Expedition* created by the Iwerks and Evans and Sutherland companies (Robertson 1994) and such advanced special-venue applications as the *Aladdin* attraction at the Epcot Center at Disney World (Reveaux 1995)—are already able to create the sensation of a more-or-less-realistic environment. The major critical limitation of virtual reality is the difficulty of synchronizing the movements of the image and the viewer. Such synchronization has always strengthened the overall impact of 3-D, even of primitive 3-D simulations like Laterna Magica and Polyecrans (Polièri 1963). It is even more desirable in virtual reality systems.

By the early 1990s most information designers understood that virtual reality was a surrogate metaphysical environment created by communications and computing systems (Wright 1990; Rheingold 1991; Heim 1992).

Since then, the quality of the interactivity in communications media has improved to the point where virtual realities have become 3-D environments in which individual users and audiences can create their own experiences.

In the research literature on virtual reality/virtual worlds (Bricken 1991; Brill 1995; Ellis 1991; Heim 1993; Jacobson 1994; Laurel 1991, among others), an overwhelming consensus has developed about the need to define and describe the theory and practice of information design for VR. From our biocybernetic information-design perspective, each art piece realized as a virtual reality (VR) represents an *information complex*. However, most of its parts (i.e., the information source, transmission conditions, and the individual receivers and their responses) are provided or heavily influenced by the users. In a traditional information complex, by contrast, most of the *information load* (the information source), is the result of the individual author's or artist's work; the receiver of the information has little or no power to alter the syntax and/or form of the information chain. Virtual reality, however, often combines both types of information cascades into a meta-complex of horizontal and vertical components (i.e., program-provided and user-chosen information). An information design approach for VR, therefore, can best be compared to the scenographic mode of thinking employed in creating a multimedia production (Polièri 1971, Laurel 1991).

Within a VR production, the consumer (receiver) becomes an important part of the art piece and his or her role within the VR domain is that of a co-creator. The information source does not, of course, disappear; it is there on a disk or in the computer's memory, but the information in it becomes specific to every viewer who interacts with it (Jacobson 1994). Thus a virtual reality experience is highly individual, highly private. In contrast to the media of mass communications that have given the name "information age" to the society of the late twentieth century, VR has the potential to bring people personal creative fulfillment in the twenty-first century.

Modeling the Information Design

The basic assumption of this section is that the information design for virtual reality must accommodate the biocybernetic framework of the human user. This calls for the designer to accept the *nature* and the *time-space axis* of the information chain. It also points to the need for a procedure to evaluate the information domains, bridges, and details of the software program designed. The biocybernetic approach also requires that the designer provide a certain degree of structure for the procedures by which the user progresses interactively within the VR program. The last point is a delicate one, since it must somehow blend the desire of the author-artist to lead the user on a previously determined path and the user's wish to freely explore the different views, avenues, and niches of the program on his or her own.

For creators it becomes very important to understand the basic design considerations and cues that will serve as effective building blocks of virtual reality. These will be far different from the knowledge of traditional arts (painting, music, film, photography, or television), even though most virtual reality will use some of the compositional structures of these two-dimensional, noninteractive media. Moreover, VR designers are unlikely to be established experts in those artistic disciplines. Their mental framework is far more likely to be influenced by analog and, especially, digital modes of thinking.

It is important to remember that digital logic and nonbiological time sequencing, which are both dominant in writing software, will clash with the biological capacities of the VR user. Human users will judge the impact and pleasure of a VR production solely on the basis of their own perceptual systems (Heim 1994). Therefore, the first basic guideline for the artistic creation of virtual realities is *to design the perceptual ramifications of space, tone, distance, spectrum, x-y-z coordinates, and divisions according to the basic measures of the human body*.

In the pioneering exercises of computer graphics, fractals, and video art, designers often found that the most effective shots were those that exploited a single cue to dimension (e.g., distance in the endless spiral of digital artist Ron Hayes's *Tristan and Isolde*, spatial proportion in Norman McLarren's animated film *Spheres*, and the audio tonal scale in Murray Schafer's 1977 exploration of the nonbiological domains of digital logic, *World*).

From the neuropsychological viewpoint, those exploitations of a single cue very often created an unusual emotional impact on the brain's neuron transfers, which makes it appropriate to label them "aesthetic surprises" (Clynes 1974). On the other hand, an overload of information on the software side can cause viewers to experience fatigue early in the pre- sentation if they are not allowed to pace the program to their own bio- logical time frame. This self-pacing attribute can easily be included in VR programs.

A second consideration for the software designer of VR art pieces is *accommodation of the user*. This is most important when creating steps, or blocks, through which the user must pass in order to continue. Although there is an easy analogy with the editing schemes of film or television (film language, television language), virtual reality differs from those media in possessing two specific facets: multidimensionality and a transhuman nature. It is a structure that merges computerized and human entities (Heim 1994). Within a VR experience, the individual user can make the story flow forward or backward, speed up or slow down. He or she can reshape time and space, focus on them, stop them, or jump over them at will. For such a program to be effective, the creator/author must take into account the rich sequencing possibilities of the design for representing different directions, times, and proportions. The most effective virtual reality is like a fluid hologram; it is not frozen in one moment of time but uses time as a multidimensional element.

The third area of creative consideration stems from the fact that *VR is a private mind space*. Its numerous contents, themes, puzzles, fantasies, and so on can be exploited without censorship, societal evaluation, or moral and ethical ramifications. Virtual reality can be as wild as the user wants it to be, as gentle and discreet, as violent, as full of beauty. Since users often do not know in advance where they may be led by the progress of the program, there is a possibility that more sophisticated VR programs may influence their health (Traub 1991, Cartwright 1994), patterns of thought, or associated motor and metabolic behavior. Without a very careful information design strategy, *there is no way to evaluate whether these possibilities will come to pass* and *whether such influences will be beneficial or harmful.*

For the first time, the technologies of virtual reality allow media designers to externalize the processes of human thought. What was for thousands of years hidden within the realm of the mind is now exposed to the laws of digital and analog processing. If a machine can create virtual landscapes and environments that are similar to the real world and produce clones of human beings, the impact of such "neurotemporary" imaginings will certainly alter human thinking and influence the shape of new human values.

A final consideration to be aware of is the fact that *VR acts as a powerful catalyst for associated thinking processes.* The person and his or her extended body (DataGlove, DataSuit, VIEWstation) becomes a synchronized hybrid and will probably eagerly repeat experiences found to be pleasurable. Repetitions of such states may lead to physiological exhaustion, on one side, and uncontrollable behavior, on the other. They could also lead to the sort of addiction or dependence often seen in children who are high users of video arcade games (Viirre 1994). On the benefit side, the art created by virtual reality has a strong potential to expand its influence beyond that of the traditional arts media and, ultimately, become a very important part of the life of a twenty-first-century person.

Influences of the Information Environment

In most industrial societies the information environment is full of visual stereotypes and symbols, but spatial cues are relatively few. Nonetheless, the amount of cortical feedback within people's brains is quite high (Breitenberg 1973). This cortical feedback is the result of imagining the spatial information that the environment fails to provide. This situation contributes significantly to the large number of barriers and prejudices mass audiences encounter in three-dimensional film or television system, especially older anaglyph (red/green filters) technologies. It also explains why some people feel uneasy when viewing holographic displays. Such responses are typical of audiences who have been exposed to the sophisticated "virtual space" of contemporary two-dimensional film and television programs. It is therefore important for designers of 3-D media not only to provide clear cues to perspective and spectral density but also to design movement parallax in a way that allows viewers to easily and quickly imagine real and deep space within the flat, two-dimensional television or film screen.

A mass audience exposed to the vast amount of information in a "virtual" three-dimensional information cascade (e.g., traditional film and TV) over years or decades develops a very firm and durable perceptual stereotype that is not easily changed when they see a stereoscopic film or television presentation. In fact, quite the opposite: audiences seem to prefer traditional two-dimensional television displays that employ space cues designed in the usual manner.

Figure 9.3 provides an overview of the diversity of possible three-dimensional media applications. Although it is not extensive or technology-specific, the figure outlines the scope and complexity that three-dimensional information design will need to deal with. Each application of a three-dimensional medium brings with it specific information design considerations that are dependent on the technology employed. To communicate effectively with their audiences producers of the software will need to understand not just how to apply the technology—as was often the case in the past—but the overall information design process as well. In all 3-D media the information chain must be respected and taken fully into account.

Conclusion

The information impact of three-dimensional media on the viewer is different from that of conventional two-dimensional media. Because they

3-D Media Applications				
TC Communication Broadcasting	Packaged Programs	Presentations & Exhibitions	Visual Databases	Digital Data Processing
R Mass & Specific Audiences	Mass Audience	Mass & Specific Audience/Users	Specific & Public Users	Specialized Users
IS Home-Theater Sports Events Still Pictures Computer Graphics	Video Games Videodiscs Electronic Cinema Movies Multi-vision	Flight Simulation Virtual Realities Public Displays Education Environmental Images Advertising	Gallery & Museum Collections Catalogues International Treasures	CAD/CAM Architecture Auto Design Satellite data imaging Medical Imaging

Figure 9.3

Current and Potential Applications of Three-dimensional Media. (TC = transmission conditions; R = receiver; IS = information source)

create more activity in the brain cortex, which is perceived as emotion, audiences report finding 3-D experiences "enchanting," more exciting than 2-D presentations, or "nauseating"—depending on the style, form, and content of the information design. The negative response can result from feedback to the vestibular mechanism (behind the inner ear), which is involved in the brain's processing of three-dimensional pictures, especially when the peripheral field of vision is employed.

The information impact of three-dimensional computer graphics and virtual realities is enriched by the addition of interactivity, giving rise to both neural and spinal information processing that creates a "true life" hodologic experience in the receiver. With three-dimensional communication media presented on two-dimensional surfaces, the major information impact stems from the careful manipulation of pictorial and aural z-axes, in which definition (i.e., sharpness) of the image is the paramount factor. Holographic 3-D information impact, on the other hand, is essentially a scenographic, theatrical experience in which viewers can experience and process a number of situations and objects without the inhibition of two-dimensional space cues.

In the next decade, as 3-D media become more ubiquitous and the perceptual stereotypes of the general public created by traditional media weaken, the role of the three-dimensional information designer will be increasingly important. Perhaps in the distant future that follows the shift toward spatial media, someone will look back on the history of the twentieth century and find that, like the fourteenth, it marked a major transition. We now sit on the cusp between the old and new media. Perhaps it is ushering in a 3-D renaissance.

References

Alkon, D. L. 1992. *Memory's Voice: Deciphering the Mind-Brain Code*. New York: Harper-Collins.

Breitenberg, V. 1973. *Gehirngespinste/Neuroanatomie für Kybernetisch Interesierte*. Berlin: Springer Verlag.

Bricken, M. 1991. Virtual worlds: No interface to design. In *Cyberspace: First Step*, Michael Benedikt, ed., pp. 363–82. Cambridge: MIT Press.

Brill, L. M. 1995. Museum-VR: Part II. More to immersive interaction than just arcade games. *Virtual Reality World* 3 (1): 36–43.

Cartwright, G. F. 1994. Virtual or real? The mind in cyberspace. *Futurist* 28 (2): 22–26.

Clynes, M. 1974. Sentics: Biocybernetics of emotion communication. *Annals of the New York Academy of Sciences* 220 (3): 55–131.

De Jonge, Derk. 1967. Applied hodology. *Landscape* 17 (2): 10–11.

Derrington, A. M. 1988. Retinal network and the cerebellum connections. *Journal of Physiology* 23: 66–67.

Ebenholtz, S. M. 1992. Motion sickness and oculomotor systems in virtual environments. *Presence* 1 (3): 302–305.

Ellis, S. R. 1991. Nature and origins of virtual environments: A bibliographical essay. *Computing Systems in Engineering* 2 (4): 321–47.

Hariharan, P. 1992. Display holography: A technical retrospective. *Leonardo* 25 (5): 431–37.

Heim, M. 1994. The art of virtual reality. In *Virtual Reality Special Report*, Kay Keppler, ed., 1 (4): 9–22. San Francisco: Miller Freeman.

Heim, M. 1993. *The Metaphysics of Virtual Reality*. New York: Oxford Press.

St. Hilaire, P.; Benton, S. A.; Lucente, M.; Jepsen, M. L.; Kollin, J.; Yoshikawa, H.; and Underkoffler, J. 1990. Electronic display system for computational holography. In *Practical Holography*, vol. 4, S. A. Benton, ed. *Proceedings of the Society of Photo-Optical Instrument Engineers* 1212, no. 20.

Jacobson, R. 1994. Virtual worlds: A new type of design environment. *Virtual Reality World* 2 (3): 46–52.

Jubak, J. 1992. *In the Image of the Brain*. Boston: Little, Brown.

Kusaka, H. 1990. Three-dimensional imaging techniques and visual depth perception. In *Three-Dimensional Media Technology*, H. Thwaites, ed., pp. 24–37. Montreal: 3-D Media Technologies Research Center (hereafter 3Dmt Research Center).

Laurel, B. 1991. *Computers as Theatre*. Reading, Mass.: Addison-Wesley.

Leventhal, A. G. 1988. Influence of the lateral geniculate nucleus on the visual system. *Science* 7–8: 21–23.

Lipton, L. 1982. *Foundations of Stereoscopic Cinema*. New York: Van Nostrand Reinhold.

Low, C. 1984. Large screen 3-D: Aesthetic and technical considerations. *Journal* of the *Society of Motion Picture and Television Engineers* (January): 14–17.

Malik, M. F. 1976. *Design de l'information*. Montreal: Société Radio Canada.

Malik, M., and Thwaites, H. 1993. *Information Design for 3-D Cultural Spaces*. Montreal: 3Dmt Research and Information Center.

Malik, M., and Thwaites, H. 1990. A biocybernetic view: A notion of spatial information impact on the human brain. In *Three-Dimensional Media Technology*. H. Thwaites, ed., pp. 75–88. Quebec: 3Dmt Research Center.

Malik, M., and Thwaites, H. 1987. *Biocybernetic Communication Research*. Montreal: Concordia University.

Martens, W. 1990. Spatial image formation in binocular vision and binaural hearing. In *Three-Dimensional Media Technology*, H. Thwaites, ed., pp. 39–60. Quebec: 3Dmt Research Center.

Nagata, S. 1990. Perceptual area of stereoscopic vision (PASV) and 3-D image displays. *Journal of 3-D Images* 4 (4): 42–49.

Nagata, S. 1989. Fusional characteristics of binocular parallax as a function of viewing angle and viewing distance of stereoscopic pictures. *Journal of the Institute of Television Engineers of Japan* 43 (3): 276–81.

Nagata, S. 1984. How to reinforce perception of depth in single two-dimensional pictures. *Proceedings of the Society for Information Display* 25 (3): 239–46.

Naimark, M. 1992. Expo '92 Seville. *Presence* 1 (3): 364–69.

Pepper, A. 1989. Holographic space: A generalised graphic definition. *Leonardo* 22 (3, 4): 295–98.

Polièri, J. 1971. *Scénographie, Sémiographie*. Paris: Denöel/Gonthier.

Polièri, J. 1963. *Scénographie Nouvelle*. Boulogne-Seine: Edition Aujourd'hui.

Pribram, K. H. 1991. *Brain and Perception: Holonomy and Structure in Figural Processing*. Hillsdale, N.J.: Erlbaum.

Pribram, K. H. 1990. Transformational realism: The optic array, the optical image and the retinal process. In *Three-Dimensional Media Technology*, H. Thwaites, ed., pp. 61–74. Montreal: 3Dmt Research Center.

Reveaux, T. 1995. Aladdin let VR out of the lamp. *Virtual Reality World* 3 (2): 40–42.

Rheingold, H. 1991. *Virtual Reality*. New York: Summit Books.

Robertson, B. 1994. Digital adventures in entertainment: Part II. Ready for a wild ride? *Computer Graphics World* 17 (2): 30–39.

Schafer, R. M. 1977. *The Tuning of the World*. New York: Knopf.

Schiller, P.; Logothetis, N.; and Charles, E. 1990. Function of the color-opponent and broad-band channels of the visual system. *Nature* 343 (4): 68–70.

Searle, J. 1984. *Mind, Brains, and Science*. Cambridge: Harvard University Press.

Smith, C. W. 1989. The Present Status of 3-D Processes. *Image Technology* (June): 224–27.

Traub, D. 1991. Neomedia: To live and learn in 3D. *Verbum* 5 (2): 22–24.

Ungerleider, G., and Mishkin, M. 1982. Two cortical visual systems. In *Analysis of Visual Behavior*, D. J. Ingle, M. A. Goodale, and R. J. W. Mansfield, eds., pp. 549–86. Cambridge: MIT Press.

Viirre, E. 1994. A survey of medical issues and virtual reality technology. *Virtual Reality World* 2 (4): 16–20.

Wright, K. 1990. The road to the global village. *Scientific American* 262: 383–94.

10 Collaborative Information Design: Seattle's Modern Odyssey

Judy Anderson

PR tells people what needs to be done. Ads tell people what to do. Art gives people the energy and inspiration to do something, based on their own ideas.
—John Koval, "Modern Odysseys"

The question the authors in this book are asking, in various forms, is What does information design do? And, more importantly, what role do designers play in the process of communicating information? Do they simply act as broadcasters of particular information, or can they design information in a way that actively facilitates the process of communication and the sharing of knowledge, ideas, and emotions?

In the communication process, when a given source has a message to convey to other individuals or to the general public, the message is first *encoded* and then transmitted to a receiver. In the design profession, this process usually translates into the *client*, who defines the message; the *designer*, who elaborates on (encodes) the message by giving it form; and the *audience*, which receives it and interacts with it. Thus communication is an interactive process in which each participant informs the others, in varying degrees, about the problem in order to create appropriate and workable solutions. These solutions can be manifested in a variety of forms, from two- and three-dimensional objects (posters, books, information kiosks, etc.) to time-based works (media works for radio television, live performances, interactive multimedia events, etc.).

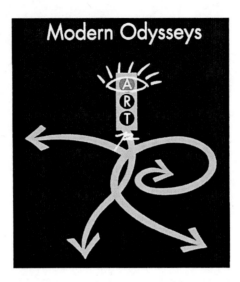

Figure 10.1
The Logo of ARTp, the Artists' Regional Transit project.

In private business settings the information designer's voice and public responsibility are limited, because the needs and message of the client predominate. Within a public context, however—where the client is also, to a great extent, the audience, and vice versa—mightn't the role of the information designer be much broader and more collaborative?

Collaboration between client and designer, designer and creative team, audience and client, or audience and designer can take many forms and be present to different degrees. Collaboration is dynamic, often messy, confrontational, uncomfortable, and chaotic. In the best case, it enriches the creative process and promotes synergistic work patterns and a product that is improved by each participant's contribution. In the worst case, it is an irritant and an obstacle to achievement. Many times, collaboration creates solutions that reinforce the old adage, "the camel is a horse designed by a committee."

Can we design the collaborative process to support the synergistic aspects of a relationship among participants and avoid the irritating obstacles? What might be the information designer's role and responsibility in such a process? Can we structure the collaboration in a way that supports each individual's expertise while integrating it with the whole? How can we hear simultaneously the individual's and the group's voices?

As designers we are accustomed to think of collaboration in a business context, where professionals from related disciplines work together creatively to solve the client's needs. Several books celebrating the usefulness of collaboration as a problem-solving process—often between architect and artist—describe the methods used and document the solutions arrived at. In the public sector, this kind of creative collaboration is supported (and to a large degree mandated) around the country by "1% for Art" programs, which specify that all publicly funded capital-improvement projects must include and fund the participation of art and artists. The mandate thus provides opportunities to integrate the informational and communications insights of artists and designers at an early stage of planning.

In the Northwest in particular, design teams have developed a useful format for these collaborations. The core of the team—artists, architects, urban designers, planners, engineers, and others—collaborate with members of the community, as well as with representatives from the public agency involved, to produce solutions that are then integrated into a project's design. In this context, the designer, first as an artist, and secondly as a citizen, enjoys a greater sense of autonomy—and perhaps a deeper sense of responsibility to the community—than when working in the private milieu. The notion of *design* in this context is expanded in the direction of *art*; and, although this is an artificial distinction, using it expands the role of the "designer/artist" in the eyes of the public and government planners.

Although at times team design is an unwieldy process, it often results in workable and imaginative solutions. It is easy to see the effectiveness of such solutions, and the contribution each team member has made to them, when they are embodied in tangible, physical objects (e.g., buildings, parks, public sculptures). But what about information, which communicates knowledge, ideas, and feelings, which don't exist in physical space? Of course, once defined, information—encoded in words, images,

Figure 10.2
The Billy Tipton Memorial Saxophone Quarter. The quartet performed its *Bus Horn Concerto* at the opening festivities of Modern Odysseys.

symbols, sounds, and so on—is broadcast in some printed, electronic, or three-dimensional form. The information designer thus plays a role in defining those informational components and integrating them into such physical products as signs, environmental graphics, printed materials, electronic kiosks, and so forth.

Are there also other ways for the informational designer to contribute to the collaborative process? Ways that create more process-based, less product-oriented solutions that both invite people to interact with the information and to share their own knowledge, ideas, and feelings? The Modern Odysseys, a public art project in the Seattle region, is one model for expanding the role of the information designer in a way that encourages collaboration with members of the public.

Modern Odysseys: Heroic Journeys We Make Every Day
A collective work designed to stimulate thinking and discussion about transportation issues among the public.

In the fall of 1991 I was chosen by Metro, Seattle's transportation agency, as the first artist member of the Regional Transit Project, a three-county plan for creating a faster, more efficient, more reliable regional transit system. The project, if realized, would become one of the largest public works systems in the United States. My commission was funded by Metro's public art program, which designated 1 percent of project expenditures for work by artists. As an artist who also works as a graphic/information designer, I was expected to help Metro communicate issues relating to transportation and the transit project to the general public. At the time, Metro's managers were having a difficult time translating their complex physical plans into understandable images, charts, and diagrams; they hoped that an artist might be able to accomplish what Metro's own design, planning, and communications teams had not been able to do. Funds were set aside to produce a "product" that would achieve this specific objective.

After spending several months meeting with the architects, planners, communication teams, and administrators, I realized that what Metro thought they wanted me to do—create images that could be incorporated into advertising and informational brochures—made little sense. Other designers and illustrators were already doing this. The kinds of publications used by Metro to communicate the issues related to the Regional Transit Project were very technical, containing vast quantities of maps, charts, graphs, and statistics. Dry in tone and produced in an unadorned official format, readers not accustomed to technical information found them difficult to understand and not very interesting. The work coming out of Metro's advertising agencies, on the other hand, was slickly produced and tried to entertain and persuade the public to take particular actions (e.g., ride the bus or carpool).

My idea was more radical. It was to use artists to translate to the public the experience of transportation in our lives in a way that encouraged people to take part in discussions of related issues. Could we, I asked myself, create solutions that would incorporate citizens into the work, not just tell them what we wanted them to hear?

The underlying premise about the impact of transportation was that we are all connected by the way we travel. We argued that, because our individual decisions about getting to work—whether to drive a car, take a bus, or ride a bicycle—affect everyone else, we need to work together to find appropriate solutions for the region's future transportation system. The challenge for me was to find ways to incorporate a wide variety of individual thoughts, ideas, and information and present them in a format that invited public interaction and discussion. Further, I wanted to interview people as they interacted with the artworks and use their responses as the subject matter of a second series of works. The project would then become a dynamic, ongoing process that reinforced the premise that the choice of transportation was a basic element of our interconnectiveness as a community.

From the outset, it was clear to me that artists should not simply duplicate in a different form what Metro's communication and public relations specialists and paid advertising professionals were already doing. Instead they should work at the fringes of art, using its communication potential in a more suggestive, experiential way. The artists' works should be integrated into Metro's public relations and advertising efforts but also be separate from them, in order to create different kinds of associations. Instead of being officious and technical or slick, the art works would be high in content, low in production quality, and diverse in nature, with all the authenticity inherent in art. Moreover, because our funding was from the 1% for Art mandate, the project itself should be a work of art—not applied design or "propaganda" from Metro. It was a formidable challenge. It meant getting the public to first think about the issues in a broad way and then become involved in carrying out the work.

I presented the preliminary idea to Metro with a request that the targeted funds be used to develop a comprehensive plan for the project that,

Figure 10.3
Bus Stop with Telephone Number of the ARTp Voice Box. Stories and limericks about travel were posted at all bus stops.

if realized, would necessitate additional funding. With their approval, I assembled a lead team—a writer, a composer, and a video artist—to work with me in planning the budget, scope, and objectives of ARTp, the Artists' Regional Transit project. This lead team, called the Mass Transformers, later served as curators of the collective work, overseeing and coordinating collaborations among artists, distributing the works to a mass audience, and creating additional works that integrated public responses. The team developed a theme, "Modern Odysseys: Heroic Journeys We Make Every Day"; a visual identity, in the form of a logo (figure 10.1) and animated figure; and a musical score. Each participating artist would "tag" his or her work with these visual and audio tags in order to give additional identity and cohesiveness to the project as a whole.

The transit authority, the mayor, and the commissioners approved and funded the plan at a wild planning session attended by the media. We presented our proposal as a performance, incorporating video, radio, print, and live improvisational elements in the style we hoped the final piece would assume. In hindsight, I think our idea was approved, in part, because public officials were swept up in the experience of the performance. And, because it was funded by 1% for Art funds, they might have been more forgiving of this nebulous thing called art than of a comparable idea presented as advertising—which it wasn't—or public relations—which it wasn't. They didn't know quite what it was but knew that the plan, and its relationship to the other, more traditional efforts of public outreach, were well thought through. Most of all, they realized that they needed to get the public more actively involved in the transit project.

The organization of ARTp integrated the individual work of approximately fifty writers, dramatists, poets, videographers, and other artists working in a variety of media. Some were National Endowment for the Arts fellows; some were just beginning their careers; and still others were children. The Mass Transformers combined the individual works and distributed them to the public as a collective work.

The Mass Transformers collaborated in a number of ways: helping create artworks, coordinating the distribution of work publicly, and facilitating collaborative opportunities between artists and members of the public. Each member of the lead team had a clearly defined role that drew on his or her individual skill as a visual designer, writer, composer, or videographer. Throughout the nine months of creating the work, weekly meetings were held; during the performance and distribution phases, meetings were held two or three times a week. As the lead artist, I directed the collaboration, making sure that each individual was clear about his or her role and taking overall responsibility during every phase of the project. The collaborative process seemed to work best when each member had a clearly defined role that maintained its separateness within the whole. Where lines of responsibility became blurred, tensions arose.

The Mass Transformers also created numerous opportunities for collaborations among the individual artists. They held meetings at which individual artists presented sketches of their work in progress; several collaborations between artists resulted from ideas presented at these meetings. At one meeting the Documentarians (the archives unit) showed a video work called "ARTp at Midterm," a twenty-minute collage of interviews with the ARTp artists that was a very powerful expression of the creative process among writers, visual artists, and performance artists.

During the fall of 1992, ARTp presented live performances throughout the region at street corners, shopping malls, and schools. Each performance was an ensemble of individual presentations related to the themes. Books of stories about transportation were distributed at coffee-houses, laundromats, beauty parlors, community centers, grocery stores, libraries, and schools. Videographers and journalists interviewed the public. Children were commissioned to work with adult artists and musicians to create collaborative works, and short stories were posted at all bus stops. Simultaneously, radio stations and commercial and cable television channels, particularly the sports network, aired audio and video artworks as public service spots. Radio stations interviewed the artists about their work, television stations and newspapers covered the performances.

We shocked shoppers at suburban malls by bringing in dancers dressed and body-painted in blue; they moved slowly through each performance space interpreting the notion of travel as kinetic sculpture. We opened Modern Odysseys at the Westlake Center, Seattle's downtown outdoor gathering place with a bus-horn concerto utilizing four saxophones and two buses (figure 10.2). We put writers on buses at opposite edges of the region and had them travel to meet at the center and write stories about their adventures en route. We videotaped and interviewed the audiences during the performances to get their input and responses to the ideas about transportation and the Modern Odysseys project.

Stories and limericks about travel were posted at all bus stops with the telephone number of the Voice Box, a free interactive art piece (figure 10.3). The artists creating their work in public spaces wore badges and distributed stickers featuring the Voice Box telephone number, and the Mass Transformers placed teaser ads giving the number in the personal sections of the daily and weekly newspapers. The Voice Box provided callers with three choices: they could listen to messages from the artists, leave a message, or listen to messages left by other callers. The Voice Box, which was constantly revised and updated during the nine months the work was created and performed, allowed the public to become active and ongoing participants in the work.

The Mass Transformers concluded the work with two pieces: a printed tabloid insert for the evening newspapers and a video for broadcast on television (figure 10.4). These final pieces, a collage of artists' works and public responses, created one final, grand collective work. In addition, the Documentarians produced a half-hour documentary film about ARTp. This film, which was premiered at the Seattle Art Museum, continues to be broadcast on television and shown in various public venues. It communicates the powerful experience—for individuals and for the public as a whole—of this collaborative project. ARTp succeeded in creating a work of art that reached and interacted with a large and diverse audience and helped facilitate discussion of the very complex issues involved in urban regional transportation planning.

a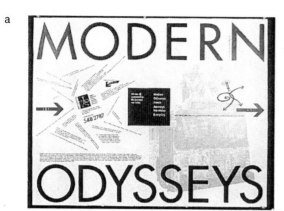

b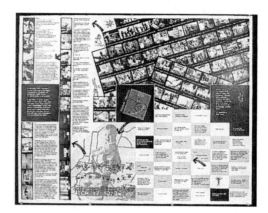

Figure 10.4a and b

Collage of Artists' Works and Public Responses. For the final collective work the Mass Transformers created a tabloid insert for the evening newspapers and a video for television broadcast.

Figure 10.5
Video Art by David Russo.

Figure 10.6
Destiny Is a Mystery, Video Art by Katie Donald and Video Associates.

Facilitating Artistic Collaboration

In any collaborative process, participants give up something to be a part of the whole. In a best-case scenario, the resulting work reflects a cohesiveness of intent, an eloquence, and a clarity that integrate each individual's contribution. In a worse-case scenario, the resulting work becomes a compromise between its collaborators that dilutes the integrity of individual works but never integrates them into a unified whole. The approach to collaboration we used for Modern Odysseys attempted to maintain each artist's voice. The whole became a collection of individual voices that, paradoxically, created cohesiveness through their diversity and complexity.

The Mass Transformers took great care to ensure that all artists incorporated the thematic devices—the verbal, visual, and sound tags—in a way that did not compromise their individual work. For example, whereas there was but one version of the verbal and visual tags, sound artists could choose from among twenty-one versions of the tag, ranging from interpretations by synthesized violins, piano, acoustic guitar, and jazz saxophone to versions featuring whistling and car horns. Each musician and

Figure 10.7
The Urban Guerrillas Performing as the Guzzler Brothers at the Opening Festivities.

a
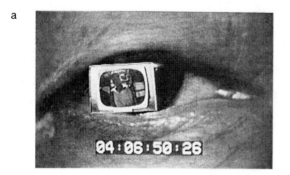

b

Figure 10.8a and b
Mrs. Yamamoto Travels to a Foreign Land, Video Art by Maria Gargiulo.

composer selected the variation that best harmonized with his or her own work.

The key to the project's collaborative process was the cohesiveness brought to the project by the Mass Transformers. Except for the creation of the tags, all the work produced by this lead team was collaborative in the traditional sense. The resulting works reflected a clarity of intent in spite of a divergence of form. It became difficult, if not impossible, to identify individuals' voice as they and their work merged into the true group voice.

In this context, my own role as lead artist was to function as a designer of information in a way that clarified the communication process and enhanced the sharing of knowledge, ideas, and emotions. After originating the concept and processing the approval and funding of the project, I acted primarily as a facilitator to different groups, both identifying important messages and organizing ways for these messages to support Metro's more traditional communication, advertising, and public relations efforts. Finally, I served as a kind of executive producer for the work as a whole to ensure that the project continued to evolve as the public interacted with it.

Figure 10.9
Performance of the Micro-rap Opera, *Hurry Up and Wait*. The opera was written and co-performed by the Billy Tipton Memorial Saxophone Quartet and Shomari Shanks.

Figure 10.10
The Billy Tipton Memorial Saxophone Quartet.

What Was Learned?

While the artists involved were unanimous in their evaluation of the project as successful, Metro officials were less sure. Even though they could clearly critique the quality of each piece of the work, they found it almost impossible to assess the results of the project as a whole. How could we measure our success in meeting the work's main objective, that of stimulating citizens' thinking and discussion about transportation issues? One of the problems resulting from expanding the notion of information design—in this case in the direction of art—is the difficulty of meeting people's normal expectations—such as the desire to assess the public response. Unfortunately, you can't measure symbolic grassroots effectiveness very well—if at all.

Nonetheless, the effort to assess effectiveness was part of project planning. The Mass Transformers kept accurate records of the distribution and reach of each component in an attempt to understand the scope and significance of the work as a whole. Perhaps the most telling, and most easily measurable element of the project, was the Voice Box. It received over twenty-six hundred calls, while Metro's public information line received only twelve hundred calls. And the cost of the Voice Box was a fraction of what was spent on the transportation agency's costly television, radio, and print campaign.

The only negative press the project received occurred during the artist-selection process, when one writer accused Metro of taking artists for a ride and using them to create cheap publicity. The article went on to state that "Metro's arts project crosses the line into the realm of propaganda ... and smacks of the socialist realism enforced in post-WW II East Germany." In fact, the opposite is closer to the truth. Not only did Metro executives not tell the artists what to say—or censor what they wanted to say—they were, if anything, anxious that the artists *not* be too articulate in their support of bus usage, which the project was not intended to promote.

Implications and Possibilities

We can perhaps best view ARTp as one approach to information design as experience—as a means, rather than an end in itself. By interacting with the work as a whole, viewers became involved in and with the subject matter. Supported by specific information—in this case, the brochures, advertisements, and reports published by Metro—they could understand the issues involved and become part of an ongoing discussion of possible solutions. The model opens up provocative possibilities for both the creators of information and the audience to initiate further collaborations. Moreover, it suggests ways for information designers to play an expanded role. Instead of serving as simply broadcasters of information, they can become active leaders and facilitators of the process of collaborative communication and the sharing of knowledge, ideas, and emotions.

III   *Designing for the Technologies of Information*

Design was once the prerogative of nobles. They alone had the means to procure artisans capable of expounding a point of view: in the Pyramids with their message of kingly immortality, in the great sculptures of antiquity proclaiming a Pax romana, in Michaelangelo's timeless paeans to papal omniscience. All the portraits commissioned, the cities designed, the buildings constructed, the paintings, the songs, the literature—for a time everything added to the natural environment by human beings was theirs.

In the physical realm, not much has changed. I thought of this while driving through a particularly arid encampment of boxlike office buildings owned by others, on broad, empty streets constructed by a government not really under my control, on my way to buy the few small personal items I could afford. In the buildings and on the streets I saw other small people who, like me, inhabited the property of others to create wealth few of them would ever own. After all these centuries, the design of the physical environment remains largely the prerogative of powerful Others. Most of us can only witness and accept.

Interactivity, however, changes things. It doesn't necessarily tip the scales enough to make our culture more egalitarian, but interactive technology does contain the seed of *commutativity*, the shared ability to affect the basic drivers that make culture what it is. Some interactive media, of course, do not reinforce this possibility. Bank ATMs and stamp machines, for instance, suggest quite the opposite: their activities are mandated and controlled by powerful owners. If we choose to participate in their processes by depositing our savings or purchasing postage stamps, we must pay a price in both cash and autonomy. Other interactive media, however, proceed in an egalitarian direction and offer the rest of us—as Apple Computer was once fond of saying—a chance to make a vital, self-rewarding difference.

In chapter 11 Nathan Shedroff, one of the first to call himself an *information designer*, elaborates an extensive theory of interactivity in which the promise of helpful participation is explicit. Working primarily with electronic media, Shedroff has invented several methods of delivering and manipulating information for the benefit of the end-user. Only a portion of his theory—the most important part—is included here. It sets forth a taxonomy and a system of shared forms of communication and understanding. Sometimes, he points out, the unintended results of an information design can create an odd and wonderful synergy among means and methods to make the consumers of information producers in their own right. Consider the case of the Internet and how it has so far eluded easy commercialization to remain a genuine vox populi of those with access to computers. Shedroff tells us why this may be so.

Does interactivity contain its own meaning? That is, does the sheer act of interacting tell us something about the nature of communication and the predicament in which we might find ourselves while immersed in the process? Sheryl Macy, Elizabeth Andersen, and John Krygier, three parts of a successful environmental graphics consultancy, take a closer look at the Shannon-Weaver model of communication and find in it clues to the human desire for interaction. The model holds that signals representing meanings are transmitted by senders to receivers through a medium of communication. The problem is that the sender and receiver of a message may not possess the same coding-decoding capabilities, which impedes the flow of information. In chapter 12 Macy, Andersen, and Krygier put a new twist on this situation, suggesting that designers' own coding-encoding paraphernalia can either confound or exemplify the successful transmission of meaning.

Jim Gasperini, who designs deceptively simple computer games and impressively complex computer art like the award-winning *ScruTiny in the Great Round*, believes that ambiguity, not common-sense, is the key to conveying meaning to the consumer of information products. He cites several examples of highly ambiguous information designs in diverse media—drama, music, and film, as well as computer-based forms—in which ambiguity makes all the difference. In chapter 13 Gasperini argues that openness to ambiguity is the designer's most important tool and that certain self-described information designers, armed to the teeth with massive desktop processors, daily practice *overdesign*. As receivers and designers of information, we all suffer the consequences. The Taoists say, "He who speaks does not know, and he who knows does not speak." We must practice our profession quietly in order to sense ambiguities we can capture and tame to the purposes of good information design.

Inherently, design and art are at odds. Designers deliberately strive to share with a target audience a particular point of view, whereas artists create only to express themselves. Or so the mythology goes. The lines are blurring, however, before an onslaught of digitalization described in chapter 14 by composer and computer scientist Steve Holtzman. Art once locked away in a private gallery or hidden in the artist's loft may now be disclosed, via the Internet for example, to a global audience of admirers and critics. Once digitally created or captured, it can circulate freely in the public domain. Easy transmission and manipulation can alter art and transform design; a passage of music can be incorporated into a composition of a very different style. Selfish art may become communal design—and communal design become selfish art. Holtzman shares with us his vision of how digital bits, the 1s and 0s that are the building blocks of information, can be shaped to a purpose—even if the final outcome is never known.

So far we have examined how design creates informational artifacts in space. In chapter 15 Simon Birrell leads us one step beyond, into spaces that are themselves informational artifacts: cyberspace, virtual worlds composed of information that is the product of imagination. The synthetic environments that exist within these worlds may be simple or elaborate, compelling or silly. As in a film, every element of the virtual world is within the producer's control—every element, that is, except the human being whose experience is the object of the producer's designs and labors. Stepping into an immersion space or figuratively projecting oneself into a screen-borne image, the individual is integrated into the imagery. The better the design of the virtual world, the better it fits with the individual's own cognitive world and the more compelling it is until, ideally, it becomes a stand-in for the material world. Though no virtual world has yet been designed with such a high level of realism, designers are becoming more and more skillful at designing these information universes. Birrell reflects on the practical and moral issues associated with the design of the virtual worlds that, perhaps in the not-too-distant future, will be the ultimate expression of information design.

11 Information Interaction Design: A Unified Field Theory of Design

Nathan Shedroff

The most important skill for almost everyone in the next decade and beyond will be the ability to create valuable, compelling, and empowering information and experiences for others. To do this, we must learn established ways of organizing and presenting data and information as well as develop new ones. Whether we do this through traditional print products, electronic means, interactive experiences, or live performances makes little difference. Neither does it matter whether we are employing physical or electronic devices or our own bodies and voices. The process of creating anything is roughly the same. The methods of solving problems, responding to audiences, and communicating to others in any medium are enough alike for us to consider them identical for the purposes of this paper. The same issues apply across media and experiences, because they directly address the phenomena of information overload, information anxiety, media literacy, media immersion, and technological overload—important problems that need better solutions.

The intersection of these issues can be addressed by the process of *information interaction design* that is described in this paper. In other circles it is called *information design, information architecture,* or *interaction design.* Some call it *instructional design,* and yet others, simply *common sense.* We all constantly create or engineer interactions, presentations, and experiences for others. Information interaction design addresses the pervasive need

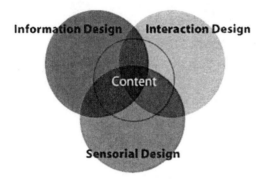

Figure 11.1
Information Interaction Design. Interface Design is a combination of three categories of disciplines: information Design, Interaction Design, and Sensorial Design (which includes all kinds of visual, auditory, written, and other sensorially-related disciplines).

to do so with one process for producing every book, directory, catalog, newspaper, or television program. We can also use it to create every CD-ROM, kiosk, oral presentation, game, and on-line service, as well as every dance, music, comedy, or theater performance. The traditions and technologies change with every venue, but the process does not—or should not.

Information interaction design is the intersection of three different disciplines: information design, interaction design, and sensorial design (see figure 11.1). *Information design's* principles originate in the publishing and graphic design worlds, although few professionals in these fields intentionally practice them. The discipline addresses the organization and presentation of data—its transformation into valuable, meaningful information. Although it is something that everyone has always done to some extent, mostly unconsciously, only recently has information design been identified as a discipline in itself, with proven processes that can be employed and taught. Unfortunately, there are precious few sources for learning about the practice of either information design or interaction design.

Interaction design (in essence, story creating and storytelling) is at once both an ancient art and a new technology. Media have always affected the telling of stories and the creation of experiences, but currently new media offer capabilities and opportunities not previously addressed in the history of interaction and performance. The demands of interactivity in particular are often misunderstood by all but the most experienced storytellers and performers. We do not yet understand precisely how these skills are expressed through interactive technologies, what interests audiences will have in them, and what demands audiences will make of these technologies. Consequently, there are few sources of information about these issues and the techniques we can use to meet them. The practitioners of this new territory are desperate for some new ideas and cogent explanations. Interaction design is also the most critical component to the success of interactive products.

Sensorial design is simply the employment of all the techniques we use to communicate to others through the senses. Most of the time we think first (right after writing) of employing the visual design disciplines, such as graphic design, videography, cinematography, typography, illustration, and photography. But the disciplines that communicate through other senses are just as important; sound design and engineering, musical performance, and vocal communication are also effective in the appropriate circumstances. In fact, sometimes they are the most creative media to employ. Tactile, olfactory, and kinesthetic senses, although rarely used (often due to technological or market constraints), are just as valid and can add enriching detail to an experience.

The professional disciplines of these sensorial media are worlds unto themselves, with their own histories, traditions, and concerns. To learn each one well would takes more time and skill than could be expected of any individual. Therefore it is important for everyone (including the general public) to gain at least an overview of the important issues and techniques of each discipline, so that they can be employed correctly in presenting ideas and communicating messages—especially within a team. Experienced experts in each of these areas, therefore, should participate in deciding how to employ the various media in support of a project's information and interaction goals and messages.

These levels of understanding are significant because they define the boundaries within which we can create and communicate. While information design is most heavily involved in the representation of data and its presentation, interaction design is most relevant to the creation of compelling experiences. When designing projects, I usually find it easier to start with the information design process if a lot of data already exists; if not, I begin with the interaction design. The following sections describe processes I have found useful for both approaches.

Information Design

While few designers have been explicitly concerned with the issues paramount to clear communication—organization, presentation, goals and messages, clarity, and complexity to name a few—these functions have been addressed, at least on a subconscious level, by everyone who attempts to organize his or her thoughts and communicate them. Information design doesn't banish aesthetic concerns, but it doesn't focus on them either. Most important to communication are the issues listed above. However, there is no reason why elegantly structured or well-architected data can't also be beautiful. *Information design isn't meant to replace graphic design and other visual disciplines but to provide the framework for expressing these capabilities.*

Our understanding of understanding must begin with the view that what most of us deal with everyday—the vast numbers of things that bombard our senses—is not information. It is merely data. Richard Saul Wurman expresses this well.[1] Data, he points out, is fairly worthless to most of us. It is the product of research or creation (e.g., writing), but it is not an adequate product for communicating. To have value, it must be organized, transformed, and presented in a way that gives it meaning—and makes it valuable (see figure 11.2).

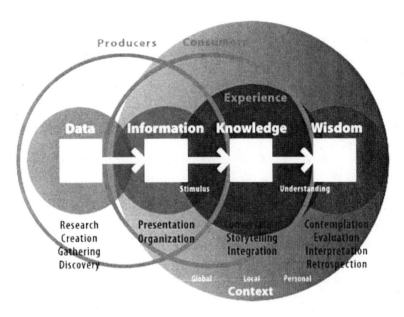

Figure 11.2
The Understanding Spectrum. Understanding is a continuum that leads from Data, through Information and Knowledge, and ultimately to Wisdom.

Information is also not the end of the continuum of understanding. Just as data can be transformed into meaningful information, so information can be transformed into knowledge and then, further, into wisdom. Knowledge is a phenomenon we can build for others, just as we can build information for others from data. This is done through interaction design and the creation of experiences, a process we will discuss further in the next section. But at this point, just think for a moment how hard it is to build a meaningful experience for someone else. It is first necessary to understanding who that person is; what his or her needs, abilities, interests, and expectations are; and how to reach them. Brenda Laurel often states that the interactive medium "is not about information, it is about experience."[2] She is absolutely correct, but I would add that in creating these experiences for others (and even for ourselves to some degree), we must understand and structure the information (and data) we use to build them.

The Continuum of Understanding

A Bit About Data   Data is the product of research, creation, collection, and discovery. It is the raw material we find or create that we use to build our communications. Most of what we experience, unfortunately, is merely data. It is fairly easy to distinguish: it is often boring, incomplete, or inconsequential. It isn't valuable as communication, because it isn't a complete message. Most of the technology we call *information technology* is, in fact, only data technology, because it does not address understanding or the forming or communication of information. Most of this technology is simply concerned with storage, processing, and transmission.

Data is useful to producers, or to anyone playing a production role. Everyone does this to some extent, whether professionally or personally—in print, electronic, or spoken forms. But data are not meant for consumers. Yet too often we deluge our audiences with data instead of information, leaving them to sort out and make sense of them. Many providers even brag of the amount of meaningless, contextless data they throw at their customers. CNN, for example, actually calls its bits of data "factoids" and slides them in between other, meaningful presentations.

Successful communications do not present data. If presenters don't bother to provide context and build meaning, audiences will have little patience for doing it themselves. As designers, we must ask ourselves constantly what service we provide.

More About Information   Information is the first level at which it is appropriate to communicate with audiences. It represents the transmission of thoughtful messages that reveal the relationships and patterns (the context) among the data presented. Transforming data into information is accomplished by organizing them into a meaningful form, presenting them in appropriate ways, and communicating the context around them. I describe these processes in more detail in the following sections.

The Experience of Knowledge   *Knowledge* is the pay-off of any experience. It is the understanding gained through experience, whether bad or good. Knowledge is communicated by building compelling interactions with others, or with systems, so that the patterns and meanings of the information can be assimilated. There are many types of knowledge: some is *personal*, having a meaning unique to one person's experiences, thoughts, or point of view; *local knowledge* is that shared by a relatively few people through their common experiences; while *global knowledge* (at the other end of the spectrum) is more general. Global knowledge is more process-based and, necessarily, more limited, because it relies on such high levels of shared understandings and agreements about communication. Effective communication, which must take into account the audience's knowledge base, is more difficult with larger audiences, whose pool of shared knowledge is less detailed and more generalized.

Knowledge is gained through a process of integration, in both the presentation and the mind of the audience. Information forms the stimulus of an experience, while wisdom is the deeper understanding of the message that can be gained through the experience. Knowledge, therefore (as figure 11.3 illustrates), is fundamentally participatory; it is the level all our communications should target, for it is the one that allows us to convey the most valuable messages. It is also the highest level that we, as designers, can affect directly, since it is still in the local or global range. Past this point, understanding is primarily the responsibility of audience members as their personal experiences are more deeply tapped.

What Is Wisdom?   *Wisdom* is the most vague and intimate form of understanding. It is much more abstract and philosophical than the other levels, and we know less about how to create or affect it. Wisdom is a kind of metaknowledge, a blending of all the processes and relationships understood through experience. It is the result of contemplation, evalua-

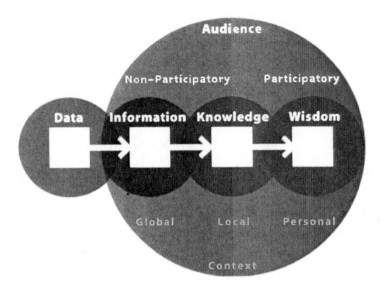

Figure 11.3
Understanding Context. Context becomes more personal as understanding becomes more complex. In addition, participation on the audiences' part becomes important and then mandatory along the same progression.

tion, retrospection, and interpretation—all of which are particularly personal processes. We cannot create wisdom as we can data and information, and we cannot share it with others as we can knowledge. We can only create experiences and describe processes that offer our audiences opportunities to find wisdom. Ultimately, wisdom is an understanding that must be gained by the individual.

Organizing Things

The first step in transforming data into information is to play with its organization. This is one of those simple, yet crucial processes that seems worthless until through it we discover something we have never seen before. We need to realize that the organization of things affects the way we interpret and understand the separate pieces. Take any set of findings: about students in a classroom, a company's financial data, a city's demographics, or the kind and numbers of animals in a zoo. How would you organize them? Which arrangement is best?

Richard Saul Wurman suggests five ways to organize everything, but seven seems clearer to me. Everything (and I mean everything) can be organized in one of these ways: according to the alphabet, location, time, continuum, number, or category. A last way of organizing things can often be randomness—in other words, *no* organization. (If you can think of another way, let me know.)

The point of this understanding is that there are usually better ways to organize data than the traditional ones that first come to mind. Each organization of the same set of data expresses different attributes and messages of the set. It is important to experiment, reflect, and choose which organization best communicates our messages. We also need to keep in mind that while these seven ways of organizing things make it easy to brainstorm new presentations, it is up to us to choose the one that is most appropriate to our audience (i.e., the method of organization that highlights the most important aspects of a presentation).

Alphabets Just about any book has an alphabetical index because, while we may know exactly what we are looking for, we often do not know where it is. Although the alphabet is an arbitrary sequence of symbols, indexes work because we were taught the sequence early and have had it reinforced throughout our lives. It is not universally useful, as you will find if you ever try to use a telephone directory in a language that uses an unfamiliar alphabet. While most indexes are organized alphabetically, very few products are (mostly dictionaries and encyclopedias). This is because few data have any great meaning based on the first letter of their respective labels. In actuality, of course, the alphabet is a continuum (from A to Z), but it is a special one for the reasons stated above.

Locations Locations are natural ways of organizing data whose importance lies in their relations or connection to other data. How easy would it be to find the exits to an airplane if they were listed and described in text with no diagram? Although many projects can benefit from locational organizations, they are seldom used, simply because their designers never experimented with the idea. Producing maps and diagrams is not as easy as simply writing text, but if you have ever used an atlas or an *Access* travel guide, you know how much better a sense of a place you get when things are oriented by their geographical relationships. Consider, for example, a subway map that simply lists all station stops in sequence, compared to one that arranges them in a layout resembling the city they serve. This may sound obvious (and it should be), but then why do car manuals not organize parts by their location on the car or medical books arrange ailments according to their location in the body—the one sure thing we know when we aren't feeling well?

Time Organizing things according to time or sequence may sound obvious for bus and train schedules or for historic timelines, but it can be just as effective for cooking, driving, or building instructions. Time need not be addressed solely in terms of minutes and hours but can also be organized in days, months, years, centuries, processes, or milestones.

Continuums Any qualitative comparison can be describe with a continuum. All ratings systems, whether numbers of stars or numbers of RBIs (runs batted in), imply a value scale. Arranging items in a continuum indicates that this value scale is the most important aspect of the data. Like other organizations of data, a continuum used as the primary organization expresses a particular message and order of importance.

Numbers I categorize number systems as a separate way of arranging things even though numbers, like alphabets, are an arbitrary continuum (usually in base 10, as our species has ten fingers). But unlike alphabets, base-10 numbers are much more universal, because they can be combined in different forms according to their mathematical relationships. It is common, but not necessary, for numerical organizations to be continuums. For example, the Dewey Decimal System used for organizing books in many libraries is a number system that does not represent any magnitude or attribute of the books but simply assigns numbers to categories and subcategories.

Categories   Categories are a common organization, and a reliable one, as they allow similar things to be grouped together according to some important attribute. The specific categories, however, are crucial, as they communicate more easily than other organizations the designer's prejudices and understandings. Like all organizations, categories affect the audience's perception of the information.

Randomness   While random or arbitrary organizations might not seem a useful way to organize things and "add value" to them, they are sometimes the best way if a challenge of some kind is involved. Think about a game in which all the pieces are already arranged or in which the sequence of moves is predetermined and carefully and logically laid out. It wouldn't be very much fun to play. There may be other times when random organizations present a better experience than an orderly one, and it is up to us to explore those possibilities and employ good judgment.

Advanced Organizations

In case these descriptions seem too dry and utilitarian, let me describe an example in which the organization of data can provide an intense emotional reaction. If you are familiar with the Vietnam War Memorial in Washington, D.C., you may know how quietly moving this monument is (figure 11.4). But you may not realize the importance of its organization. The names of all of the U.S. military personnel who died in Vietnam are inscribed on the surfaces of two long, black, granite walls. The walls at the beginning of the monument are short (around twelve inches tall) but they increase in height to more than nine feet at the center where they meet. They are constructed this way for a special reason. The names of the men and women are arranged according to the time of their death, beginning with the first who died during the "police action," mounting as the death

Figure 11.4
Advanced Organizations. The organization of information can effect more than merely legibility and understanding, it can be the basis of powerful, emotional reactions. The Vietnam War memorial in Washington, D.C., is an example of an organization of data that drives form, space, and ultimately, emotions.

toll rose at the height of the war, and trickling down as the United States pulled out of the country. The names thus chart the pattern of the United States's involvement and the personal stories of the people involved and most affected by it. Imagine how different the monument would be without this organization. Suppose the names were listed alphabetically (which was actually proposed when the design was accepted). While it might be easier to find a particular person, the search (like the names themselves) would be reduced to a mechanical process, a granite White Pages. Lost would be the individuality of each name and life. And in a list of seventeen John Smiths, which one is yours?

An alphabetical organization would have completely depersonalized the monument and diminished its emotional power. So would most other organizations. Imagine an organization by categories: pilots listed here, infantry listed there. How about a continuum based on rank or, for that matter, height: the tallest men and women at one end, the shortest at another?

What is key to this emotional experience is that those who died are found among those with whom they died. Without this organization, in fact, there is no longer any meaning to the wall's gradual growth and dwindling height. Any other organization would have created a different memorial entirely, one, most likely, without the power and emotion created by the one built. Yet all of this is somewhat subliminal. When you visit the monument, you aren't much aware of the mechanics of its structure, but it works nonetheless. And this is true of any project, whether it is a sensitive and emotional monument, a powerful, inspiring museum, a useful and concise catalog, or a thrilling and interesting performance.

Multiple Organizations

Almost all organizations are really nested, multiple organizations. Most directories, for example, list people's names by division or location, then by department or title, and then by alphabet. Catalogs may break products into categories first, then arrange them in a continuum based on price (highest cost to lowest perhaps). Be aware that the primary organization is just that and that large groups of things may need secondary or even tertiary suborganizations. Each of these subcategories, of course, needs to be clear and meaningful as well.

It is also useful to include indexes that organize the same items in different ways. This allows people to find things in the ways they are accustomed to or in the ways they learn best. All people learn differently and have varying skills. Some may be comfortable with maps, while others prefer lists. Some may not understand the alphabet, while others can't relate to a continuum. Multiple organizations help everyone find things more easily. In addition, even if people understand the organization, they may not have the correct information. For example, they may know the street they need to go to, but not where to find it on a map (this is where street indexes come in handy). They may know that they want a recipe for a low-calorie dessert but don't want to search through every recipe in the dessert section to find one.

Lastly, it is precisely the ability to see the same set of things in different organizations that allows people to uncover the patterns of relationship among them. If possible, a design should let people rearrange things themselves or provide them with alternative organizations so that they can discover the patterns for themselves.

Metaphors

Much has been made of the ability of metaphors to help people understand things quickly. While a metaphor can be generally helpful, it is a false crutch to cling to. Metaphors (which are usually similes) are not required; nor are they always the best approach. Too many interactive projects, for example, start with the question "What metaphor should the interface use?" Most often, the interface shouldn't use any metaphor at all—at least not as the word is narrowly defined.

Metaphors are simply one way of establishing context (i.e., transforming data into information). It is important that the context implied be the one intended and that it match the desired understandings. Too often, metaphors establish the wrong context and help create inaccurate expectations that cannot be met.

Metaphors are especially useful when they fit well into a user's or reader's experience. But to be used well, they must be abandoned when they begin to fail, or when they are asked to do more than they are capable of. A good example is the desktop metaphor used by many personal computers. The strength of this idea was that it used common objects to indicate relationships by analogy (a trash can for discarding files, files for individual projects, folders for keeping groups of files together, etc.). Fortunately, the designers ignored the metaphor when it broke down (for example, in inventing dialog boxes) and didn't try to take it further than was convenient.

Recently, a colleague of mine suggested that metaphors could be another way of organizing data. She may be correct, and more thought should be devoted to this question. But I generally feel that metaphors are more about representation than about organization or presentation. They seem to me to relate more to the cognitive orientation (i.e., the meaning) than to the structure of a presentation.

Goals and Messages

All effective communication involves defining the goals of the experience being created and the messages to be conveyed as early as possible in the development process. These two objectives drive all decisions—from information design, through interaction design, and including all aspects of sensorial design. Every decision, no matter how simple or mundane, should support the goals and messages. This is a way of ensuring that inappropriate data, techniques, technology, or styles will not be used. At every decision point, the choice should be the solution that best meets the goals and messages decided on at the beginning of the project. While this sounds obvious, too often the ideas that drive the presentation are at odds with the messages presented.

Very often the goals and messages stipulated by a client will not be correct. The client is often too close to the problem to see the solution clearly. To be successful, we need to uncover one or two layers of fundamental goals that underlie the stated goals and agree to present these. Otherwise, we may find ourselves unable to satisfy the client or communicate the correct messages to our audience.

Clarity

The most important goal of effective communication is clarity. Clarity is not, however, the same as simplicity. Often a simple organization is clear if the intended message is brief and limited in scope; but if the message is about a complex relationship, it may necessitate presenting a large amount of data. This complexity can be made clear through effective organization and presentation and need not be reduced to meaningless "bite-sized" chunks of data, as simplifying it usually does. Clarity is best accomplished by focusing on one particular message or goal at a time and not attempting to accomplish too much all at once. Simplicity, on the other hand, is often responsible for the "dumbing down" of information rather than the illumination of it.

Interaction Design

Think for a moment about what experiences are. How do you create them? How do you know when they are successful? What are the most satisfying experiences you can remember? Unfortunately, few people are ever taught how to create wonderful experiences for others. I believe that one of the nicest experiences you can have is to enjoy a stimulating conversation with another person over a great meal. I would rather do that than watch television, read a book, or use any interactive product I have ever seen. But how do you set up and maintain such an experience? We are taught history, science, mathematics, languages, and many valuable processes but hardly anything about having a great conversation, though this can be one of the most satisfying things in life. Why?

While some people seem to have natural abilities for creating wonderful experiences for others (think of the "life of the party," that great instructor, your friends, etc.), most of us must learn the hard way, through trial and error. Wouldn't it be great if we could be explicitly taught how to create meaningful interactions for each other? This is what interaction design addresses. Unfortunately, it is still a new field and has few texts, fewer classes, and almost no curriculum—even less of these than information design. The best sources for learning the skills critical to the success of *any* interactive project or presentation are the performing arts. Indeed, the most successful people now practicing interaction design in new media seem to have a background in some type of performance: dance, theater, singing, storytelling, or improvisation.

Because of the history of interaction in the performing arts, the fields of scriptwriting, storytelling, performance, and instructional design provide some of the only sources of guidance. Each of these disciplines attempts to communicate varied stories and messages through the creation of interesting and wonderful experiences. As we look to these disciplines for knowledge about interactivity, we must also keep in mind the limitations of the technologies and media through which our messages are transmitted.

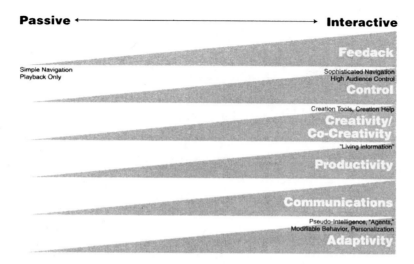

Figure 11.5
Interaction Spectra. There are several aspects to experiences that audiences tend to fell make an experience more "interactive." Some of the most important are these six.

Continuums of Interactivity

One way to consider the meaning of interactivity is to envision all experiences (and products) as inhabiting a continuum of interactivity. On one side are such passive experiences as reading or watching television. While some have held that even these activities involve an interaction between the mind and the device, or the imagination and the story, this argument seems weak and overly philosophical to me. By comparison with experiences like painting, conversing, or producing a television program, these activities offer the audience no choice, control, or incitements to productivity or creativity. The difference that defines interactivity, then, can include the amount of control the audience has over the tools, pacing, or content; the amount of choice this control offers; and the audience's ability to use the tool or content to be productive or creative.

All products and experiences can, therefore, by placed along a continuum (as shown in figure 11.5). It is important to note that there is no good or bad side of this continuum. The only value judgment should be whether the level of interactivity (place on the continuum) is appropriate to the goals of the experience or the messages to be communicated.

Interactivity is different from production values or richness of content. Television programs and films can have incredibly rich stories, technical qualities, and narrative presentations but offer almost no opportunities for interaction (except changing the channel or leaving the theater). Compare this situation with the experience of improvisational comedy, in which the audience is involved by offering suggestions or actually joining the action as the story is created.

Control and Feedback   The first two spectrums of interactivity involve how much control the audience has over the outcome (i.e., the rate, sequence, or type of action), and how much feedback the interface supports. Typically, experiences with high interactivity offer high levels of feedback and at least some control. Examples of these kinds of experiences are games in which the play depends directly on the player's involvement and choices—unlike television, in which the experience plays out whether anyone is there or not.

Productivity and Creative Experiences   Productivity is another spectrum that can coincide with other interactivity spectrums. Creative experiences allow a user/creator/participant to make, or share in making, something. Some experiences can be used more productively than others (as opposed to being merely entertaining), and productivity is traditionally more valued in business products than in entertainment devices. Nonetheless, most people find creating and producing something interesting, entertaining, and fulfilling—even in leisure activities. Tools of creation are therefore extremely important components of the meaningful, compelling, and useful experience. Creative products require users to participate in shaping the experience or manipulating components instead of merely watching and consuming what the product brings forth.

Technologies that are *co-creative* (a term coined by Abbe Don) offer the user or audience assistance in the creation process.[3] People are naturally creative and are almost always more interested in experiences that allow them to create instead of merely participate. While many situations can create anxiety in people not accustomed to performing with the tools or techniques provided, this anxiety can be lessened through careful design or by offering assistance that helps people express their creativity. This could take the form of recommendations, guidelines, advice, or actually performing certain operations for users.

Another attribute of interactive creative experiences is the ability to add new content or tools to the initial set so that a product, toolset, or database becomes a "living," evolving project. As yet, few products are designed to grow or become more valuable over time with the active participation of the audience. Future products that help users structure their experiences and share their knowledge are certain to become more valuable than those that do not.

Adaptive Experiences Adaptive technologies are those in which the behavior of the user/reader/consumer/actor changes the experience. These changes can result from agents, modifying behaviors, and pseudo-intelligences. *Agents* are processes that can be set to run autonomously, performing specific, unsupervised (or lightly supervised) activities and reporting back when finished. *Modifying behaviors* change the tools and/or the content in different ways, depending on the actions and techniques of the user. Some games, for example, do this by becoming more difficult as the player becomes more proficient. Others may modify the content to reflect a user's point of view, level of proficiency, or desire for varying amounts of detail. Both agents and modifying behaviors, as well as other techniques, can make a device or character in an interactive presentation (e.g., game) appear to be intelligent (*pseudo-intelligence*). Of course, this appearance of intelligence alludes to a much larger question about intelligence, life, and how these are defined. Suffice it to say that making certain kinds of choices to change behavior based on the actions of others (whether random, instinctive, or algorithmic) can create the appearance of a sophisticated system or process and imply a kind of independent intelligence.

Communicative Experiences Like other productive and creative experiences, opportunities to meet others, talk with them, and share their personal stories and opinions are always viewed as valuable and interesting. Because these experiences involve two or more people, they also inherently involve high levels of control, feedback, and adaptivity. The telephone is a great example of such a communicative device. So are chat lines, discussion bulletin boards, and cocktail parties. Some of these are so valuable and enjoyable for some people that they become virtually indispensable to their lives.

The Experience Cube

Each of the six attributes described above can be plotted on a diagram (figure 11.6) in order to visualize how typical interfaces and products are related to each other by these attributes. Unfortunately, it is difficult to create a clear six-dimensional diagram; however, we can produce a close approximation by combining the feedback and control attributes into one dimension (height), the creative, productive, and communicative attributes into another (width), and envisioning the adaptive attributes as a third, depth dimension. This gives us an experience cube that gives us some idea of the general relationships among the kind of experiences we can learn from.

One of the first lessons to note is that all life experiences (whether mediated by technology or not) fit into this cube. This is important, because it reminds us that the experiences we create in our designed products are viewed within a much wider context by our audiences. Unfortunately, most producers of interactive media or multimedia don't realize this fact. It must be remembered that a reader/user/consumer has access to many media and, most likely, is not as enamored of the technology of any particular medium as its developer might be. This means

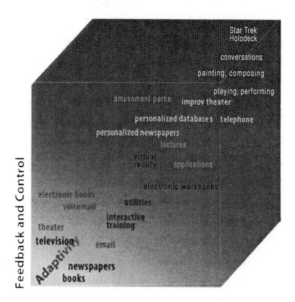

Figure 11.6

The Experience Cube. By combining the six interaction criteria into three axis and arranging in a cube, a clear progression toward more elaborate and interactive experiences emerges.

that the competition for interactive media products is as big as all of human experience. In other words, your competitors for that CD-ROM on tropical fish are not only other tropical fish CD-ROMs, or even laser discs, but also television documentaries, narrative and reference books, aquariums, scuba diving, travel, and so forth. If the experience you create is not a compelling one (whether justified by the bounds of the technology or not), you will never find a large audience.

This is probably why we have seen only a few categories of successful interactive media products: children's books and lessons, games, reference works, and pornography. Both games and reference works use interactive media appropriately and create experiences that cannot be duplicated easily in other media. While some children's books and products do this too, even those that don't have been successful, probably because the market (parents) can justify any expenditure—on both the products and the systems to run them on—that contributes to their children's education.

Curiously enough, even though current pornography uses interactive technologies particularly poorly, the market thrives. There seems to be an overlap between sexual curiosity and technology.

So, we come back to the question: How do we as designers create meaningful experiences and interactions for others? As noted above, we must first revisit our goals and messages and re-evaluate the kinds of experiences we want our audience to have. We must also ask them what they need and want from these experiences. This inquiry is what market research is supposed to be about. It is not user testing (which needs to be done later once some possibilities have been developed), but it is nonetheless a crucial step. The process of development must involve brainstorming various alternatives for meeting these goals, messages, and audience interests and abilities (in whole or in part) until possible solutions emerge. We must then give shape to the solutions with the tools of sensorial design and test them before we approve them or label them successful.

Sensorial Design

Sensorial design is simply an all-encompassing category comprised of the many disciplines involved with the creation and presentation of media experiences (figure 11.7). These include writing (text); graphic design, iconography, map making, calligraphy, typography, illustration, and color theory (graphics); photography, animation, and cinematography (images); and sound design, singing, and music (sound). We should probably also include perfumery and cooking in this category, as these involve the purposeful stimulation of the senses—even if the senses of smell and taste are not very widely utilized as entertainment media. Each of these disciplines have deep traditions and detailed procedures. It is not pertinent to focus on them individually at this point; but while they are different in many ways, they all share some common attributes and concerns. The latter include the appropriate use of media, style, and technique; concern with media literacy and bandwidth application to a particular technology; and an understanding of the human senses.

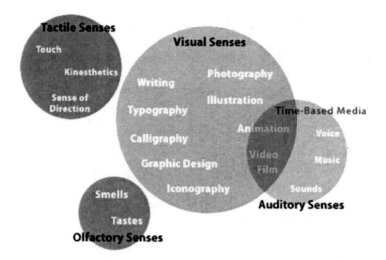

Figure 11.7
Sensorial Media. All "presentation" media stimulate the senses in some way. While visual, auditory, and written media are the most common for computer interfaces, they are not the only important media available.

Media Differences

Each medium has different strengths and weaknesses. Each excels in different capabilities and different types of communication. These are intricately related to the way we perceive the world through our senses (figure 11.8). Think for a moment about our senses and how we as designers use sight, hearing, touch, taste, and smell. To do so more effectively, we need to develop a better understanding of our senses, how they operate, how they relate to each other, and how to create for them.[4] Gaining this understanding will be but the first step toward learning to imagine more compelling experiences.

Style and Meaning

Using the media appropriately is not always easy. Many times, one person or group involved in a project demands that a particular component be

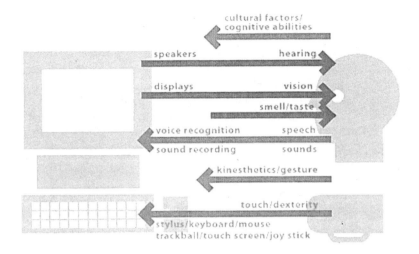

Figure 11.8
Media Differences. Each medium has its own strengths and weakness regarding interfaces between people and machines. These must be chosen wisely to be used effectively.

used when another would be better. The same is true of style, which conveys meaning, whether implied, accidental, or deliberate. Choosing the appropriate attributes and implementing them consistently is essential to development of a cohesive audience experience. On large projects, this cohesion can easily get lost as many people implement various parts according to their own standards and preferences. There are few details that do not affect the presentation, legibility, and understanding of a message. Even a detail like whether to set text flush left, flush right, centered, or justified on both margins changes the legibility and perception of the paragraph, and, therefore, affects the text itself. All sensorial details must be coordinated, not only with each other but also with the goals and messages of the project. The better integrated and careful the synthesis of these design processes is, the more compelling, engaging, and appropriate the experience will be and, consequently, the more successful the interactive communication will be.

Conclusion?

Designing an interface for any audience experience, whether technological, physical, or conceptual, begins with the creation of meaning and the development of an appropriate type of interactivity. These decisions influence further decisions about the type and style of sensorial media needed to present the experience to the audience in an appropriate and supportive way. Addressing one factor in the equation while ignoring the others can lead to an incomplete or unbalanced experience. In many cases, simply understanding the concepts of interactive information design can lead to development of better experiences. More often, it is necessary to address explicitly ways of integrating these concepts into the components of the final design.

This is really not a conclusion as much as it is a beginning. There is still much for all of us to learn and share about these issues. Both information design and interaction design are extremely new disciplines and will grow and improve as we experiment and create. The concepts formulated so far, however, represent the beginning of a better understanding of communication and will serve us well over the next phase of our development.

Notes

1. Richard Saul Wurman is one of the most renowned information architects. His *Information Anxiety* (1989) is one of the few instructional sources available on information design. His issue of *Design Quarterly, Hats* (1989) also provides a condensed version of his most important understandings.

2. Brenda Laurel, one of the ablest interface designers in the industry, is a major proponent of the design of experiences. Her edited anthology, *The Art of Human-Computer Interface Design* (1990) is a great place to start, and her *Computers as Theatre* (1991) is a good place to continue.

3. Abbe Don, another talented interface designer, specializes in interfaces for personal narratives. Her address is Abbe Don Interactive, 618 Sanchez, San Francisco, CA 94114.

4. Diane Ackerman's book, *A Natural History of the Senses* (1990), offers an inspiring discussion of our sensorial experiences.

References

Ackerman, Diane. 1990. *A Natural History of the Senses*. New York: Random House.

Laurel, Brenda, ed. 1990. *The Art of Human-Computer Interface Design*. Reading, Mass.: Addison-Wesley.

Laurel, Brenda, ed. 1991. Computers as Theatre. Reading, Mass.: Addison-Wesley.

Wurman, Richard Saul. 1989. *Information Anxiety*. New York: Doubleday.

Wurman, Richard Saul. 1989. *Hats*, a special issue of *Design Quarterly*, no. 145.

12   *Interactivity and Meaning*

Sheryl Macy, Elizabeth Anderson, and John Krygier

Meaning is a community of understanding. The transfer of meaning is the basic purpose of language, and the association between language and meaning is indissoluble.
—Mario Pei

All human communications are an attempt to transfer meaning. Written and spoken languages traffic in semantic content. Music and art expand the concept of meaning to include emotional, visual, or aural experiences one person wishes to share with another. Interactive programming, a new communication medium combining language, images, and sound, creates a new dimension of information manipulation. If its developers thoroughly understand the new environment's demands and possibilities, interactive communication will enhance the process of exchanging meaning still further.

Why Is the Communication of Meaning So Difficult?

Whatever the method of communications used, humans have always found the transfer of precise meaning problematic. Language is fundamentally error-prone, because our immensely complex human thought processes make the symbolic representation of any single idea a daunting task.

Human brains are a matrix of neurological, cultural, environmental, and experiential memories, the product of each individual's cumulative personal observations. Every message, because it is derived from many experiences in the sender's past, requires the receiver to draw on a similarly broad range of information in order to understand it clearly. Concepts are not self-contained, free-standing crystals of meaning but are integrated into a much larger context. Imagine, for example, the different images of the symbol *tree* that might be constructed by English-speakers from southern India, northern California, or a colony on Mars. Similarly, a current (1998) Internet compilation states that there may be ten or more words for ice and snow in the Labradoran Inuit language and as many as forty-nine words for snow and ice in the language of western Greenland. Linguists have noticed that geographic locations afflicted by wind, rain, or other harsh weather elements generally weigh in with high word counts to describe the relative degrees of these phenomena.

Given the vast and varied supporting data that surround the symbols we use to communicate ideas, it is amazing that humans are able to communicate at all. In moments of frustration, most of us have felt certain that no two people on earth understand anything in exactly the same way and that our belief in human communication is no more than a comfortable delusion.

Fortunately, perfect communication of meaning is seldom necessary; imperfect or incomplete transmission is often enough to achieve the desired result. When one person must quickly communicate to another the message, "Run, that tree is falling," the subtleties of the tree's structure, shape, or emotional associations are irrelevant. It's enough to know that the tree is large, dangerous, and moving rapidly downward. We can define human language as a set of agreed-upon conventions that make such rapid exchanges of information possible in spite of our differences.

The pioneering linguist Leonard Bloomfield observed, "Each person must necessarily refer language symbols to his or her own experience, and no two of us have the same background of experience. Even where the term represents approximately the same concept in two different minds, the reaction may be altogether different. Meaning, like its carrier, language, is subject to human variability and human differences ... but areas of general agreement permit the business of semantic transfer to go on and function" (1933: 92).

Aristotle was the first to understand language as an arbitrary convention —a social contract that assigns a name to an object or an action on the basis of broad social agreement. This understanding has become an accepted foundation of modern linguistics, although subject to many academic subtleties.

Nineteenth-century neolinguists like Benedetto Croce held that language is sound whose purpose is self-expression rather than communication; he believed that it is the individual's creative urge that is the ultimate arbiter of change and innovation in language. In Ferdinand de Saussure's early-twentieth-century view, language is a sociological phenomenon shaped by its speakers and their psychological processes; this explanation was a natural precursor to the Marxist school of linguistics that stresses language as a class phenomenon. But virtually all modern students of communications would agree with Mario Pei that "The purpose of language is absolute. It is the transfer of meaning from one human mind to another. If the form of communication used fails in this one respect, no true language can be said to exist ... if there is no semantic transfer from one mind to another, speech resolves itself into a series of noises ... incapable of being referred to the thought centers for interpretation" (1962: 109).

Expanding the Richness of Our Communications Environment

Not content with the scientifically measurable details of a tree's height, diameter, and color, human observers wish to communicate their observations in considerably more depth and detail. Is it a dead and barren hulk buffeted by the harsh winds of January? Or is it a stately, ancient oak spreading protective arms over a family picnic on a warm summer's evening? What emotional response does the tree evoke in the observer? Do its leaves whisper in a voice that speaks of other days? These things matter, as the tellers of tales and the painters of pictures have long realized as they searched constantly for more effective ways to communicate subtle shades of meaning.

We could reasonably argue that each increase in the complexity of our communications vehicles—the moves from pictographic languages to abstract alphabets or from cave painting to digital image manipulation— has been motivated by a desire to improve the range and richness of meaning we can share. Incomplete communication of meaning may be adequate for everyday life, but humans appear driven to find more complete expressions of their experiences.

The introduction of each innovation in communications has brought new potential for realizing this aspiration. Advances in the subtlety and complexity of language have been followed by technologies that, in turn, vastly extended the reach of human minds. New capabilities, however, may also introduce new limitations. For example, face-to-face human speech provides speakers with an opportunity to express themselves visually as well as verbally, by using facial expressions, body language, and tone of voice to enhance the richness of the semantic content. Books and telegraph wires extend the physical distance across which a person may express semantic content but eliminate visual and aural information that may be integral to meaning. The telephone preserves changes in the tone of voice but disembodies the speaker and precludes the exchange of visual information. Even two-way video communication, which reintroduces the visual element across long distances, is unable to convey the subtle and undefinable meanings sometimes discernible by such sophisticated human senses as taste, smell, or tactility.

The Potential of Interactivity

Interactive programs running on personal computers provide a singular combination of new tools to enhance the communication of meaning. They can present visual, verbal, and aural information and have the added advantage of giving users access to huge databases of supporting information. Nonetheless, they too have their limitations. They still lack the true interactivity of two independent intelligences exchanging ideas. Because they cannot yet replicate direct human-to-human interactions, we must classify interactive programs with books and cave paintings. It is possible, however, that algorithms sophisticated enough to endow computer programs with some level of "intelligence" will be developed in the future. Rather than permitting them to simply parrot the content installed by their human authors, programs will be able to combine new input with existing data, reach independent conclusions, and create original ideas—making them truly interactive.

Even today's (early) versions of interactive programming greatly enhance the possibilities for human communication. By adding more powerful tools for writers, artists, and musicians, computers have increased the potential for sharing meaning. By offering users access to a superset of information and a richer context for an author's message, interactive programs improve readers' ability to understand the intended meaning. And, if the authors of interactive programs are willing to make information easily available, these programs can give users the freedom to explore a world of new ideas.

Access to such a wealth of information, therefore, is affected by at least two gating factors: the thoroughness of authors' identification and inclusion of relevant information; and, even more important, their willingness to share control of the ultimate result.

Sharing the Control of Meaning

If we define the spoken communication of meaning as a process that includes the situation in which the speaker utters a sound, the sound itself, and the hearer's response,

Speaker's situation $\rightarrow$ Speech $\rightarrow$ Hearer's response

then a similar exchange between an interactive program and its user should also include these elements—plus the numerous other possibilities

for simultaneous communication of the message presented by the interactive medium.

Author's intention   →

    → Visual message   → User's response

    → Verbal message   → User's response

    → Musical message   → User's response

    → Symbolic message   → User's response

    → Aural message   → User's response

The introduction of this expanded potentiality can place an increasing
responsibility for reaching decisions about the program's meaning on the
shoulders of users. Each added level of informational richness may explain
the author's context more fully, or it may increase the possibility that
users will reach a conclusion about the program's meaning that is entirely
different from what the author intended. Early in the design process,
therefore, authors of interactive programs must make decisions about the
level of control they wish to maintain over their program.

Highly structured interactive environments allow the author to maintain rigid control over meaning by allowing the least flexibility and the
smallest potential for user-supplied meaning. Although this type of programming can take advantage of some of the richness of the interactive
medium—primarily through the use of full-motion video or sound to sup-
plement written material—it restricts its full potential. This approach may
be essential, however, when an author needs to communicate a sequence
of narrowly defined, tightly controlled ideas with little or no input from
the user. However, a linear presentation that allows the user to do nothing
more than turn the page is actually less interactive than a printed book,
which at least lets the reader skip to the end to find out "who done it." As
in all things, unwillingness to relinquish control can result in limited
gains.

For creators willing to share the creative process, and for authors wishing
to communicate abstract concepts that require user participation to define
their meaning, interactive programs offer broader horizons. The potential

for user freedom in interacting with the information provided is almost unlimited. The heightened freedom may mean loss of author control; or it may increase the likelihood of users getting lost in the program's complex interior structure; but it also allows users to take full advantage of all the available data.

Instead of marching through a linear series of data chunks and reaching an inevitable conclusion, individual users can choose where, when, and how they approach the information. At its best, the data supplied can be a model of the larger matrix of information and experience that surrounded the idea in its author's mind. And in the same way that we explore our own past experiences for information to make sense of a new event, users of an interactive program can explore its informational structure in search of the supporting data needed to understand it.

Interactive computer programs have the potential to convey meaning more accurately than any other communications medium yet devised. They offer a richness and range of data that mimics, on a small scale, the matrix of information that surrounds our own ideas. When we attempt to communicate meaning by using such a program, we are no longer forced to launch our thoughts into the unknown, alone and unsupported. Instead, we can find the ideas we seek to understand surrounded by familiar sights, sounds, and friends and supported by a wealth of data that validates and confirms their meaning.

References

Bloomfield, Leonard. 1933. *Language*, 2nd ed. New York: Holt, Rinehart and Winston.

Pei, Mario. 1962. *Voices of Man: The Meaning and Function of Language.* New York: Harper & Row.

13 Structural Ambiguity: An Emerging Interactive Aesthetic

Jim Gasperini

In recent decades various literary and dramatic artists have experimented with ways to make the role of the audience more active. Although computer technology now makes it possible to develop a true interactive aesthetic, grafting interactivity onto earlier forms of narrative is like making a movie with a fixed camera: it fails to take advantage of the essential power of the medium.

Interactivity in Literature and the Theater

The first interactive work I remember hearing about was a French novel of the 1950s. It originally came in a box, printed one chapter per page, with instructions to shuffle the chapters and read them in any order. Intrigued by the concept, I hunted down a copy at my college library, only to find the pages firmly bound together like every other book, a victim of the indiscriminate efficiency of a library binding service.

Since then we have seen such partially interactive works as Julio Cortazar's *Hopscotch* (1966), a novel with a number of "optional" chapters that readers can read or skip at their own discretion, and, more recently, Milorad Pavic's "lexicon novel," *The Dictionary of the Khazars* (1988), whose many short chapters may be read in a variety of sequences. Numerous reader-active books, the first and best known of which is

Edward Packard's *Superbike* (1995) in the Choose Your Own Adventure series, allow children to choose from among several different plot lines at the end of each chapter.

In the theater, this century has seen numerous attempts to alter the aesthetic distance between audience and performer. As part of a play within a play in his *Six Characters in Search of an Author* (1922), Luigi Pirandello placed a simulated audience within the real audience to reinforce the emotional link between audience and actors. In his theory of epic theater, Bertolt Brecht continually fought the notion that people in the audience were simply observers of an aesthetic object. He searched for ways to break down the veil of illusion, make the experience of theater instructive as well as entertaining, and stir the audience to action in the here-and-now. Toward the end of his life, asked whether the theater was still an adequate means of representing the modern world, Brecht replied yes, the world can be represented on the stage, but only if it is portrayed as *veranderbar* (changeable).

Playwrights and directors continue to experiment with ways of altering the distance between actors and audience. In the theatrical version of *The Mystery of Edwin Drood* the audience is offered the opportunity to select one of a number of endings (a device Brecht used several decades earlier). The Living Theater, among others, continues the Brechtian antitradition into our times. At performances of several recent plays (*Tamara*, *Tony'n Tina's Wedding*), the audience mingles with the actors, choosing what aspect of the story they want to observe at what time.

Limitations

Interactivity in book form suffers from a severe technological limitation: the page does not change. Readers' decisions can have very little impact on the way the story unfolds. Varying the order in which a story's chapters are printed may affect readers' perceptions of individual chapters; but as reading a particular chapter has no effect on how later chapters read, the author's ability to build contrasting chains of choice and consequence is very limited.

Interactivity in the theater suffers from different practical limitations. The choice of endings in *Edmund Drood*, coming at the very end of the play, is more of a gimmick than a true effort to involve the audience in the writing process. While the audience walking around the set of *Tamara* undoubtedly experiences the characters' world differently than it would in a conventional play, the essential plot structure is unaffected by anything audience members do. Though these works allow an unusual degree of audience participation, they are not truly interactive.

Actors' improvisational workshops, of course, call for a high degree of interactivity. So, in a more limited way, do the skits of certain comedians and the performances of improvisational troupes. Giving the audience control over the plot development of a full-length commercial production, however, would mean advance preparation for a dauntingly broad range of possible audience suggestions. The enormous expense involved—not to mention the extraordinary demands such a production would make on the actors—ensures that the theater will remains dominated by linear plot lines and audiences that quietly watch the spectacle unfold.

Performance in a Computer-generated World

Enter the computer. Computer technology allows us to create elaborate simulated worlds within which players have considerable freedom of action. They are given the general outlines of a character and told to improvise their reactions to a simulated environment, simulated props, and other (sometimes simulated) characters. Although a computer-generated interactive simulation is a performance medium, it differs from other performance media in that the audience is also the protagonist. An interactive work, by definition, first presents a player with some sort of choice, then with the consequences of that choice. It therefore takes place over time and allows for construction of a plot, which gives it at least some kinship with other forms of narrative. Like drama, the interactive work may also provide encounters with simulated characters, although, as we will see later, "characters" may take unusual forms.

While analogies to the theater and to literature are useful, they are inexact. By erasing the distinction between audience and performer, stories told using computer technology have made a radical break with both traditions of storytelling. But what is it about these technologically sophisticated role-playing exercises that make them more like short stories than, say, like a game of charades? One answer may be found by taking a close look at one of the key techniques of narrative: ambiguity.

Structural Ambiguity

The depth of a narrative work's ambiguity is a good measure of its quality. The richer the work, the more it resonates with ambiguous meanings. In any work, we can distinguish three different levels of ambiguity: two familiar levels and one that is quite new.

The first level, *textual ambiguity*, appears in texts presented on a printed page or on a screen. A *metaphor*, a word or phrase with a surface meaning that also points to something else, is this sort of ambiguity; it means at least two things at once. The celebrated definitions in William Empson's *Seven Types of Ambiguity* are all variants on textual ambiguity. According to Empson, ambiguity is "any verbal nuance, however slight, which gives room to alternative reactions to the same piece of language" (1947: 1). In some forms of writing (e.g., technical writing, journalism) the opposite of *ambiguous* is *precise*. In creative writing the opposite of *ambiguous* is *dull*.

Another level of ambiguity, *interpretive ambiguity*, comes into play when words appear as part of a theatrical performance. The same role may be interpreted in radically different ways. One actor may portray Hamlet as an indecisive introvert, another as an impotently raging victim of Oedipal conflict, and a third as a suicidal misanthrope. The contributions of the director, set designer, and others also influence the way the audience understand the work. One way to distinguish a great play from a merely good one is by the degree to which it lends itself to different interpretations, so that actors and audience alike will wish to experience the play again in a different guise.

A truly interactive work offers a third level of ambiguity, *structural ambiguity*, which arises from the role the audience plays in creating the plot. Rather than building a nuanced experience from the meanings of words and phrases, or from a dramatic interpretation, structural ambiguity constructs meaning from alternative possibilities of choice and consequence as they are played out over time.

There are two types of this structural ambiguity: closed-ended and open-ended. In the former, certain "apparent" ambiguities are first raised in the player's mind and then resolved. The work becomes less and less ambiguous as play progresses. In the latter, ambiguity deepens as the work unfolds. The open-ended type of ambiguity has the greatest potential for creating richness of meaning. However, as closed-ended ambiguity is used in most current computer game narratives, we will discuss it first.

Closed-ended Structural Ambiguity

Typical "twitch" games, including most Nintendo and arcade-style computer games, depend principally on learning to perform a hand-to-eye coordination task. The game presents players with a series of obstacles, sometimes stringing them together into a simple story and sometimes not bothering with plot at all. The player learns when to zig, when to zag, where to put the falling trapezoid, how to kill the bats, how to deal with endlessly sprouting mushrooms. It's stretching a point to call this process a resolution of ambiguity, so let me quickly pass on to firmer ground.

A better example of closed-ended ambiguity may be seen in the type of game known as *adventure* or *interactive fiction*, stories that proceed according to what I call a *resistant plot*. The player takes on a role within an imaginary world filled with apparent ambiguities that he or she must resolve. By overcoming obstacles or solving puzzles—for example, discovering the hidden usefulness of simulated objects or learning how to change the behavior of a character—the player advances the plot. Since the original *Adventure* was invented by a pair of computer scientists named

Crowther and Woods in the mid–1970s, the genre has seen considerable refinement in graphical imagery and application to varied subject matter.

One problem with resistant-plot stories is that they demand a great leap of faith. The player must spend a considerable amount of time struggling to make something happen without being sure that the end result will be interesting. Many people are understandably reluctant to spend a good chunk of their lives beating their heads against imaginary walls. As a former writer and player of interactive fiction, my own current feeling about this kind of computer game is best summed up by a line from Voltaire: "Life is too short to learn German."

Even in the best interactive fiction, once all the puzzles have been solved the plot is revealed in all its naked linearity. A finished closed-ended work is like a punctured balloon, empty of all ambiguity. There is little reason for anyone to go through it again.

Open-ended Structural Ambiguity

By contrast, an open-ended work becomes more ambiguous, not less so, the more it is played. It is through repeated experiences, comparing the different plots chosen through the same web of potential plots, that a work becomes most meaningful. This can be most clearly seen in the genre known as *simulations*. Here, again, we must distinguish between different uses of a term.

Classic computer simulations are designed as serious analytical tools, or as a means for training people in specific tasks. Setting up a model of a real-world system (e.g., a power plant, an airport control tower, an all-terrain vehicle) allows players and designers to examine the workings of that system. They can test modifications on the model before putting them into actual practice, identify potential problems, or learn their jobs in an environment where mistakes cause no real damage.

Narrative simulations, however, are designed with more broadly didactic and expressive goals in mind. By playing a role within a simulated system, players can explore the system the author has modeled and experience the underlying conflicts, powers, and constraints that are peculiar to that role in the real world. Two examples of this type of simulation are *Sim City* by Will Wright and Maxis Software and my own *Hidden Agenda*, written with TRANS Fiction Systems.

Sim City puts the player in control of a landscape, which begins as a bucolic stretch of riverbank seen from the air. As you create residential areas, roads, power plants, and industrial districts, the city quickly comes alive. Little houses start to appear once people (the *sims*) move in. Soon the sims may be seen going back and forth to work in cars and commuter trains. Opinion polls tell you how they feel about your skill at managing their city. They complain about taxes, demand that you spend more on police and fire protection, and plead for emergency aid in the aftermath of floods and earthquakes.

Hidden Agenda also puts the player in a position of power, this time as the president of a fictitious Central American country (figure 13.1). The action takes place as encounters with various characters, who are represented by photographic images and bits of dialogue about policy choices you must make. These characters—representing political parties, Army factions, social groups, professions, economic classes, other nations, and international agencies—all try to convince you to follow their policy agendas (figure 13.2). If they grow impatient or disillusioned with your leadership, they may take action on their own.

These two games present the world very differently—one through a graphical representation of a growing metropolis, the other through words and background graphics that express the changing positions taken by various characters (figure 13.3). They are alike, however, in inducing players to feel increasingly responsible and ambiguous about the effect they can have on a virtual culture. Players inevitably measure each city they build in *Sim City* against the variant cities they might have built had they made other choices. The city itself—"your" city, which you may name for yourself if you so desire—becomes a kind of character for whose growth, problems, and personality you feel directly responsible. Since you can save and copy the city at any point, you can build two or more

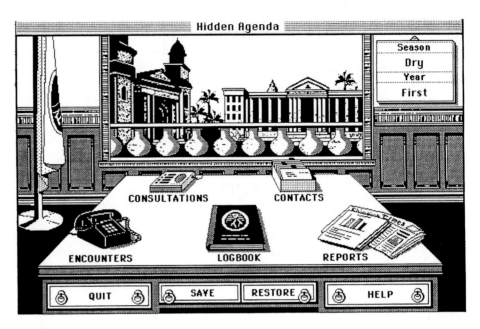

Figure 13.1
Hidden Agenda, An Interactive Game of Political Choices.

variants on the same city and observe the effects of even minor modifications of policy.

In *Hidden Agenda* the player's choices incrementally construct one plot out of an extremely varied number of potential plots. For example, midway through the game, El Presidente can decide to hold elections; depending on other choices made along the way, various things happen during the election season. Sometimes events play out as they did in El Salvador's 1982 and 1984 elections: with terrific violence, assassination of leftist candidates, strong right-wing army control of the process, and proclamations by the United States that the results are a triumph for democracy (figure 13.4). Sometimes they play out more as they did in the 1984 Nicaraguan elections: with minimal violence, withdrawal of rightist candidates, strong left-wing army control of the process, and U.S. officials denouncing the results as fraudulent.

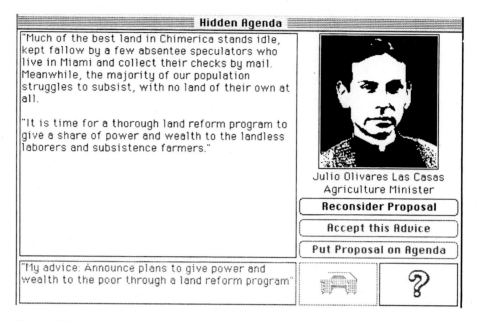

Figure 13.2
The Agriculture Minister, A Character in *Hidden Agenda*.

As the author, I am of course making several ironic points in this example, points that the interactive structure amplifies and sets in context. Each time a player completes the election campaign, he or she naturally compares what happened this time and what happened during earlier elections. These comparisons serve to deepen the player's awareness of the range of available structural possibilities.

In both simulations, it is up to you to decide whether you have "won" or "lost." *Sim City's* extremely open-ended format lets you follow the progress of your city through the centuries, whereas in *Hidden Agenda* your term as president is limited to three years (if you are not overthrown in a coup or voted out of power). Regardless of how your term of office ends, the simulation concludes with an encyclopedia entry supposedly written far in the future. This "Verdict of History" details what you tried to do and describes the results, but it is up to you to interpret this verdict and eval-

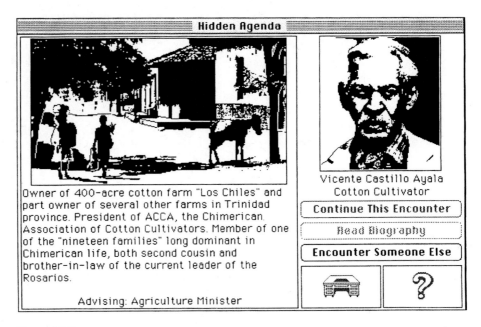

Figure 13.3
A Prominent Chimerican Land Owner, A Character in *Hidden Agenda*.

uate your successes and failures according to your own set of priorities (figure 13.4).

Authored Interactivity or Game?

The author of a novel or play, of course, does more than string together sequences of ambiguities. The ambiguous elements must have at least a surface coherence and be informed by some encompassing vision. Can the designers of simulation games do something similar? Can we describe these works as "authored"?

I believe we can. Though most simulation games offer schematic renderings of the essential processes of real-world systems, exactly which processes are incorporated into the model and exactly how they play out is a matter of artistic choice that reflects the author's own understanding and

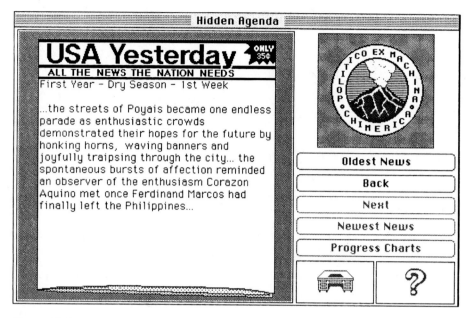

Figure 13.4
A News Report Screen from *Hidden Agenda*.

passions. The schematization allows players to participate in and understand within a short time processes that in the real world take place over years, decades, or centuries. It also allows the designer to impose his or her personality on the work as a whole. Although designers may honestly attempt to model reality accurately and present controversial issues in a balanced light, they inevitably construct works that at bottom represent their own vision of the world.

A term already exists, of course, for imaginative exercises that ask a player to actively perform a role: it is *game*. But this word covers so many different activities, from charades to baseball to Monopoly, that using it in this context tends to trivialize interactive programs. To many people the word *game* suggests something entertaining but not serious—and certainly not artistic. (Of course you could consider baseball, say, as a form of dance with a set, familiar choreography on the theme of conflict, and a certain range of interpretive freedom for individual performers. I suspect, however, that few ballplayers would define themselves as movement artists.)

The assumption seems to be that since a game requires the player to take some sort of action, it is inherently less dense with meaning than forms directed toward a relatively passive audience. This assumption arises, quite naturally, from our long familiarity with many types of games. From earliest childhood we use games to amuse and instruct ourselves, starting with the simplest and moving on to those of increasing complexity.

Whatever the main point of interest—which players win or lose, how well they play the game, how much fun they have along the way, or how much money they make—most games are simple sets of procedures for taming and managing conflict and can be repeated over and over again. Most interactive game designers have ceded so much control over outcomes that players can have very little sense of participating in someone else's artistic vision.

Yet here I am, arguing that new technologies allow such exceptional authorial control over an interactive experience that a "game" may be designed with enough precision and depth to be considered a form of narrative art. How can that be?

Wanted: Term for a New Category

Part of the difficulty is semantic. Once we find a name for this distinctive category of experience, it will be easier to evaluate it on its own merits, instead of endlessly distinguishing it from other things. Unfortunately, all the words we use to describe authored interactive works—*game, simulation, interactive fiction, multimedia presentation*—are too broad; they point (ambiguously!) in too many directions at once.

Take *simulation*, for example. If defined very broadly, a simulation of human behavior presented by actors on a stage is called a *drama*, a *play*, a *theatrical experience*, the *stage*, or *histrionics*. A simulation of human behavior we experience by reading words in a book or a periodical is a *narrative*, *literature*, a *novel*, a *short story*, or *fiction*. A simulation of human behavior experienced by watching patterns of flashing lights on a screen is called a *cinematic presentation*, a *motion picture*, a *movie*, a *television show*, or a *video*. Similarly, a simulation of human behavior experienced by interacting with computer technology is called ... *What?* We sorely need a new term or two. Interactive works are not subgenres of drama, fiction, or cinema— they are a fourth thing entirely.

Strengths of the Medium

Every medium has its own peculiar strengths. Because simulating human behavior interactively is so new, there are vast numbers of subjects that have not yet been addressed. It is already clear, however, that one of the medium's great strengths is its ability to show us the world from another person's perspective. What does the world look like to a Latin American? What powers come with the role of leader of a small country? What are its limitations and constraints? There are interactive works that enable a player to experience a day in the life of an Israeli, a typical Australian neighborhood barbecue, and the life of a French gentleman during the Enlightenment.

So far, most of these works have been designed for instructional purposes, offering players insights into sociology, language, and history. As time goes on, we may use the interactive medium to help players develop more personal insights. A game might explore, for example, what it is like to be a woman on the edge of madness or a man in the midst of a midlife crisis. Another might simply examine "what it is like to be me." There will undoubtedly be propagandistic uses, with interactive Leni Riefenstahl's creating strongly biased simulated worlds. Some interactive artists may decide to use the new medium to look at subject matter traditionally associated with narrative art. On the other hand, the interactive medium may be able to deal with some aspects of human experience better than traditional forms can. Questions of economic theory and political philosophy, for example, can be more easily woven into the narrative structure in a medium that casts the audience in the role of protagonist.

Novels, plays, and films about men and women in public life usually focus on the tension between the public and the private person. They do so in part because these forms (at least as they are conventionally used) work by inducing the audience to identify with and care about the principal characters. Because the audience of an interactive work no longer sits to one side judging the way the protagonist meets various challenges, authors can use the player's sense of direct responsibility for the character's actions to build emotional resonance.

That a work is built with structural ambiguity does not preclude the use of other levels of ambiguity as well. I believe we will soon see an increasingly poetic use of textual ambiguity in interactive works and will recognize that interpretive ambiguity is a natural consequence of collaboration between author and player. The effects of this collaboration may already be seen in the tendency of complex simulated systems to behave in ways their designers did not explicitly plan—a phenomenon known as *emergent behavior*. For example, in some enactments of Sim City mature slums begin to appear as the result of the choices made by some players.

Simulation games have the potential to accomplish some of the purposes Brecht sought to achieve in his experimental theatrical forms. The interactive medium can inform while entertaining, make the audience an active and aware participant, and illuminate the political and cultural context within which audience and performance exist. In some games, interactive players can choose to examine information in many different formats (for example by viewing charts or newspaper reports), which is arguably analogous to Brecht's technique of underlining the significance of events by placing placards inscribed with statistics on stage.

Not all of Brecht's theatrical innovations were designed to break down aesthetic distance. In fact, he fought against the idea that theatergoers should lose themselves in the characters on the stage. By contrast, the appeal of many computer games is precisely that they induce players to lose themselves in a character—or, worse, in a sequence of pointless aggressive actions. What Brecht would have thought of the interactive medium is idle speculation. I suspect, however, that he would have hated most current computer games.

Interacting with the Future

Although I firmly believe that computer games can be serious works of art, I do not argue that the works produced so far do much more than hint at that possibility. Serious art not only evokes emotion, it also embodies its creator's own authentic emotions. Just how deeply the interactive medium will probe into the human psyche and the human condition remains to be seen. Are we witnessing the birth of a new art form, one that holds out the promise of expressing the tenor of our times? Or will interactivity develop into a new kind of hype, a way to sell us the illusion of control while packaging a safely neutered rebellion against the enforced passivity of so much of our current culture? It may well be both.

Most members of the audience remain unprepared to look beyond the immediate gratification of closed-ended games devoted to trivial themes. As the generations growing up with interactive entertainment mature, however, the medium will mature along with them.

Moreover, the medium is very new, and still cumbersome to work with. Designers face a constant struggle simply to keep the logical nature of our primary tools from dominating our thought processes. After all, computers really only know how to count to one; everything else is illusion. The challenge is to build works that aspire to some artistic purpose in a context set by the binary thinking of computer programs—to somehow use logical computers to recreate human fuzziness.

Perhaps it is inevitable that this new form of narrative arose in the age of quantum mechanics. Physicists tell us that what we take to be solid matter is only a reflection of our limited perceptions; that time may be bidirectional; that things can be simultaneously true and untrue; and that it is entirely possible to create and destroy alternative universes. Maybe the way the interactive medium plays with ambiguities in the structure of experience mirrors the way we have come to view our universe. Perhaps our cultural imagination is only following, in crude and timid fashion, our innate sense of the ambiguity of existence as it molds the structure of our dreams.

References

Cortazar, Julio. 1966. *Hopscotch*. New York: Pantheon.

Empson, William. 1947. *Seven Types of Ambiguity*, 2nd ed. New York: New Directions.

Packard, Edward. 1995. *Superbike*. Milwaukee: Gareth Stevens.

Pavic, Milorad. 1988. *The Dictionary of the Khazars: A Lexicon Novel in 100,000 Words*. New York: Knopf.

Pirandello, Luigi. 1922. *Six Characters in Search of an Author*. In *Three Plays by Luigi Pirandello*. New York: Dutton.

14 *Sculpting in Zeroes and Ones*

Steve Holtzman

Sculptors are taught to respect the material they work with. If the material is clay, the sculpture should look like clay. If it is stone, the sculpture should have the weightiness of stone. If it is steel, it should reflect the strength of steel. Sculptors also learn to take into consideration how light, heat, cold, and the environment interact with their material, knowledge that helps them unleash its expressive potential. The sculptor Henry Moore believed that "Every material has its own individual qualities. It is only when the sculptor works direct, when there is an active relationship with his material, that the material can take its part in the shaping of an idea" (quoted in Burnham: 95).

The grandeur of Michelangelo's sculptures reflect the color and scale of his massive blocks of marble. Rodin's sculptures emerge from slabs of rough unpolished stone to harness the raw power of their weight and immobility. Present-day sculptors such as Richard Serra slice through open space with massive sheets of steel whose surfaces—when exposed to the air—are thickly coated with layers of red-brown rust.

The information designers of the future will also need to consider the materials they work with as they sculpt their digital worlds. Peeling back the layers of structure from the surface of digital worlds ultimately reveals the lowest level of abstraction in digital form: the 0s and 1s of binary code. Creation in the world of digital media is a process of designing information—in the sense of *information* defined by Claude E. Shannon some sixty years ago.

Information Theory

Claude Shannon was a precocious research student at the Massachusetts Institute of Technology when, in 1937, at the age of twenty-one, he made the breakthrough that laid the foundation for the digital computer. He demonstrated in his master's thesis that both the 1s and 0s of Boolean algebra and the various Boolean operations that could be applied to process them (e.g., addition, subtraction, and the logical *and*, *or*, and *not* operations) could be represented by electrical switches that were either on or off. Using webs of electronic relays and switches and following the rules of Boolean logic, he could create a binary string—the input—that could be processed to create another string—the output. With this insight, the binary world of digital technology was born.

Eleven years later, Shannon, who was then working at Bell Laboratories, published "A Mathematical Theory of Information." He suggested that, while science after Einstein had come to focus on the relationship between energy and matter ($E = mc^2$) measured in electron volts and grams, it had overlooked information. He proposed that information was a phenomenon as fundamental as energy and matter that could also be quantified and studied as a thing in itself (Shannon and Weaver, 1949). His theory outlined how information could be measured in *bits*—the number of 0s and 1s required to represent a piece of information in binary code.

Shannon's Bell Labs research was focused on finding the most efficient way to send messages through wires or space that prevented them from being garbled by random noise. When he considered the problem of quantifying information, he was thinking, in particular, of information in the form of words and numbers.

How many bits does it take to represent a (text) message? For example, if you want to distinguish among 128 different symbols—say, the 52 upper- and lower-case characters of the alphabet, the ten numeric characters 0 through 9, all the punctuation marks, and the various other symbols you might need for a message—you can represent each one by a unique combination of seven bits (2^7 equals 128). Thus a word made up of five characters (or symbols) would require thirty-five bits of information, and a sentence of a hundred characters would require seven hundred bits of information. The more information there is, the larger the number of bits needed to represent it.

In Shannon's definition, information is derived from the structure of the bits. It is the inverse of randomness: if there is no structure to the arrangement of the bits—that is, if the bits are randomly organized—there is no information. To the extent that there is structure, there is information. In Shannon's information theory, information is the structuring of bits. In the digital context, therefore, when the computer becomes a tool of human expression, that expression is a product of designing information-as-it-was-defined-by-Shannon. Anyone creating structure in any digital form is, literally, an information designer.

Chameleons of the Julia Set

The fundamental materials of today's information designer are strings of 1s and 0s. The material of digital worlds is digital information—nothing else. Only the sequence of bits turns it from incomprehensible data—strings of 1s and 0s that we cannot interpret directly—to the vivid experience of a digital world. Only the form of the data distinguishes information from random noise.

To better understand how the work of today's digital sculptors is shaped by this ethereal material, I visited the studio of J. Michael James in the rolling hills of Sunol in northern California. I asked him why, given his training in traditional sculpture, he chose to work in a virtual medium. James replied, "My drive for self-expression requires digital media. I have a fascination with fractal structures. All sorts of fractal forms fly around inside of my head all the time. Yet, even though nature creates fractal forms, there's no way outside of the virtual for me to work with them for personal self-expression. I can't actualize my ideas in any other medium" (James 1996).

The view out the window—a red-tailed hawk circling above the dry brown grasses and craggy oaks—is a stark contrast to the interior of his studio, which is cluttered with technology. James creates his virtual sculptures on a network of Intel Pentium computers. He has removed the covers of the machines and stacked them to one side. Exposing the computers' guts facilitates the removal and insertion of various components. James is constantly adding faster graphics cards, bigger disk drives, more RAM, and new motherboards, along with upgrades of the latest processor, in his continuing attempt to satiate the demands of his virtual art. A tangle of cables connect graphics tablets, scanners, joysticks, and other devices to his computers.

Yet James's studio isn't so much what I see scattered across the room but, rather, what sits within his computers—in cyberspace. I peer into this virtual studio through a twenty-one-inch color-correct monitor and see his *Chameleons of the Julia Set* (figure 14.1). Iridescent chameleons hang from a wall in virtual space, and I see that they are structured in the form of a fractal spiral I recognize as the Julia set.[1] As I push the joystick to view it from the side, the three-dimensionality of the sculpture becomes evident. The chameleon-vine clings like ivy to the polished white sheet of a wall (figure 14.2).

The Digital Design of a Chameleon

Rather than using a hammer and chisel, James shapes his chameleons with computer software for digital design. His tools include software for creating three-dimensional forms, utilities for digitally scanning photographs and graphics, various "plug-in" modules for processing digital images, and programs that perform the complex calculations required to simulate even the simplest lighting effects.

The structure of James's unnatural sculpture originates with a single chameleon clinging to a branch. He peels back the texture-mapped veneer

Figure 14.1
Chameleons of the Julia Set by J. Michael James.

of one chameleon to show me the "wireframe" that maps its contours (figure 14.3). To demonstrate how he creates a chameleon, James begins by scanning in a picture of a chameleon seen in profile. He then takes the scanned image and digitally processes it to create a vector representation— that is, a representation of the profile as a series of connected straight lines. This gives him a two-dimensional outline of a slice down the middle of his chameleon from nose to tail.

To create a three-dimensional form, James then uses his mouse to make a copy of the profile and to point to, click, and drag the connecting points of the vectors of this second outline to form a profile of the chameleon as seen from half way between the center and its side. He creates a third

Figure 14.2
Side View of the Three-dimensional *Chameleons* Sculpture.

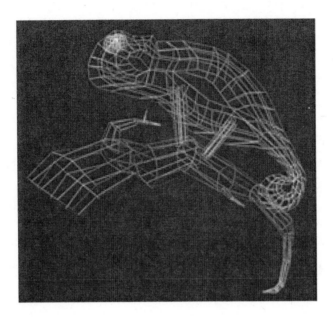

Figure 14.3
The "Wireframe" of a Single Chameleon.

profile half way again between the second profile and the side and, lastly, a fourth set of vectors outlining the chameleon's side.

After positioning the slices parallel to one another in layers, James instructs the computer to stretch a virtual skin across the two-dimensional profiles, producing a transparent three-dimensional mesh surface of connecting polygons. Each one of James's chameleons is made up of hundreds of polygons.

Within the computer, the wireframe itself is a data structure defined as a series of numbers representing the vectors that make up its form:

. . .

VERTEX

−238.767624 20 −234.272858 30 242.820145 70 192 0

VERTEX

−230.624588 20 −248.100037 30 246.640839 70 192 0

VERTEX

−230.777878 20 −262.700500 30 254.805893 70 192 0

VERTEX

−239.422287 20 −272.456177 30 264.313049 70 192 0

VERTEX

−251.660660 20 −271.826385 30 272.149475 70 192 0

VERTEX

−264.454071 20 −262.115295 30 275.486694 70 192 0

VERTEX

−269.094482 20 −247.592529 30 269.839233 70 192 0

VERTEX

−270.672424 20 −233.822052 30 262.358734 70 192 0

. . .

As James sculpts in virtual space, the computer processes the vector data to redraw the morphing forms.

Having created a three-dimensional wireframe model of his chameleon perched on a branch, James next digitally scans photographs of the skin of a chameleon and the bark of a branch into the computer. He uses image-processing software to manipulate the hues and saturation of the chameleon's skin colors to give it an unnatural iridescence. He adjusts the contrast of the tree bark only slightly. He then wraps the flat plane of digital surface onto the naked wire structure in a process known as *texture mapping*. He has now created the digital representation of his kernel chameleon (i.e., the basic form he will replicate to produce the complete sculpture).

Creating the Julia Set

To create the larger structure of his sculpture, James forms a mirror image of the chameleon by giving his computer a few simple instructions. He then performs an *affine linear transformation* to produce a Julia set; that is, he applies the quadratic iteration $Z2 + C$ to each of the two chameleons again and again until the representational image has been transformed into an abstract form.

Rendering a single view consumes hours of computer time. Vector lists must be processed for size and position and flat textures wrapped around wireframes. The sculptor must direct the computer to calculate the lighting reflections, taking perspective into account. The complex array of binary numbers that represent the texture-mapped surfaces is processed by a series of other computer instructions to *ray trace* the translucent lighting—a process that is extremely computation-intensive.

Finally the computer presents the results of its computation. As we study the virtual structure, rotating it, zooming in and out, I ask him what would be involved in making a minor change—perhaps shrinking the chameleon's width or tweaking its skin tones. After confirming that I was only posing a hypothetical question, he smiles as he describes the flexibility of his virtual medium. "If this were, as they say, carved in stone, making changes would be a major production, especially if you wanted to restore a part that had already been cut away. That, of course, would be impossible. But the virtual material I'm working with is incredibly malleable. In the end, my sculpture is only made up of a string of bits, each of which represents a dot of the image that creates the illusion of a virtual world."

He types a series of instructions to the computer to show me the internal binary representation of the sculpture within the computer. Hundreds of thousands of zeros and ones fly across the screen.

... 0010101000000000000000001000000011000000010001000100000001000001000001101000000001000000010011110101010001110011100000000000000000000000110111101010000011001011100000000011000101110000000111100010001010000000 0010101100001010000 ...

He then goes on to explain, "My sculpture is a unique structure of 0s and 1s. At its essence, it's only digital information. To make a change, all I have to do is instruct the computer, in effect, to reprogram it, to recompute the sequence of 0s and 1s. It's when I want to make a change that it's most clear to me that creating virtual sculpture is nothing like working in stone or clay."

Virtual Substance

Digital technology has made possible new media that could not exist without it. The sculptures of J. Michael James's virtual worlds are not made of clay, or marble, or steel; they are the stuff of cyberspace. Their digital representation, the binary data that define their structure, are nothing but rows of numbers in a vector list. James sculpts his worlds out of 0s and 1s.

Yet, though he creates his works in a world that exists exclusively in the digital domain, they are not without substance. They are made of information, which is now, in this Information Age, taking its rightful place beside energy and matter as a fundamental shaper of the world we live in. Of the three, only information is at the heart of who and what we are. It is a manifestation of our humanity that, in digital form, is sculpting new worlds. Self-expression in digital form is, literally, a process of information design.

Notes

1. A fractal is a "self-similar" structure that is repeated perfectly within itself over and over and with endless resolution to create a larger complex and beautiful structure.

References

Burnham, J. 1987. *Beyond Modern Sculpture*. New York: George Braziller.

James, J. M. 1996. Author's conversations with J. Michael James, May.

Shannon, C. E., and Weaver, W. 1949. *The Mathematical Theory of Information*. Urbana: University of Illinois Press.

15 Personal Reflections on the Development of Cyberspace

Simon Birrell

The recent arrival of real-time three-dimensional graphics for low-cost personal computers appears to have been a boon for enthusiasts eager to construct multiuser cyberspace—the Holy Grail of the Virtual Reality community. There has been a flood of 3-D chat worlds released on to the Internet, based around the various software-only rendering libraries, including my own effort, MILENA. I was very proud indeed of its cool 3-D graphics, created by artist Jose Maria Gonzalez. Jose spent a great deal of time rendering images of moodily lit streets and buildings in 3-D Studio and then importing them into the RenderWare scenes as textures. We played with the transparency and wireframe features of the renderer in the "rave" zone. And, grudgingly, we tried to cut down on our polygons to keep the scene running in real time on hardware we liked to think of as modest.

I'm therefore being a little perverse in this essay, as I would like to argue that 3-D is *not* the key technology for cyberspace and that the emphasis in our industry on flashy 3-D may actually be leading us down the wrong technological paths. I think that our attention as a community should be focused on other areas, and that we may be making hardware demands on the end-users that are misguided.

Because, face it, 3-D graphics need a LOT of power. Many people reading this book are computer professionals—whether programmers or design-

Figure 15.1
A Virtual Teapot.

ers—and are used to having their equipment upgraded at least annually. But home users still using their 386s will be getting a very different impression of the cyberspaces we are building them.

A Different Approach

Let us think about what is important in the development of cyberspace. Let's take a specific example, that of a virtual teapot. What is the most important thing we have to consider when constructing a virtual teapot (figure 15.1)? I suspect that typical answers from the VRML (3-D software) community might be

- It should have a nice decorative texture wrapped around the model, so it looks like my aunt's old teapot.

- It should have gourard shading to give it a rounded, chinalike surface.

- It should have a low polygon count, so that it can run in real time on normal PCs.

These are all interesting answers. And all wrong. The most important thing about a virtual teapot is that it should make tea.

A teapot is not a teapot because it is red, blue, textured, or even round. A teapot is a teapot because it makes tea. It may be a square teapot. It may

Figure 15.2
A Platonic Teapot.

even be modeled in the shape of a human head with a long nose acting as a spout. It is still a teapot, providing that we can make tea with it. The point is that we should consider virtual objects by what they are and what they do, not by what they look like. The physical model or representation of our virtual object should be a secondary characteristic.

Let us consider an alternative way to represent a virtual teapot (figure 15.2). Plato believed that all the objects that we see in the world around us are but reflections, or imperfect versions of a perfect "divine" object inhabiting some celestial nonphysical realm. In other words, all teapots on earth are but imperfect versions or variations on the single divine, essential teapot. The essence of this divine teapot is its ability to make tea. It is quite clear that Plato had in mind the intricacies of cyberspace development, as this is a useful and practical way to think about the problems we are trying to solve.

Plato's most famous analogy was that of The Cave. Consider a cave with a fire in the center, and imagine that there are animals and people moving around the fire. They cast great moving shadows on the walls of the cave. Now imagine that we, as terrestrial observers, are also in the cave. Our faces are turned to the wall, facing away from the beings moving around the fire. In our ignorance, we imagine the moving shadows to be the real thing and forget that they are cast by real, "essential" objects out of our sight.

The real objects moving around the fire are the "real" virtual teapots, and the shadows are their 3-D representations. VRML-like software simply renders the shadows, ignoring the real objects, and, even worse, is now

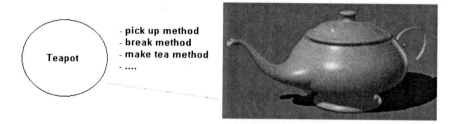

Figure 15.3
A Platonic Teapot and Its Physical Model.

trying to push the shadows around by adding "behaviors." Behaviors are not something that should be tacked onto a 3-D model as an afterthought; behaviors define what that object is. The 3-D model is thus "attached" to the real object (figure 15.3).

What does all this buy us?

First of all, it is clear that we can have multiple types of representation for users who all share the same world. The lucky Silicon Graphics user can see a beautiful 3-D, zillion-polygon rendered teapot. Other users might have a simpler model, or even a two-dimensional icon on their desktops. Yet others might see the same teapot on their terminals as the message "There is a teapot here" (figure 15.4). Intel is working on this project.

Second, focusing on the essence of an object simplifies many of the problems we may come across in simulating worlds. Certain aspects of physics can be modeled as a graph of relationships connecting objects with methods, ("the teapot IS ON the table"), rather than having to worry about perfectly reproducing all the dynamics of the real world.

Thirdly, this solution allows for different types of representations for different problems. Many of the arguments that have flared across the mailing lists are of the type "if we implement feature X then my game won't run fast enough," or "if we don't implement feature X then I won't be able to make my virtual wind tunnel work properly." The underlying assumption behind these arguments is that there exists a single representation suitable efficient for both a wind tunnel and a game. Perhaps we

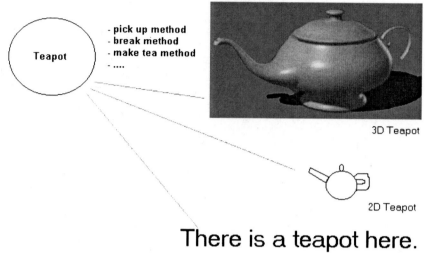

Figure 15.4
Multiple Physical Representations of a Teapot.

should work on multiple graphical solutions that are optimized for different problem domains.

Finally, with the ever-increasing demands on our hardware from 3-D graphics removed (or at least put to one side for a while), we could turn our attention to all the other, burning issues of multiuser consistency, data availability, and behavior modeling.

Pioneering Work

As an example of what can be achieved in cyberspace development, I'd like to describe a computer game made four years ago that I helped work on and show that it implements many of the technologies that we should be concentrating on today.

The game in question, called *Jekyll & Hyde*, was made at the now-defunct Palace Software in London. It was designed and programmed by a brilliant

Figure 15.5
A Screen Shot of the Jekyll & Hyde World.

young programmer called Chris Stangroom and was an example of what we then called *adventure games,* and that are now called *interactive fiction.*

Most modern interactive fiction has followed the same path as current cyberspace work and concentrated almost exclusively on adding ever-more-sophisticated graphics to a fairly simple core program. They are usually based on tree structures of decision points, in which the user chooses from among a set of predetermined paths through story space, each one accompanied by flashy multimedia presentations. In no sense can we consider this type of game to be a "world."

Jekyll & Hyde worked on a different principle (figure 15.5). It was a simulation of a small, sixty-zone world that contained autonomous characters (today we might say *"agents"*) who moved from zone to zone and interacted with each other. Some characters were controlled by their own internal programs—written in a custom-built interpreted language called Character Control Language, (CCL)—while others were controlled by human players through a menu interface. The descriptions of where you, the player, were and what you saw were represented mostly as text.

Characters had basic behaviors, such as "defend yourself if attacked," and different people had more specific behaviors. They had goals, such as "work out the antidote to the magic potion," for Dr. Jekyll or "make lots of money through theft, blackmail, and extortion." for the criminals. They had emotional states and relationships with other characters that numerically reflected levels of friendship, lust, suspicion, and so on. These values were dynamic, altering the characters' behavior toward each other and being modified by external events. Somebody might begin the game as your friend but, if you persistently treated him badly, his feelings and his behavior toward you would soon change.

From the point of view of the world simulation, there was no difference between a character controlled by a user and a character controlled by a CCL program; in current terminology, the *avatars* were treated in the same way as the *agents*. This meant, for one thing, that it was trivially easy to implement a command to switch characters at any point in the game. This was fun, but we had to restrict the shifts to give the game some degree of challenge. Otherwise, you could win a fight with an enemy by becoming the enemy, killing yourself, then swapping back to your previous character.

It also means that things are going on in the background. While you as a user are playing in one zone, two computer-controlled characters may be fighting (or making love) in another zone. This made the game difficult to test. As Dr. Jekyll, you might send the CCL-governed delivery boy off to fetch a much-needed ingredient. On the way back from the chemist, however, he might be mugged by a CCL-governed thief, who sells the ingredient and spends the money down at the pub. All the game tester would see is that the delivery boy has gone off and not returned. It was hard to tell what was a bug, and what was a legitimate twist of fate (figure 15.3).

That problem also threw up fascinating challenges to the way we could provoke story situations for the player (although this is less relevant to cyberspace development and ought to be the subject of another essay). In *Jekyll & Hyde* we did not impose a story upon the world; all we could do was set up the characters' initial relationships and goals and let them get on with it. It was rather like trying to program an ant colony, and our characters led us a merry dance.

It seemed important—particularly after early testing with volunteers—to stop players running amok throughout the world. We decided to do this within the world system by simulating a police force rather than by mechanically restricting players' freedom of action. With his cheerful disregard for what was generally assumed to be possible, Chris invented an entire system of crime detection and investigation in which the police could be either computer or user controlled. When a criminal act occurred in the game, an "atom" of knowledge, which had attributes referring to the aggressor, victim, time, and so on, was "instantiated." Any witness to the crime would have a copy of that atom, or memory, and could pass it on to other characters by gossiping or reporting it to the police. The police, who were told these knowledge atoms, or who could partially construct them from examination of the scene of a crime, would move through the world, questioning suspects and verifying their alibis. Notice that this atom of crime knowledge is a first-class object within the world design, although it is totally nonphysical. In no way does it represent the "behavior" of a physical object.

Jekyll & Hyde also featured such inanimate objects as safes, jewels, money, fire, and teapots. Everything was represented by text, with the occasional spot graphic. But we could still model basic physical relationships and properties in the manner described at the beginning of the essay. "The teapot is on the table" can be modeled as two abstract objects with a relationship between them. You could put an object inside another objects—so that weighing the container would correctly return their combined weight—set fire to objects, break them, and so on.

Chris implemented liquids made by mixing of chemical ingredients together. So ingredients such as mercury, acid, and water could be mixed into a single liquid that would additively combine the properties of all three. One day a games tester discovered an interesting side effect of this capability. There was a pub in the game with a CCL-controlled barman who served the other characters when they came in for a drink. The tester discovered that you could pour the potion that turned Jekyll into Hyde into the pub's beer barrel. This meant that from then on every character who came in for a nice glass of beer would instantly turn into a raving maniac and that within a few minutes the game world would be littered with dead bodies.

It's important to understand that this outcome was not explicitly programmed into the game; it emerged as an unexpected consequence of the way a high-level abstract physics had been programmed into the game. It surprised and delighted the hell out of the programmer. This chance appearance seems such a fundamental aspect of any really rich simulated world that I believe we can offer it as a necessary condition for a virtual reality:

A virtual world is not real unless it can surprise its own creator.

This all sounds great, but is it cyberspace? Surely one of the defining characteristics of cyberspace is that it is multiuser?

Jekyll & Hyde was, in fact, a multiuser adventure. Up to four PCs, Amigas, and STs could be connected into a ring by an eccentric use of the serial port, and a player at each computer could control up to three characters—all other characters being CCL-controlled. In designing *Jekyll & Hyde* Chris met with, and resolved, many of the issues still being debated today in discussions of multiuser world consistency. In summary then, *Jekyll & Hyde* had:

- A high-level abstract representation of the world, including relevant physics
- Autonomous agents with emotions, relationships, and goals
- Avatars that could do the same things as agents, and vice versa
- Multiuser consistency
- The ability to surprise its own creator

This, to me, is a cyberspace, even if its interface is text-based and not 3-D. It is richer, more interesting, more sophisticated, and more "real" than anything I've seen on the Internet, or indeed anything I've seen on- or off-line in my three years in the VR industry. I know of no other project,

Figure 15.6
Chris Stangroom.

before or since, of equal scope. Chris's world seethed with a bizarre crowd of madcap characters living out their brief existences according to their own logical and moral precepts. They fell in love, got drunk, fought, robbed, became sad, and got high on opium. Crimes were committed, investigated, and solved. Clandestine encounters between adulterous characters were witnessed, gossiped about, and published in the newspaper. And when they slept, you could read their dreams.

It was written, and it ran, on a 286 processor in one megabyte of RAM.

In the summer of 1995 Chris Stangroom was robbed and killed while on holiday. Shortly before then we had begun discussing the revival of the *Jekyll & Hyde* world engine as the basis for a new, on-line 3-D cyberspace environment. It is maddening to think that such a person can be taken from us for the sake of a few dollars. We can only guess at what he would have achieved had he lived (figure 15.6).

The Way Forward

Describing in hindsight why a particular information architecture was used is a lot easier than instructing others how to design in the same way. The design process seems to consist of endless reevaluations of what each software entity *really* is, which is another way of saying what it has to do. I know another talented programmer who once spent days anguishing over what the cursor in the word processing program he was writing *really* was. Suddenly it came to him in a flash. The experience is like emerging from a complicated mathematical problem and seeing a beautiful, simple result. Steve Jobs once said that hard software problems always appear easy at first glance. Then the programmer thinks about it for a bit and begins to realize that it's actually much more complicated than he or she thought. Most people stop there. However, if you keep thinking about the problem long enough, it eventually becomes simple again.

It is critical that we develop a high-level, abstract way of modeling our virtual worlds and use 3-D, or 2-D, or text as a window onto them. It's a lot harder intellectually than spinning a few 3-D objects in a browser, but the results will be cleaner, more beautiful, and more powerful in the end. Surprisingly enough, it's feasible to do this on very modest platforms.

Exciting, rich multiuser environments over the Internet are achievable today. My suspicion is that they will not be invented by the experts currently pontificating about which kind of scripting language should be used to push around their 3-D models. I suspect they'll be invented by some brilliant kid without the money for a 3-D accelerator card who, with youthful disregard for what ought to be possible on his machine, will dream of making sophisticated, interesting, and fantastic worlds where we can all work, live out our fantasies, and make tea.

Epilogue

16 *Presenting Information*

Jef Raskin

When Bob Jacobson asked me to write a chapter for this book, I hoped to be here, batting in the clean-up position. On reading the other chapters, I find that they accurately represent the diversity of the field—from fuzzy New Age touchy-feely rantings to thoughtful studies. I believe that most readers will find the practical pointers in the form of heuristics developed by experienced practitioners to be especially valuable. Overall, although some of the material is rather vague, at least the reader is always pointed in the right directions.

One of the ways we increase the returns we receive from understanding the world is by adapting our vocabulary to reflect our increasing knowledge. Humanity never would have progressed beyond building the most primitive of mechanical engines if careful thinkers had not learned to distinguish between *energy, force, work,* and *power*. These words are still used loosely in everyday speech, but professional mechanical designers and physicists use them carefully and with well-defined meanings. Professionals in the field of information-related design will have to learn to be equally careful. We must not allow sloppy thinking to muddy the deep waters we find here at the meeting place of art, psychology, and electronic technology. Things are difficult enough as it is.

I was embarrassed to see a few of the authors in this book abusing terms such as *information, digital,* and *binary*, seemingly unaware of their precise meanings and implications. If our field is to advance, we must, without displacing creativity and aesthetics, make sure our terminology is clear.

There Is No Such Thing as Information Design

As a curmudgeon, I am delighted to point out that the very title of this book, *Information Design*, is a misnomer. Information cannot be designed; what can be designed are the modes of transfer and the representations of information. This is inherent in the nature of information, and it is important for designers to keep the concepts of *information* and *meaning* distinct.

Information is an abstraction from any meaning a message might have and from any particular form a message might take. In the 1940s, the founder of information theory, Claude Shannon, moved information from the realm of philosophers to that of physicists by showing that the term could be given a clear definition. Not only could we define it, but, he demonstrated, we could quantify information and treat it as a part of physics, something I found amazing and eye-opening when I first read his works. One of the ideas that Shannon established is that any piece of information can be represented by a sequence of the elementary particles of information, which we now call *bits*. The unit of information presents us with a two-way choice: we can model a bit mentally as yes or no, green or red, on or off, zero or one, and so on. The word *bits* was coined by the mathematician John W. Tukey as a contraction of *BInary digiTS*, that is, zeros and ones, the most commonly used mental model of the smallest unit of information (Shannon and Weaver 1949: 9).

We can represent any piece of information as a sequence of bits or, equivalently, as a sequence of characters in a text or a string of numbers in base ten (or any other base). These mechanical rearrangements do not change the information in any way. There is nothing special, with regard to the content, about the binary (base two) representation of information, although some people (even in this book) treat numbers in base two as something almost mystical.

Similarly, there is nothing special about the digital representation of information. If I take some information and translate it into a nondigital (i.e. analog) form—say, voltages on a conductor or the frequencies of a radio signal—that information remains unchanged. We can convert it back and forth between analog and digital representations at will. In fact, every time we use a modem to send e-mail over a telephone line we convert digital information into analog form; yet nothing happens to the information from losing its digital cachet. The information is the same however it is represented, and the identical message eventually appears on the recipient's display, showing no evidence of ever having been in analog form.

Readers should therefore disregard any use of the term *digital* in this book when it is used to imply that the digital nature of some information affects its the content or impact. The form of information storage or transmittal—whether digital or analog, binary bits or decimal digits, or in some other guise—is irrelevant to the issue of conveying meaning to people. It is this issue that is the proper subject of this book.

You might ask: If any information can be represented as a finite sequence of symbols, can we represent other aspects of the world, such as a one-centimeter cube of pure gold or an infinitely long, nonrepeating decimal like the square root of two, as information? We can. I just did. That information can take the form of a bunch of numbers—or even the form of words on a page—does not limit the content the information might convey.

Even though information is an abstraction independent of form and therefore cannot be designed, the way in which we represent information to others is of crucial importance in communicating the meaning of the information. The representation of the information is the plastic medium with which we work. It would have been more appropriate to name this book *Designing Information Representation*.

So, how do we represent particular information so that it has a desired effect on the recipient? That it is possible to define the issue (and the field) in this way depends on the fact that we can represent the same information in different ways and that some representations are more effective than others. In addition, the particular effect we want to achieve can vary a great deal.

This is where we—graphic designers, computer-interface specialists, artists, musicians, sound technologists, lighting directors, cognitive psychologists, type designers, ergonomicists, and even mathematicians and physicists—come in. It is our job to design the representation of information for human consumption.

Theory and Practice

Learning how to represent information effectively requires us to travel along two complementary paths. One is the apprenticeship route, on which we learn from the example of current and past practitioners. The other path is the theoretical route, since understanding some theory—and how to apply it—can shortcut much trial and error. I use *theory* in the sense that scientists usually do, to mean an established body of knowledge, rather than in the everyday sense of a tentative idea.

Some of the chapters in this book provide concrete examples of the practice of representing information effectively. They represent the apprenticeship path. To leverage further our designing efforts, we can build on the foundations of information theory and cognitive psychology that underlie the theoretical path. The right place to start on the second path is with an examination of the audience for our information: people.

Ergonomics and Cognetics

In spite of technical advances, our access to external information has not expanded beyond that provided by our senses of sight, hearing, touch, smell, balance, and taste. Therefore, the first responsibility of the designer is to know the limitations and capabilities of the human senses, a body of knowledge usually considered part of ergonomics and the study of human factors. A practitioner should know or have immediately to hand, for example, the angular resolution of the human eye and how large lettering must be for various colors, light levels, distances, and contrast ratios. We need to know, for example: How fast can the eye move from point to point? How long does it take to find a target visually? Under what conditions can we hear and understand speech (e.g., in terms of signal-to-noise ratio), and what range of frequencies are easiest to hear? Which typefaces are most readable? How much or how little pressure can we feel on our fingertips and elsewhere on our bodies? How much force can a human hand exert? In addition, we must know how all this data is affected by human variables such as age and health.

At times, common sense and established practices are sufficient guides to this knowledge. But be careful. Time and again, hallowed practices have turned out to be less than optimal, and designers ignorant of ergonomics have often failed to create products that work within the physical and mental limitations of human users. Don Norman's delightful book, *The Design of Everyday Things*, is full of examples of designer disasters.

As a designer, you may be called upon to create a computer kiosk or a web interface. Doing so efficiently and effectively is difficult if you are not familiar with the pertinent research in cognitive psychology and with quantitative methods such as those explained in the classic book, *The Psychology of Human–Computer Interaction* by Stuart Card, Thomas Moran, and Allen Newell (1983). Hundreds of millions of computers have unpleasant interfaces (Microsoft Windows comes to mind) because they require abilities humans simply do not possess, proving that their interface designers were ignorant of fundamental facts about the human mind. The sheer volume of jokes about computers reflects our near-universal dissatisfaction with their interfaces.

Of course, it is not only cognitive psychology that is useful. When our representations of information have emotional content, it is helpful to have studied what little is known about human emotions from an engineering point of view. For example, there is no direct correlation between color and emotional content; the meaning of color is culturally mediated. Red is not universally seen as a sign of danger; in some oriental cultures it is white, not black, that is associated with death; and so on. Naive designers who rely on their intuition (i.e., cultural biases) in these regards are likely to find that creations intended to work for a variety of users unexpectedly fail.

I am not suggesting that designers should study the neurophysiology of the brain. While such studies can lead to useful knowledge about how people absorb and react to representations of information, how the brain functions internally is not directly relevant to our field. We can treat the brain as a black box and safely ignore all the twaddle about the parts of the brain and what they do. Even when this physiological information is technically correct (which is not always the case), it is of no direct use to us. As information presenters, our only interest in the human brain is how it reacts holistically, that is, how people respond or behave.

The currently fashionable right brain–left brain distinctions are particularly silly. Does it matter to us, as designers, that certain abilities are located at such and such a location? Would it make any difference if the right brain–left brain abilities were localized in the top and bottom of the brain rather than the right and left halves? I think not. Useful information takes an operational form.

Art or Science?

Every major field of human activity is a mix of art and science. Theoretical physicists and professional mathematicians speak of the aesthetics of their work and are driven by concerns about elegance and beauty. Is a painter any less an artist for knowing perspective, understanding Josef Albers's elegant experiments and demonstrations about color, or being aware of chemical incompatibilities between various kinds of paint?

Designing the presentation of information, by the same token, partakes of the nature of both art and science. Edward Tufte's books reflect such a blend of knowledge. In one of them he outlines his five principles for designing graphics (1983: 105):

- Above all else show the data
- Maximize the data-ink ratio
- Erase non-data ink
- Erase redundant data ink
- Revise and edit

The first four principles are (mostly) science-based. But the last, "revise and edit," tells us not only to check repeatedly that the first four conditions are met, but also to apply our aesthetic judgment to the final work. Describing electronic displays in terms of numbers of pixels no more makes our work technical than the fact that the frequencies of consecutive notes of the tempered chromatic scale have a ratio of the twelfth root of two makes musical composition a hard science.

Summary

This book presents a cross-section of the art, science, and personalities involved in representing information effectively. As I have pointed out, some practitioners try to drape themselves in the mantle of technological modernity, recklessly pinning the drapery together with abused jargon and misunderstood concepts. The gaps that are left prove more revealing than they know. This does not mean that their work as designers is bad; it just means that we cannot learn much from what they say about their work.

I predict that, just as astronomy moved from the ancient tales of how the constellations were formed (lovely, but totally fictitious) to the modern scientific models of the universe (breathtakingly beautiful and even more awe-inspiring), the most valuable improvements in the effectiveness of representations of information will come from scientific analyses of human performance. I do not imply any abandonment of art and the artistic impulse. I used to spend hours tediously learning the formal motions used in conducting the various musical meters so that those actions would become automatic; now, when I conduct an ensemble, I do not spend any mental energy on technique but can focus entirely on communicating the music through the baton. For the same reason, a designer who works with information should have a firm grasp of human factors. Once mastered, that knowledge can be swept into the unconscious, where it can guide you unobtrusively, leaving you free to concentrate on the emotive and aesthetic sides of your work.

The designer must, to use Wittgenstein's words, "throw away the ladder after he has climbed up it" (1961: 151). It has been the role of my chapter to point out that it can be dangerous to dispose of the ladder any sooner.

References

Card, Stuart, Moran, Thomas, and Newell, Allen. 1983. *The Psychology of Human–Computer Interaction*. Hillsdale, N.J.: Lawrence Erlbaum.

Norman, Donald. 1988. *The Design of Everyday Things*. New York: Basic Books.

Shannon, Claude, and Weaver, Warren. 1949. *The Mathematical Theory of Information*. Urbana: University of Illinois Press.

Tufte, Edward. 1983. *The Visual Display of Quantitative Information*. Cheshire, Conn.: Graphics Press.

Wittgenstein, Ludwig. 1961. *Tractatus Logico-Philosophicus*. London: Routledge & Kegan Paul.

Contributors

Elizabeth Anderson, a member of the Society for Environmental Graphics Design, has over nineteen years of experience designing signage systems, logos, typefaces, and all kinds of graphics. Her educational background includes work in literature, typography, fine arts, and graphic design. Elizabeth attended Whitman and Reed colleges and has taught at Portland State University and the Pacific Northwest College of Art. She is a partner, with John Krygier, in Anderson Krygier Inc.

Judy Anderson is a professor in the School of Art at the University of Washington. She has received numerous public art commissions and served as lead artist for collaborative works involving writers, video artists, musicians, performers, visual artists, architects, and urban designers. As a design consultant, Ms. Anderson creates comprehensive identity programs, publications, and information/exhibition design systems. Her work creating special edition books in experimental formats is supported principally by grants and awards.

Her special edition books have been exhibited worldwide and are in the permanent collections of the Walker Art Gallery, Getty Museum, New York Public Library, and several universities. She has received numerous regional, national, and international awards for her print and book designs and has published in *Print*, *CA*, *Idea*, *AIGA Graphic Design Annual*, *ID*, *Print Casebooks*, *Typography 4*, and the *New York Art Directors Annual* (which awarded her a Gold Medal). As a 1995 fellow of the Northwest Institute for Architecture and Urban Studies in Rome, she explored the expanded role of public and private communications in the vitalization of key public gathering places.

Simon Birrell's fate was sealed at the age of seventeen when his parents bought him a BBC microcomputer. Since then he has worked in the videogame industry, first as a programer at Virgin Games, then as head of development at Palace Software. On moving to Madrid, he joined Realidad Virtual, Spain's pioneering virtual reality company. Birrell programed MILENA, one of the world's first Internet-based chat spaces. He now heads the E-Spaces studio in Madrid, where he develops three-dimensional and multimedia worlds for the Internet. His paper in this volume is based on a lecture given at the CyberConf in June of 1996.

Mike Cooley has studied engineering in Germany, Switzerland, and England and holds a Ph.D. in computer-aided design. He has held director-level design and technical management posts in the public and private sectors and currently directs several high tech companies and the European Union's Technology Exchange ("The Product Bank").

Dr. Cooley is an international authority on human-centered systems design and has been a visiting professor at universities in Europe, Australia, the United States, and Japan. He is a member of joint EU/Japan Commission on New Technologies and has directed major EU projects in advanced technology. His software work includes tools for *Learning and Earning Organizations*, which utilizes Dr. Cooley's "Curiosity Generator." He has published over 120 scientific papers and is the author or joint author of 15 books in English and German on technology and its consequences.

Brenda Dervin received her Ph.D. and M.A. degrees in communications from Michigan State University and her bachelor's in journalism from Cornell University. She has worked as a public information officer, journalist, and researcher and has taught at Syracuse University and the University of Washington. She is currently a professor of communications at Ohio State University. Her teaching and research focus on the design of responsive communication and information systems and the use of interpretive methodologies to incorporate users and their needs into the design of such systems. She is past president and a fellow of the International Communication Association and a member of the governing council of the International Association for Media and Communication Research. For a decade she served as editor of *Progress in Communication Sciences*. Dr. Dervin is the author of numerous scholarly articles and book chapters.

Jim Gasperini at the time of writing was a partner with Tennessee Rice Dixon in ScrutTiny Associates, a New York–based developer of aesthetically sophisticated multimedia. Their interactive CD-ROM artwork, *ScruTiny in the Great Round*, won the Grand Prix du Jury at MILIA '96 in Cannes. They also collaborated with J. Carter Brown on the CD-ROM adaptation of his international art show, *Rings: Five Passions in World Art* (Calliope Media) for the Atlanta Cultural Olympiad. For the past twelve years, Gasperini has worked at the intersection of writing, design, and programming, using interactive media to create new forms of storytelling and make complex ideas entertaining and comprehensible. He explores the aesthetic possibilities of structural ambiguity in works like *Hidden Agenda*, his political role-playing game, and has designed interactive works in CD-ROM, CD-i, and 3-DO for publishers around the world. Gasperini's latest accomplishment is a complete redesign of SimCity, the popular urban-planning simulation game. His critical and theoretical articles about interactivity have appeared in *Wired*, *Interactivity*, *Eloquent Interfaces*, and *Talkback*. He holds a B.A. in literature from Williams College.

Yvonne M. Hansen holds a Ed.D. and an M.A. in organization development from the Fielding Institute of Santa Barbara. She is the founder and principal of Consulting in Human Interaction and of Geminideas Press. Dr. Hansen is the author of *Think Visually!* and *V.A.S.T.: Visual Approach to Systems Thinking*. She has taught art in the United States and abroad and, at the college level, has offered courses in organization theory and behavior and leadership and group dynamics. In her passion for enhancing visual, conceptual thought to generate whole-brain creativity and enable systemic thinking, Dr. Hansen created Graphics Tools, a system of real-time visual notation to give visible form to ideas, nonlinear phenomena, planning ideas, and other abstractions. A consultant to entrepreneurs,

Yvonne resides in Austin, Texas, where she is involved in professional and community groups. Sometime in the next few years she intends to build a house out of straw bales and earth.

Steve Holtzman, an advocate of "new content" for the digital age, was the author of *Digital Mosaics* (Simon & Schuster, 1997), a preview of future digital worlds. His earlier work, *Digital Mantras* (MIT Press, 1994), has been critically acclaimed as "a philosophy of creativity for the digital age." Holtzman was a guest commentator on National Public Radio's *All Things Considered* and wrote for, among others, *Wired*, *HotWired*, *Technology Review*, and *Digital Media*. Over the past fifteen years, he held various executive positions in the high technology industry. Most recently he was CEO of Perspecta, Inc., a software company developing new ways to navigate the Web and find information on the Internet, and was on the boards of directors of Liquid Audio and The Motion Factory, also Internet software companies. Steve held a B.A. in philosophy and a Ph.D. in computer science from the University of Edinburgh, Scotland.

Robert Horn's professional work has concentrated on developing the research and systematic foundations of information design. He is chairman of Information Mapping, Inc., an international consulting company located in Waltham, Massachusetts; the company specializes in making complex information understandable. He is also president of the product-design group, MacroVU, Inc. Horn has taught at Harvard and Columbia universities and is currently a visiting scholar at the Program on People, Computers, and Design at the Center for the Study of Language and Information of Stanford University.

His information design projects have included an information database and retrieval system for all federal programs in education, training, and research and the design and development of the standard reference work on simulations and games for education and training. He is the author of eight monographs and books, including his recent *Mapping Hypertext*, which describes how the precise structuring of information can solve many of the problems of the on-line display of information. He has completed another book, *Visual Language*. An earlier work, *How High Can It Fly?* summarizes the research on structured writing.

Bob Jacobson, editor, has a long history of involvement in the design of information environments. As a community-media activist, he gained an early appreciation for the power of information technology as a tool for individual and collective learning and activation. He served on the city of Los Angeles's first cable television commission and was a founding member of the Los Angeles Public Access Project and, later, Sacramento Community Radio. As a principal consultant and staff director with the California State Assembly, Dr. Jacobson wrote California's Universal Telephone Service Act; it provides low-cost telephone service for low-income individuals (and in 1996 was incorporated in the federal Telecommunications Reform Act). He also wrote California's Telephone Privacy Act and the pioneering Electronic Commerce Act of 1984. Dr. Jacobson was a cofounder and associate director of the Human Interface Technology Laboratory at the Washington Technology Center and the founder and CEO of Worldesign Inc., an award-winning virtual-worlds design studio, both in Seattle. He founded and from 1990 through 1995 comoderated the USENET newsgroup, *sci.virtual-worlds*, the main "meeting place" for the nascent virtual worlds industry. Most recently, he has been a senior consultant with SRI Consulting in Menlo Park, California, and a strategic technology planner with IBIS Consulting in San Francisco. He currently consults to leading Internet and design firms on strategic and information-design issues.

Dr. Jacobson is the author of *Municipal Control of Cable Communications* (New York: Praeger/Ablex, 1977) and *An "Open Approach" to Information Policymaking* (New York: Ablex, 1989), and coauthored *Access Rights to the Electronic Marketplace* (Sacramento: Assembly Office of Research, 1981). As a Fulbright Scholar and with support from UNESCO and the Nordic Development Bank, he helped to organize a multinational policy study of regional telecommunications in the "Nordkalott," the region of Scandinavia north of the Arctic Circle. Dr. Jacobson holds an M.A. (Television Studies) from UCLA's Theater Arts Department, an M.A. (Communications Management) from the Annenberg School of Communications at the University of Southern California, and a Ph.D. in Information Systems Planning from UCLA's Graduate School of Architecture and Urban Planning.

John Krygier, a graduate of the Art Center College of Design in Los Angeles, brings over thirty years of industrial and graphic design experience to his work. He has worked in transportation design, architectural design, product packaging and marketing, and graphic design for a wide variety of national and international clients. In his work for Anderson Krygier, Inc., he developed numerous environmental graphic design projects and computerized interactive displays.

Sheryl Macy is an author and producer of interactive programming. Noted for her lively intellect, insatiable curiosity, and highly developed ability to make connections, she puts words to paper for a variety of clients. Macy is a 1976 graduate of the University of Oregon School of Journalism and has a lifelong interest in the arts and technology.

The teaching and research activities of ***Romedi Passini***, a professor in the School of Architecture of the University of Montréal, bridge the topics of environmental psychology and architectural design. After completing his architectural training at the Eidgenövssische Technische Hochscule in Zurich in 1964, he spent the five years designing large buildings. Attracted by the emerging interdisciplinary field of environmental psychology and armed with a grant from the Canada Council, Passini embarked on graduate studies in that field and received his Ph.D. from Pennyslvania State University in 1977. His first book, *Wayfinding in Architecture* (Van Nostrand Reinhold 1984, 1992), introduced the concept of wayfinding and its application to building design. With graphic designer Paul Arthur, he has also published a reference work entitled *Wayfinding, People, Signs, and Architecture* (McGraw-Hill 1992). Passini has explored various research issues in environmental perception and cognition and the problems of mobility and wayfinding among the visually impaired. His current research focuses on wayfinding and diorientation in dementia and spatio-cognitive deficiencies caused by brain lesions, specifically topographical amnesia and agnosia.

Jef Raskin is best known for having created the Macintosh computer project at Apple Computer, where he was manager of advanced systems. Earlier, he was a professor of visual arts and director of the Computer Center at the University of California, San Diego. He has served as CEO of several companies, including his own, Information Appliance Inc, and is presently a writer and consultant on human–computer interaction and system design.

Raskin has published three volumes of chamber music and exhibited his artworks at several prominent museums and galleries. He has also been a conductor of the San Francisco Chamber Opera Company and has represented the United States at the International Festival of the Arts in Edinburgh, Scotland. He is currently attempting to build a pipe organ from corrugated cardboard.

Throughout a long career, **C. G. Screven** has combined university teaching and research in learning, perception, and motivation with consulting in interpretive planning, evaluation, and design for informal public environments. He has worked for thirty years in museums and public settings that have served as laboratories for examining the limitations and potentials for generating voluntary attention and learning in public settings. Dr. Screven is professor emeritus of psychology at the University of Wisconsin-Milwaukee and has taught and conducted research at Colorado State University, the University of Geissen (Germany), the Institute of Design at Illinois Institute of Technology, and the Office of Museum Programs of the Smithsonian Institution.

He has published over eighty-five journal articles, monographs, and book chapters and conducted symposia, hands-on workshops, and forums all over the world, including, among many others, the TVA Energy Center; the Institut für Museumkunde, Berlin; the National Museum of Natural History, Smithsonian Institution; the Louvre, Paris; the Powerhouse Museum, Sydney, Australia; the Seneca Rocks Visitor Center, U.S. Forest Service; and the Desert Botanical Gardens, Phoenix. He is the principal of Screven & Associates, Chicago, the editor of *Visitor Studies Bibliography and Abstracts* (published by Exhibit Communications Research), and a board member of the Education Foundation, Society for Environmental Graphics.

Nathan Shedroff has been an information and interface designer for over ten years. He is currently the Chief Creative Officer at vivid studios, which he cofounded eight years ago to develop online brand strategies, online products and services, and online events and communities. He earned a BS in Industrial Design, with emphasis in Automobile Design, from Art Center College of Design in Pasadena, California.

Before co-founding vivid, he worked with Richard Saul Wurman as a senior designer at TheUnderstandingBusiness. Throughout his career, he has worked in many different media and authored several books on multimedia, computers, and information. His electronic experience spans CD-ROMs, kiosks, published titles, application development, and online experiences.

Nathan is actively defining and developing new understandings of all aspects of information and interaction design, communication, visual design, and online brand development.

Nathan was nominated for a Chrysler Innovation in Design Award in 1994 and, while a student, received an Honorable Mention in the 1987 Unisys Industrial Design Competition.

Nathan teaches and speaks often at both international colleges and professional seminars. He has written and designed several books and maintains a website with resources on Interaction Design at *http://www.nathan.com/thoughts/*.

Hal Thwaites has over ten years of professional work with the Canadian Broadcast Corporation to inform his ongoing research and teaching at Montreal's Concordia University, in its Communication Studies Department. He has served as a consultant in the areas of communication research, media information design, and analysis for private companies and government departments. Professor Thwaites's work focuses on the areas of media production, children's television, computers and new media, communication programming, information design, virtual reality, and three-dimensional media. He is the founding Director of the 3Dmt Center, a nonprofit organization devoted to three-dimensional and new-media technologies based at Concordia University. Thwaites has organized two international conferences on three-dimensional media, 3Dmt '89 and 3Dmt

'92, and has recently served as a co-organizer of several related conferences in Japan. He has lectured internationally in Belgium, Germany, Japan, Taiwan, and the United States; and coauthored two texts on communication analysis and biocybernetic research. He is a tenured faculty member at Concordia and serves on the boards of the *International Journal of Virtual Reality* (USA) and the International Society on Virtual Systems and Multimedia. (Japan).

Roger Whitehouse is one of the world's leading experts in the design of universal and accessible information and wayfinding systems. Trained as an architect and graphic designer, he has been responsible for many landmark projects for institutions and corporations in the United States and abroad, including the research and design of a visual, audible, and tactile information system for low-vision and blind users at The Lighthouse Inc. in New York. He is president of Whitehouse & Company a New York design consultancy.

Whitehouse is a fellow of the Society for Environmental Graphic Design and an associate of the Royal Institute of British Architects. He is the author of *New York: Sunshine and Shadow* (Harper & Row 1974) and *A London Album* (Secker & Warburg 1980). He has taught at the Architectural Association, London, the School of Architecture of Columbia University, and many other schools in the United States and the United Kingdom. His clients include the Lincoln Center for the Performing Arts, the Metropolitan Museum of Art, Sotheby's, the Knoll Group, Herman Miller Inc., and IBM.